MISSING LINKS

IN THE JFK ASSASSINATION

"Evidence Of Conspiracy & Coverup"

By: Ralph D. Thomas

Copyright: 1992, Thomas Investigative Publications, Inc.
All rights reserved.
ISBN: 0-918487-60-9

Other Works By Ralph Thomas

HOW TO FIND ANYONE ANYWHERE
FINDER'S FEE: The Skip Tracer's Text
PHYSICAL SURVEILLANCE TRAINING MANUAL
LEGAL INVESTIGATION TRAINING MANUAL
HOW TO INVESTIGATE BY COMPUTER
PRE-EMPLOYMENT INVESTIGATION
PRE-MARITAL INVESTIGATION
BUSINESS INTELLIGENCE INVESTIGATION
HOW TO MAKE MONEY AS A PROCESS SERVER
HOW TO MAKE MONEY IN AUTO REPOSSESSION
INVESTIGATOR'S DIVORCE COURSE
ADVANCED SKIP TRACE TECHNIQUES
HOW TO FIND CASES ANYWHERE
ELECTRONIC SKIP TRACE TECHNIQUES
INVESTIGATOR'S INTERNATIONAL ALL-IN-ONE DIRECTORY
INVESTIGATOR'S GUIDE TO ONLINE SEARCHING
THE PRACTICE OF PRIVATE INVESTIGATION
INSURANCE DEATH CLAIMS INVESTIGATION

For a catalog of hundreds of books on private investigative techniques, online information services and investigative equipment, send $2.00 to:

Thomas Investigative Publications, Inc.
P O Box 33244
Austin, Texas
78764

MISSING LINKS IN THE JFK ASSASSINATION
Evidence Of Conspiracy And Coverup
By: Ralph D. Thomas

TABLE OF CONTENTS

INTRODUCTION: APPOINTMENT FOR ASSASSINATION

John Kennedy's trip to Texas was a political trip needed to mend fences within the democratic party. Kennedy, even with Johnson on his ticket, barely won the state in 1960. The next Presidential election was less than one year away. The democratic party within Texas was fractionalized. The gap between democratic liberals and democratic conservatives was profound. Senator Ralph Yarborough was considered the leader of the Texas liberals within the democratic party. John Connally is often given credit at the time for holder of the leadership position of the democratic conservatives in Texas. Kennedy was clearly caught in the middle. Although he tried to wear two hats, he tended to be thought of as outside the boundaries by each fraction. Perceived as a liberal by the conservative block, many conservative democrats were threatening to vote republican. The liberal block was unhappy with many of Kennedy's programs and perceived him as a conservative. Kennedy was hoping that this trip would smooth the ruffles of some of these problems as his eyes were on the next Presidential race in which he felt he needed to carry Texas.

Many of Kennedy's advisors didn't like the idea of Kennedy going to Texas from the standpoint that they felt it would be a dangerous trip, especially Dallas. On April 10th, 1963, someone attempted to assassinate conservative General Edwin Walker. On October 24th, 1963 Ambassador Adlai Stevenson visited Dallas. He was spat on and hit on the head with placards. Recently, Vice President Johnson had been to Dallas and encountered a very angry crowd. But Kennedy felt that any trip to Texas must include a stop in Dallas.

The Presidential party arrived in Texas on November 21st, 1963 in San Antonio. Kennedy gave a speech in San Antonio and flew on to Houston. The Presidential party left Houston during the evening hours of November 21st and traveled to Fort Worth. The next morning, the President got up early and read the Dallas Morning News. He saw a copy of a black bordered ad that appeared in the paper that was very unfavorable to the President. He remarked to Mrs. Kennedy how easy it would be for someone to assassinate a President. The time was 10:30, just two hours away from the assassination. Kennedy walked outside the hotel and addressed a small crowd. He then attended a breakfast with Mrs. Kennedy sponsored by the Fort Worth Chamber Of Commerce. The President and his party left Fort Worth in Air Force One for a very short flight to Dallas Love Field. The day was cloudy, gloomy and rainy. When Air Force One landed at Love Field, the sky had cleared and the sun was out. It was determined that the bubble top of the Presidential car would not be needed.

Plans called for a motorcade in Dallas, a luncheon at the Dallas Trade Mart and departure from Dallas to Austin, Texas. Kennedy had planned to spend that evening at the LBJ Ranch near Austin.

The Dallas motorcade consisted of a pilot car that drove several miles ahead of the motorcade on the lookout for any accidents or events that would require a switch in the planned route. The lead car contained both Dallas Police Chief Jesse Curry who was driving, Sheriff Bill Decker who sat in the back seat and Secret Service Agent Lawson who sat next to the police chief in the front. Three motorcycle patrolmen followed the lead car. Following the lead car and motorcycle patrolmen was the open presidential limo known as SS 100 X. Six passengers were in the open vehicle. Secret Service agents Kellerman and Greer sat in the front seat. Governor and Mrs. John Connally sat in the rear jump seats. The President and first lady sat in the back seat. Following the Presidential limo was a secret service car that contained half a dozen secret service agents. Following the Secret Service vehicle was an open convertible carrying Vice President Lyndon

Johnson, Mrs. Lyndon Johnson and Senator Ralph Yarborough. Following the Vice President's car were several cars for the mayor and local congressmen along with press cars and a bus carrying the Presidential staff.

It had been raining during the early morning hours. Officials were concerned about the motorcade. If the rain continued, the bubble top would have to be put on the Presidential vehicle and the crowds along the motorcade route would be very thin. Although the bubble top was not fully bullet proof, it might have prevented the assassination.

The presidential motorcade in Dallas left Love Field and traveled through downtown Dallas. The crowds were heavy. The reception was good. Kennedy had the motorcade stop twice so he could shake hands with the citizens. As the motorcade approached the other end of the downtown area, Mrs. Connally turned around to the President and said, "Mr. President, you can't say that Dallas doesn't love you." The president replied, " No, you certainly can't." That sentence was the last words spoken by the President.

The motorcade was on it's way to a luncheon at the Dallas Trade Mart. The motorcade had come down Main street which is the major street through the middle of downtown Dallas. It made a right hand turn onto Houston and then a sharp left turn onto Elm Street entering a city park area called Dealey Plaza. Elm Street sloped down a small grade through the plaza. Just ahead was a railroad bridge Elm Street passed under. To the right was a grassy knoll that sloped upward to a wooden fence that was landscaped with bushes and small trees. Behind the fence on the top of the grassy knoll was a dirt parking lot and the railroad yard. To the right rear was a seven story building called the Texas School Book Depository Building that was the last tall building the motorcade passed on it's way to the Trade Mart. On top of the building was a clock that indicated the time as 12:30. The motorcade was running about five minutes late because of the stops the President had made to visit with the crowds. Halfway between the Texas School Book Depository Building and the wooden fence at the top of the grassy knoll, Abraham Zapruder was perched on top of a concrete wall with his 8 mm movie camera.

As the Presidential limo approached the railroad bridge called the Triple Underpass, shots rang out and Kennedy slumped down in his seat. Early witnesses said they saw part of the president's head get shot off and saw Governor Connally fall into his wife's lap. Presidential aide David Powers was riding in the Secret Service car directly behind the President. He said that the last shot caused the " sickening sound of a grapefruit splattering against the side of a wall," as it hit the President's head. Mrs. Kennedy jumped out of her seat and tried to climb onto the trunk. Secret Service agent Clint Hill ran from the rear Secret Service car and climbed onto the trunk to help Mrs. Kennedy get back into her seat. By the time he got into a position to see the President he said that he noted the, "right rear portion of the President's head was gone."

Police Chief Curry, who was driving the lead car, picked up the police microphone and said:

> *Go to the hospital, officers, Parkland Hospital, have them stand by. Get men on top of the underpass, see what happened up there, go up to the overpass. Parkland stand by.*
>
> *Notify station five to move all men available out of my department*

back into the railroad yards and try to determine what happened and hold everything secure until homicide and other investigators can get there.

One of the motorcycle patrolmen looked to his right and drove his motorcycle halfway up the bank of the grassy knoll, got off his motorcycle and ran the rest of the way up the hill to the fence. Spectators fell to the ground for cover. Two motorcycle patrolmen, Bobby Hargis and B. J. Martin, riding on the south side and just to the rear of the presidential limo were splattered in the face with blood and a fine mist of brain. Hargis was hit so hard in the face with bits of bone and flesh that he first thought he had been shot.

Both Sheriff Decker and motorcycle patrolman Staruis Ellis saw a bullet hit the pavement as the shots rang out. Secret Service Agent Paul Landis, riding in the follow up car, stated that he thought the shots had come from the front right hand side of the road, the area of the grassy knoll and wooden fence.

(Note that seconds after the shots, the police chief indicated that he thought the shots had come from the overpass or the railroad yard behind the fence and a motorcycle patrol officer got up to the fence area as fast as he could)

(Note also that a Secret Service Agent thought the shots had come from the grassy knoll area and two policemen saw a bullet hit the pavement that, as you will understand later, would rule out the lone gunman theory)

Four minutes after the shots rang out, the UPI newswire began to issue flashes of what had happened:

DALLAS. ....THREE SHOTS WERE FIRED AT
PRESIDENT KENNEDY'S MOTORCADE........

FLASH
KENNEDY SERIOUSLY WOUNDED...........

(News wire instructions)
STAY OFF ALL OF YOU STAY OFF AND KEEP OFF

DOWNTOWN DALLAS TODAY......PERHAPS FATALLY.

BULLETIN:
(DALLAS) SNIPER SERIOUSLY WOUNDED PRESIDENT
KENNEDY IN DOWNTOWN DALLAS TODAY....PERHAPS
FATALLY.

The presidential vehicle roared out of the area and traveled at a high rate of speed to Parkland Hospital. The Secret Service men in the follow-up car directly behind the Presidential car pulled out high powered rifles.

It only took a few minutes to reach the hospital. Connally was pulled from the vehicle. He was covered with blood. Mrs. Kennedy was bent over the President and wouldn't let go of him. A Secret Service agent handed Mrs. Kennedy his coat to put over the President's head. Mrs. Kennedy and the President were also covered with blood. The president had to be pried out of the hands of Mrs. Kennedy. The right section of his head was missing. His eyes were wide open. Kennedy and Connally were rushed into the emergency rooms. Connally was taken to surgery.

Doctor Perry was the first doctor to look at the President. Dr. Perry noted a small wound in the President's throat. He thought it was an entrance wound. He cut open the wound to get a breathing tube down the President's throat. The right section of the head was an open gaping wound. Blood covered the floor and the stretcher and was oozing out of the wound.

Mass confusion persisted. The Vice President was escorted into another room of the hospital closely guarded by Secret Service Agents. Early television reports concerning Vice President Johnson stated that he may have suffered a heart attack as he was observed holding his chest as he left his vehicle and entered Parkland Hospital. However, these reports were in error.

The white leather seats of the Presidential car was covered with blood. Secret Service agents placed the hardtop on the car and kept the news media away from it. Some attempted to wash the back seats of the vehicle which may have provided vital evidence.

About ten minutes after the assassination, local Dallas television station WFAA broke into it's regular program with the news that Kennedy had been shot. The announcement came from a newsman who had been a block from the assassination site and had heard the shots. The newsman ran back to the station which was only a few blocks away just a few minutes after the assassination to report the events. The newsman stated that he heard some reports that he had thought were firecrackers. He said that, by the time the third shot rang out, he identified them as gun shots. The newsman ran into the Plaza area and evidently spotted the Newman family on the ground.

WFAA first reported that shots had been fired from the grassy knoll area or from the Triple Overpass, the railroad bridge that goes over Elm Street. Within a few minutes, WFAA had Mr. and Mrs. William Newman, the first eyewitnesses on the air making statements that the shots had come from behind them, the area of the grassy knoll and picket fence. Both Billy Newman and his wife had been standing on the curb on the north side of Elm Street and stated that they were caught in the line of fire as shots rang out and they fell to the ground.

At 12:40 Walter Cronkite broke into a soap opera that was airing on CBS with a news flash that the President had been shot in Dallas. At this very minute, one of the Secret Service agents at Parkland Hospital asked for a priest. At 1:00, the President was pronounced dead. At 1:13, a Secret Service Agent told Lyndon Johnson that Kennedy had expired and called Johnson "Mr. President" for the first time. At 1:26, Johnson was escorted from Parkland Hospital to Air Force One in an unmarked police car. Local Dallas authorities started planning for an autopsy on Kennedy's body. Secret Service agents objected. Kennedy's body was placed in a coffin and whisked away with Mrs. Kennedy by Secret Service Agents against the advice of local Dallas officials. When Kennedy's body left Parkland Hospital with Mrs. Kennedy and Secret Service agents, Dallas authorities had assumed the body was being taken to the local morgue for an autopsy. Instead, the body was driven directly to Air Force One. At 2:38 Johnson took the oath of office. By 2:47, Air Force One was airborne on it's way back to Washington with Kennedy's body, Mrs. Kennedy and Lyndon Johnson.

At 1:16, a citizen announced that a police officer had been shot in the Oak Cliff section of Dallas on a police radio. At 1:50, Oswald was arrested in a movie theater for murdering the police officer. He quickly became the prime suspect of the President's assassination. He was taken to Dallas Police headquarters and interrogated for a total of twelve hours over the weekend and charged with both the murder of the President and the murder of the police officer.

Sunday, November 24th, Oswald was bein_ .ransferred from the Dallas police station to the county jail. He was being escorted by several police officers in handcuffs in the basement of the Dallas Police Station when he was shot by Jack Ruby at 11:21 A.M. Oswald was rushed by ambulance to Parkland Hospital and expired at 1:07.

(Note: The exact times were taken from time logs of the historical book, *The Death Of A President* by William Manchester.)

THE GOVERNMENT INVESTIGATIONS

Within hours after JFK's assassination, speculation arose concerning the possibility of a conspiracy concerning the murder. In fact, confusion concerning where the shots came from were present only seconds after the shooting. At first, spectators and police officers ran up the grassy knoll as this is where they had thought the shots had come from. Dozens of police officers swarmed the parking lot and railroad yard behind the fence. However, focus of the investigation quickly turned to the School Book Depository.

Rumors about the President's assassination and about a conspiracy were broadcast throughout the world by the news media. J. Edgar Hoover, the director of the FBI, stated within hours that the assassination was the result of a lone gunman by the name of Lee Harvery Oswald although the investigation of the murder was actually under the jurisdiction of the Dallas Police. The body of the President had already been illegally hijacked out of Dallas by the Secret Service without a local autopsy.

As the Dallas police began to conduct it's investigation, they began to obtain pressure from Washington to turn all evidence over to the FBI. A Senate Intelligence Committee determined years later that both President Johnson's office and Hoover's office issued internal statements that said:

> A) *The public must be satisfied that Oswald was the lone assassin.*
> B) *Speculation must be cut off about a conspiracy.*

According to Curt Gentry in his book *J. Edgar Hoover: The Man And The Secrets*, Deputy Attorney General Nicholas Katzenbach sent an internal memo to Bill Moyers, Johnson's press secretary on November 24th a few hours before Oswald was murdered by Jack Ruby. On page 547, Gentry quotes the memo which stated:

> *"It is important that all of the facts surrounding President Kennedy's Assassination be made public in a way that will satisfy people in the United States and abroad that all the facts have been told and that a statement to this effect be made now. The public must be satisfied that Oswald was the assassin; that he did not have confederates who are still at large; and that the evidence was such that he would have been convicted at a trial. Speculation must be cut off."*

Gentry also states on the same page that Hoover placed a call to White House aide Walter Jenkins the hour of Oswald's murder in which Hoover said:

> *"The thing I am most concerned about, and so is Mr. Katzenbach, is having something issued so we can convince the public that Oswald is the real assassin."*

After Oswald's murder by Jack Ruby, President Johnson ordered the Dallas Police to stop it's investigation and turn all evidence over to the FBI. According to a book put out by the Dallas County Historical Foundation called, *The Sixth Floor*, 52% of America believed that the assassination was a plot after Oswald was murdered. At first, Johnson appears to have wanted the

FBI to conduct an investigation and issue it's findings to the public. But on November 29th, 1963 President Johnson created a commission to study the assassination of Kennedy chaired by the Chief Justice of the Supreme Court Earl Warren. The Commission became known as the Warren Commission. Although publicly, the Warren Commission was supposed to have looked into all aspects of the Kennedy assassination, the internal statements made by both Johnson's office and Hoover's office before it's creation would tend to indicate that the real purpose of the Warren Commission was to:

> A) *Issue a report to the public that Oswald was the lone assassin.*
> B) *Cut off speculation that the assassination was the result of a conspiracy.*

Deputy Attorney General Nicholas Katzenbach was the first person to ask Earl Warren to head up an investigative commission concerning the President's assassination but Warren said he would not. The same day, President Johnson summoned Warren to the White House in which he stated that rumors concerning the assassination needed to be dispelled and only the Chief Justice could dispel them. Warren accepted the assignment and left the White House in tears.

Other plans for an investigation of Kennedy's assassination had apparently been changed. On November 25th, Texas Attorney General Waggoner Carr announced that an investigation of the assassination by the state of Texas would be done after the FBI report was completed. After the FBI report and the state of Texas report were in, the President was to appoint a blue ribbon commission to review the findings of both the FBI and the Texas Attorney General's office.

On November 26th, Senator Everett Dirksen issued a statement that said that the United States Senate would investigate the assassination. A few days later, Congressman Charles Goodell stated that the House Of Representatives would conduct an investigation. It was at this point that President Johnson formed the Warren Commission by executive order to apparently put an end to the various investigations. The Warren Commission asked Texas Attorney General Carr to hold off on his investigation until Jack Ruby's trial was over. Carr's office never did conduct an official investigation but Carr was permitted to sit in on the Warren Commission hearings.

The FBI became the investigative body of the Warren Commission. It appears that Hoover had reached his own conclusion about the assassination within hours of it taking place and issued a statement to that effect. This was the crime of the century and Hoover was known throughout America as the number one US crime fighter. Hoover had a reputation for always being right. Naturally, once Hoover made a public statement that Oswald was the lone assassin, he could not go back on that statement. Thus, the FBI started it's investigation with a presumption from the director that Oswald was the lone gunman.

"CLOAKING" THE EVIDENCE STARTS: According to an interview given by Dallas F.B.I. Agent James Hosty to *Investigative Reports* (a cable television documentary on the JFK assassination), the original inditement of Oswald by the Dallas District Attorney's office first stated that Oswald murdered the President in what they termed, an international communist conspiracy. The White House and FBI contacted the district attorney's office and had them change the inditement omitting any reference to a conspiracy. Hosty also stated in the same interview that Oswald's prior trip to Mexico was "cloaked" (covered-up) by the federal government because the government did not want the public to know about the Cuban connection fearing it could spur a world war.

A suspicious statement, then retraction was made to the news media by the Dallas Police Chief Curry concerning prior knowledge of Oswald being in Dallas. In his first remarks he stated that the Dallas Police Department did not know Oswald was in Dallas but it was his understanding that, "the FBI did know." Curry later made a specific verbal statement to the news media retracting his first statement saying that he actually had "no knowledge" concerning whether or not the FBI had known Oswald was in Dallas. Years later, it became public knowledge that FBI agent Hosty not only had an open file on Oswald, not only had interviewed him and/or his wife several times in the months prior to the assassination, he was ordered to destroy a handwritten note Oswald had given him after Oswald was murdered.

The FBI became the investigating arm of the Warren Commission. The FBI went forward with it's investigation based on the presumption that Oswald was the lone assassin which is obvious from the director's first public remarks. It's obvious from the above two paragraphs that the FBI was, at best, attempting to control the information that was released on the assassination. When the Texas attorney general came to the Warren Commission with information that Oswald was an FBI informant, the commission relied on the FBI to investigate itself in this matter and the FBI, of course, stated that Oswald was not an informant. A filtering process seemed to develop in the information gathered by the Warren Commission since it relied on the FBI to develop much of the information.

Members of the Warren Commission were:

> *Earl Warren: Chief Justice (Chairman)*
> *Richard Russell: Democratic Senator: Georgia*
> *Gerald Ford: Republican Congressman: Michigan*
> *Hale Boggs: Democratic Congressman: Louisiana*
> *John S. Cooper: Republican Senator: Kentucky*
> *Allen Dulles: Former Director: C.I.A.*
> *John McCloy: A well known businessman*

The actual commission did little of the investigative work except hold hearings with some of the key witnesses involved in the assassination. The Warren Commission had a staff of several dozen people who assembled the basic facts and interviewed witnesses.

A careful review of all the evidence known today shows that any type of evidence or any type of witness testimony that did not go along with the lone gunman theory was simply ignored by the commission. As you will learn in this investigation, several witnesses who did testify that had testimony that didn't meet the lone gunman theory were either cut off or had their testimony changed in the official transcript. Other witnesses were threatened. The bulk of the witness testimony and evidence that didn't go along with the lone gunman theory was either suppressed or ignored.

According to the *J.F.K. Quick Reference Guide* compiled by Martin Brizil, the only time the complete commission was together all at once was for picture taking ceremonies. None of the seven members of the commission had all been present at any one time during the hearings. The *Quick Reference Guide* gives the following breakdown percentages of members being present:

EARL WARREN: 94%
GERALD FORD: 70%
ALLEN DULLES: 61%
JOHN COOPER: 50%
JOHN MCCLOY: 35%
HALE BOGGS: 20%
RICHARD RUSSELL: 6%

If you read the transcripts of the Warren Commission, you'll learn that the members would continually walk in and out of the hearings.

The commission reports were released in September and October of 1964. Their conclusion was:

> *Acting alone, Lee Harvey Oswald fired three shots from the sixth*
> *floor window of the School Book Depository. No other shots*
> *were fired.*

The Warren Commission report was, at first, hailed as the final conclusion of the assassination. Within weeks, however, people began to find inconsistencies in the report. Two commission members themselves later claimed that the conclusions in the report were not right:

> *SENATOR RICHARD RUSSELL: Said in a television interview*
> *that he never did believe that Oswald acted alone.*

> *CONGRESSMAN HALE BOGGS: Had serious doubts about the*
> *lone assassin theory and called for the resignation of Hoover.*
> *Boggs later died in a plane crash over Alaska.*

Although President Johnson publicly supported the conclusions of the Warren Commission, he cast doubts of his own about it after he retired from public service. In President Johnson's last television interviews before his death with Walter Cronkite, he indicated that Oswald had some suspicious connections of an international nature implying that he didn't completely believe the Warren Commission. In an *Atlantic Magazine* article by Leo Janos in 1973, Johnson is quoted as saying, "I never believed Oswald acted alone."

> *PRESIDENT LYNDON JOHNSON: "I never believed Oswald*
> *acted alone."*

THE CLARK PANELS: Because the Warren Commission relied on drawings of the autopsy performed on Kennedy, public opinion in the US demanded that further investigation be conducted. In 1967, Attorney General Ramsey Clark developed two panels that reviewed various pieces of the medical evidence of the Kennedy assassination that became known as the Clark Panels. These panels determined that the Warren Commission had placed the back wound of the President four inches lower than it should have been. No photographs were provided in their report. When the bullet wound is moved up to it's correct position, the trajectory of the bullet wounds doesn't line up to support the lone assassin theory. Speculation about a conspiracy began to intensify.

THE ROCKEFELLER COMMISSION: In 1975, the Rockefeller Commission was set up to study and investigate illegal activities of the CIA. Although the finding of the Rockefeller Commission supported those of the Warren Commission, it concluded that the CIA had withheld information from the Warren Commission and disclosed illegal domestic intelligence activities the CIA was engaged in which was outside it's official charter.

THE CHURCH COMMITTEE: In 1976 a Senate Committee was formed to study intelligence activities that was chaired by Senator Frank Church. This committee concluded that the intelligence community was not involved in the assassination but concluded several other related points. It determined that the CIA was using members of organized crime in plans to assassinate Fidel Castro. It said also, that the CIA, Secret Service and the FBI all withheld information relevant to the Kennedy Assassination from the Warren Commission. Demand for another formal investigation into the Kennedy assassination grew even more.

THE HOUSE SELECT COMMITTEE ON ASSASSINATIONS: In 1976, thirteen years after the fact, the House Of Representives formed a committee to investigate both the Kennedy and the Martin Luther King assassinations. The committee was actually formed as a result of building suspicion of the American public.

At first the committee looked like it was going to support the Warren Commission findings. Toward the end of the hearings, acoustical experts determined from a radio recording of the assassination that at least four shots were fired and one of those shots had been fired from the top of the grassy knoll behind the wooden fence.

In the late 1970's the Select Committee on Assassinations of the United States House of Representatives published their findings concerning the assassination of John F. Kennedy. The most significant finding can be found in their summary that stated:

> A) *Scientific acoustical evidence establishes a high probability that two gunmen fired at President John F. Kennedy.*
>
> B) *The committee believes, on the basis of the evidence available to it, that the President John F. Kennedy was probably assassinated as a result of a conspiracy.*

After several official government investigations solid evidence is finally established that pointed to more than one gunman which means that the assassination of the President was indeed a conspiracy. The evidence used by the Select Committee was not available in the other investigations, and the technology to make an analysis of the evidence was not known to mankind in the 1960's. The evidence might never have come to light if it had not been for assassination researcher Mary Ferrell. Ferrell is a private citizen of Dallas who has spent her spare time since the event researching the assassination. She knew of a police recording from a motorcycle in the motorcade that was in existence. The events on that day in November had been recorded due to a stuck microphone from a police motorcycle that was in the motorcade. Because of Mrs. Ferrell's efforts, the committee became interested in the recording, obtained possession of it and submitted it to the acoustical sciences firm of Bolt, Beranek, & Newman.

For years, this firm has been established as the top acoustical firm in the United States. This was not the first time the federal government has had a contract with them. They analyzed the gap found on Nixon's famous White House tapes and also recordings made of the National Guards' shooting in the Kent State incident.

In 1978, the acoustical firm made a reenactment of the assassination in Dealey Plaza, the assassination site. The experts established a 95% probability that four shots were fired that day in Dallas. Three of those shots came from the School Book Depository Building. The other shot came from the grassy knoll area. Yet, for years, those who saw puffs of white smoke and thought they saw men lurking with rifles behind the fence on the grassy knoll were judged as having been victims of their own imaginations. At last physical evidence surfaced to prove their memory.

Other related findings by this congressional committee included:

> A) The Federal Bureau Of Investigation failed to investigate adequately the possibility of a conspiracy to assassinate the president.

> B) The Federal Bureau Of Investigation was deficient in its sharing of information with other agencies and departments.

> C) The Central Intelligence Agency was deficient in its collection and sharing of information both prior to and subsequent to the assassination.

> D) The Warren Commission failed to investigate adequately the possibility of a conspiracy to assassinate the President. This deficiency was attributable in part to the failure of the Commission to receive all the relevant information that was in the possession of other agencies and departments of the government.

Although the Select Committee was the government agency that finally and officially stated that JFK was assassinated as a result of a conspiracy, it recommended that the Department Of Justice continue the investigation. The Department Of Justice found that the acoustical evidence was not valid so we are right back were we started as far as official government investigations go.

Going back to the original government investigative body, the Warren Commission, one finds that only information that points to a lone assassin theory is covered. This investigation attempts to cloak the other evidence.

THE KNOLL AND PICKET FENCE AREA

Dealey Plaza is a peaceful place on the outskirts of the busy downtown area of Dallas. Prior to the assassination, it was a quiet place were people could come at noon time to eat their lunch or walk around the park. It is a very beautiful place with three roads coming together like the top of a fork that go under a bridge known as the Triple Underpass. The area is landscaped with grassy knolls, trees and shrubs. The three roads that come together and go under a railraod bridge slope downward with grassy knolls on each side. These three streets are Commerce, Main and Elm Streets. The middle road is Main Street which is, as the name implies, the main street that cuts right through the center of downtown Dallas. Main Street actually runs east and west. Houston Street runs north and south through the west side of the plaza. The street on the north side of Main Street is Elm Street. Elm Street slopes downward and curves around from the intersection of Houston Street. Commerce Street has the same slope and curve as Elm Street on the south side of the plaza. On the north side of Elm Street, a grassy knoll slopes back up to meet a wooden fence. On the other side of the fence is a parking lot and railroad yard. The other side of Dealy Plaza, south of Commerce Street, the same sloping grassy knoll and fence is present but our area of focus will be on the north end of the plaza.

On the north west corner of the plaza sits the School Book Depositoy Building, the last tall building in Downtown Dallas. Between Elm Street and the Book Depository Building on the north side of the plaza, a roadway cuts through the area seperated by a concrete monument and landscaping. This two lane roadway gives one access to the parking area behind the picket fence.

I have spent a great deal of time in Dealey Plaza as many other people, writers, investigators, tourists and researchers have done. The plaza appears just like it did in November of 1963. People linger around smelling and sensing a taste of history. People point around usually at the sixth floor window of the School Book Depository Building and the top of the knoll on the west side of the plaza. Photographs are taken by the hundreds. No one smiles. Everyone has, what appears to me, a puzzled look on their face. It seems to be a place were people come to heal the emotions within them. More serious researchers comb the ground area looking for undiscovered evidence and even open manhole covers and jump inside. Many can be observed with notebooks and legal pads. The serious ones get up on top of the Triple Overpass and gaze back towards the School Book Depository. Most go behind the wooden fence gazing out onto Elm Street.

If one stands behind the fence on the grassy knoll, one finds that not only would a gunman have excellent protection with the fence, you can almost reach out and touch any vehicles going by out on the roadway on Elm Street. If you were behind the fence on the day of the assassination and looked to your rear, you would find a sea of cars that, in about 10 seconds, would provide you with excellent cover. It would be very easy to keep down avoiding detection as you moved your way through the sea of vehicles out of the assassination site. The fence makes you feel as if you are almost in a different place. Besides, you could fire at almost point blank range. Besides the acoustical evidence now developed that points directly toward a conspiracy, is there any other evidence concerning the gunman on the knoll?

ASSASSINATION WITNESSES AROUND THE KNOLL AREA

Dozens of eyewitnesses to the assassination reported seeing people and activity around the picket fence area but were never called as witnesses before the Warren Commission.

JULIA ANN MERCER: MERCER was on her way to work on the day of the assassination. She lived in Dallas and was employed in Fort Worth. About 11:00 A.M., one and one half hours before the assassination, she was traveling through the assassination site. MERCER, although never called as a witness before the Warren Commission, has given the following revealing information to just about every assassination researcher since Mark Lane.

Traveling west on Elm Street in the right hand lane, she came to a stop just before the Triple overpass. She has stated that a green panel truck was stopped with two of it's wheels up on the curb. She described a man that got out of the passenger side of the truck as:

White male, late 20's or early 30's
wearing a grey jacket, brown pants
and a plaid shirt.

MERCER stated that this man came around to the side of the panel truck and opened a compartment. He pulled out a brown case that MERCER thought appeared to be a gun case. She described the case as:

About eight inches on one side tapering down
to about 3 1/2 inches on the other side, brown in
color and about 3 1/2 feet long.

After obtaining the case, MERCER said that this man walked up the embankment of the grassy knoll area. After three or four minutes, MERCER was able to pull around the truck in the inside lane. In doing so, she made eye contact with the other man sitting behind the wheel of the truck. She described him as:

Heavy set, middle aged white male
with a round face wearing a green jacket.

MERCER continued on her route to Fort Worth stopping at a Howard Johnson's for a meal. MERCER stated that she stopped at this location on regular occasions to eat before going on to work. MERCER commented about the men she had just seen to several people including some police officers making a statement to the effect that the Secret Service was not very secret. She left the Howard Johnson's after finishing her meal and was stopped by two police officers who informed her of JFK's shooting. The police officers told her that she would have to come down to the police station with them so her statement could be taken. MERCER has stated that she was questioned by several police officers and several men dressed in suits. After about five hours, they drove her home.

At 4:00 A.M. in the morning, several men identifying themselves as F.B.I. agents woke her up and told her they wanted her to take a look at some photos. The men gave MERCER about twelve photos and asked her to pick out the men she had seen during the green tuck incident. She picked out two of the photos.

The following day, she witnessed RUBY shoot OSWALD on television and she has stated that these were the two men she had seen around the assassination site. MERCER has also stated that these are also the two men in the photos she picked out from the men who identified themselves as F.B.I. agents the day before. The F.B.I. has no record of agents interviewing her and showing her photographs.

DALLAS POLICEMEN CONFIRM GREEN TRUCK: The Warren Commission confirmed the story of a green truck parked on the side of the road. Two police officers stated that they had thought the truck had broken down. However, this event was never reported in the Warren Commission's final report.

JULIUS HARDIE: HARDIE has stated to newspaper reporters that he saw three men on the Triple Overpass as he drove through the area between 9:30 and 10:00 A.M. on the day of the assassination. Two of these three men were carrying "long guns."

PHILLIP HATHAWAY: Hathaway was walking a short distance from the plaza area on Akard Street toward Main Street an hour or so before the assassination. He stated that he saw a man walking toward the plaza area carrying a gun case. He described this man as:

Very Tall, 6' 5", 250 Lbs.
30's with dirty blond hair, crewcut

ERNEST JAY OWENS: Owens stated that he was driving on Wood Street a few blocks from the plaza just an hour or so before the assassination. He also noted a man walking toward the plaza area carrying what appeared to be a "foreign-made rifle." Owens described this man as:

White male, Heavy build
Dark Colored Suit

LEE BOWERS: Bowers was setting up in the railroad tower that was fourteen feet above the ground behind the wood fence as he always had done. He was a towerman for the Union Terminal Company. BOWERS stated that the area behind the fence, which was, at the time, a parking lot for the police department was sealed off to the public at about 10:00 A.M. BOWERS testified before the Warren Commission and was interviewed by assassination researcher Mark Lane. BOWERS described three vehicles moving in the parking lot area just before the assassination. The first vehicle appeared about two hours before the assassination. The vehicle appeared in BOWER'S sight from the corner of the School Book Depository Building. He described the vehicle as a 1959 Olds blue and white station wagon. Bowers noted it had out of state tags, a Goldwater for President bumper sticker and was covered with red mud. The car came into the parking area right near the School Book Building. It circled the area as if it was looking for ways back out of the parking lot. The second car made its appearance a few moments later. This second vehicle was a 1957 Black Ford. BOWERS said the second vehicle "probed" the area three or four minutes and then left the area. A little while later Bowers noted a third vehicle moving in the parking area. This vehicle was a Chevrolet with the same out of state tags, bumper sticker and mud as the first. Bowers said that the driver of this vehicle appeared to be talking on a two way radio as he drove through the parking lot. The last time BOWERS noted the third vehicle he stated that it was pausing right around the picket fence area.

Just before the assassination, Bowers said, that he saw two men standing near the fence area. He described one as:

middle aged-fairly heavy set and
wearing a white shirt with dark pants.

The second man Bowers described as:

a white male in his mid 20's
with a plaid shirt.

BOWERS stated that these men where standing about fifteen feet apart on his side of the fence facing the motorcade as he first noted the motorcade coming into his line of sight. BOWERS also noted that these were the only two strangers in the area as he could identify everyone else as railroad employees.

At the time of the shooting, Bowers said that his eyes were drawn to this area behind the fence. He described what he caught out of the corner of his eye as " a flash of light or smoke." When he looked he did not see anything.

SAM HOLLAND: Holland was on the railroad bridge as the shots rang out. HOLLAND was employed with the Union Terminal Railroad Company and stated before the Warren Commission that he went up on top of the Triple Underpass about 11:45 A.M. to watch the motorcade. HOLLAND stated that there were two Dallas policemen and a plain clothes officer on the overpass. The policeman asked him to identify other people on the overpass which he did. Anyone who was not a railroad employee had been sent away. He told police that he heard four shots, thought they had come behind the wooden fence and saw a puff of white smoke come from some bushes on top of the knoll. Holland ran into the area behind the fence on the grassy knoll after the shots. He said that he noted some footprints in a "tight-grounding" that must have belonged to at least more than one person. Also noted were fresh cigarette butts and mud on a bumper of a station wagon backed into the fence as if someone had just cleaned the mud off their shoes. HOLLAND told assassination researcher Mark Lane back in the 1960's that it took him one or two minutes to reach this area behind the fence after he heard the shots. He stated that the parking lot was "a sea of cars." By the time he reached the area where he saws "puffs of white smoke", there were about fifteen policemen and plain clothesmen in the area.

JAMES L. SIMMONS: SIMMONS was another witness who worked for the railroad and was on the overpass. He stated that when he heard the first shot he was talking to Dallas police officer Foster. He heard a noise that sounded like it came from behind the fence. As he looked up and to his left he saw smoke come out of the bushes at the top of the knoll in front of the picket fence. SIMMONS stated that, like Holland, he ran around behind the fence were he thought the shots had come from. Like Holland he saw mud on a car bumper and lots of footprints. He noted the smell of gunpowder in the area behind the fence.

RICHARD DODD: DODD was also on the Triple Overpass. He stated he also saw puffs of white smoke in the trees on the grassy knoll area and had thought the shots had come from that area. In researcher Jim Marr's book *Crossfire*, he confirms three other witnesses who saw puffs of white smoke come out from the trees on the grassy knoll area.

OTHERS ON TRIPLE OVERPASS: Including Simmons, Dodd and Holland, there were fifteen witnesses on the Triple Overpass. Of those fifteen witnesses, twelve gave statements that at least one of the shots had come from the grassy knoll and picket fence. One two stated that all shots came from the School Book Depository Building and one stated gave no opinion as to the directions of the shots.

JESSE C. PRICE: PRICE was a building engineer for the Union Terminal Annex building that is on the corner of Houston & Commerce. Price stated that on the day of the assassination, he went to the roof of the building to get a better view of the motorcade. He watched the President's limo as it moved into the plaza. As the limo approached the Triple Overpass, he heard shots which he thought had come from behind the picket fence. PRICE signed a statement for police that described a man running behind the fence and had something in his hands which could have been a rifle. He described this person as:

> *young white male,*
> *wearing a white dress shirt*
> *with no tie and khaki colored pants.*

This person ran from the picket fence area into the "sea of cars" described by Holland. In Jim Moore's book, *Conspiracy Of One*, he states that the man Price saw was most likely a witness running in the area after the shots rang out. Moore goes on to point out that asassination researcher Mark Lane got Price to say this for his book *Rush To Judgment*. Price is dead now so he cannot comment on Moore's statement. However, Moore fails to back up these statements by not stating which witness Price would have seen running and fails to mention the statement Price gave to the police. Lane did not get Price to make the statement, Price made the statement of his own free will to law enofrcement officers long before Lane ever interviewed him.

JEAN HILL: HILL had positioned herself halfway between Houston and the underpass on the south side of Elm Street. Moments before the Presidential limo arrived, she saw a van with a sign on the side of the truck that said, "UNCLE JOE'S PAWN SHOP" pass through a police line on a road that goes directly in front of the School Book Depository Building that ends up behind the wooden fence. As the Presidential limo came to the nearest point to Hill, she stated that she stepped out into the street as Kennedy was looking away from her toward the other side of the street. She yelled, " Mr. President..look this way....we want to take your picture." JFK started to turn toward Hill. HILL stated that it was just then that he was first hit and a few seconds later another shot hit him that took off the top of his head. HILL stated that almost everyone fell to the ground but she didn't. She saw a puff of white smoke and flash of light around the bushes at the top of the knoll. She also stated that she noted a person walking very fast in front of the School Book Depository a fraction of a second after the shots were fired. She thought he looked funny or out of place because everyone else was frozen at this second. Hill noted that this man was going toward the area that was behind the wooden fence and she attempted to follow him. She dashed across the street and up the grassy knoll when a man in a business suit stopped her. HILL stated that this man showed her Secret Service identification. The last she saw of this person, he was running toward the railroad tracks where they connected to the Triple Overpass. The following Sunday, she identified this man on television. The man was JACK RUBY.

In November of 1991 I had the opportunity to interview Mrs. Hill. Over the years, Mrs. Hill's testimony has been distorted and impeached. However, she had consistantly stuck to her orginal story. Some researchers have stated that Hill indicates she saw a man behind the picket fence fire the last shot. Hill told me that she has never told anyone this and it is a misquote. She also asked me, "Are you going to tear me apart," before I started the interview. I told her that I would not and that I just wanted to know the truth as I noted many inconsistencies in her statements over the years by various researchers but I believed that these inconsistencies were the result of misquotes on the part of the interviewers. I believe that Hill is sincere when she states that she has been misquoted about seeing a man fire the last shots behind the knoll. She did point out however, that she is certain she saw a puff of smoke and a flash of light and that her impression was that the fatal head shot came from the knoll and picket fence area.

Jim Moore, in his book, _Conspiracy Of One_, attempted to discredit Hill's statements about seeing the man behind the picket fence after the assassination. Moore stated that Hill could not have observed a person walking behind the picket fence area from her location. I have stood on many occassions in the same position that Hill stood during various times when people were behind the fence and I could see the top portion of their body moving along the other side of the fence. I guess if it was a short person, a child or a midget, this might be possible but no one has ever indicated this to be the case. Photographic evidence of the general location of Hill indicates that you can certainly see the top of the fence and, of course, Moore does not present any sort of evidence other than his own impression that would support his statement.

In my interview with Hill, she stated that it was her impression that there were between four and six shots, some of which were very close together. Hill stated that the shots that were very close together were almost on top of each over. Her impression was that the shots were coming from different places, but the headshot, she distinctly recalls, came from the picket fence area. Hill indicated that when the shots first rang out, she thought it was a matter of, "good guys and bad guys." She indicated that she thought others were firing back at the bad guys. This is based on the number of shots and the spacing of the shots. However, as we all now know, no "good guys" fired back at anyone. In Jim Moore's book, _Conspiracy of One_, he states that the plaza is an echo chamber and that the accounts of the number of shots fired above three by many witnesses are because of the echoes. In my interview with Hill and other minor witnesses in November of 1991, the basic impression as to the echoes is that echoes did occur but they were very distinct from the actual shots.

I was present in the area during the re-enactment made for the Oliver Stone movie and I did note echos in the plaza. Over a number of days, I positioned myself in various locations all around the plaza and noted carefully the sounds of the echoes. The echo sound was present from every location. However, the echo sound was very low in volume and completely identifiable from the actual shots. All of the witnesses I have spoken with, including Hill, stated that they also noted echoes with each shot and that the echoes were very distinct from the actual shots. At no time did any witness ever seem confused as to which sounds were the actual shots and which sounds were the echoes. I have also interviewed another witness, Frank Upchurch, who was present at the Warrren Commission re-enactment and Mr. Upchurch stated that he too noticed the echo sounds but they were very low in volume and very distinguishable from the actual shots.

19

On the day of the assassination, Hill was taken to a building for interrogation by two men dressed in suits. Hill reported to these men then that she had heard between four and six shots. One of these men, whom Hill assumed were law enforcement officers, told her that she would be wise to "keep her mouth shut" about hearing between four and six shots.

Hill has been hounded for interviews about the assassination for twenty-nine years. She has given thousands of them. Her story account has remained the same. Hill's story about her being the closest witness to the headshot will be told by Bill Sloan in a new book called *JFK: The Last Dissenting Witness* which will be out in early 1992.

MARY MOORMAN   Hill had been standing in the area with her friend, Mary Moorman. Moorman was taking photographs with a polaroid camera. As each photo was snapped and pulled out of the camera, Moorman would hand the photographs to HILL who would put a fixative on the photograph and place them in her pocket. Just a split second before Kennedy was hit by the first shot, Moorman had snapped a photograph. This is one of two photographs taken that reveal a figure located just behind the fence. In photos made just seconds later, this image is gone. The House Select Committee had a computer enhancement done of this photograph by experts who confirmed that the image reveals tones of color that indicate it to be a human figure. The computer enhancement reveals what looks like a photograph of a man holding a long object in his hands. Assassination researchers have coined this mystery, "The Badgeman photograph," because the image looks like a photo of a man dressed in a police uniform with a badge. (We will get into this photograph under the Arnold caption.)

MOORMAN has been interviewed on local television stations in Dallas, Texas and by prominate assassination researcher and attorney Mark Lane. I obtained recorded remarks made by MOORMAN through the video newsclips made of local television interviews in the Dallas area and with interviews recorded in Mark Lane's video *The Plot To Kill JFK: Rush To Judgment*. I conducted Reverse Speech tests (which we will go into later) on all of Moorman's remarks and found her to be telling the truth.

JOHN MARSHELL SMITH   Smith was a police officer stationed in the area. A woman came running up to him yelling that someone was shooting the President from behind the wooden fence on the knoll. Smith ran to the area and smelled gun powder behind the fence. As he moved from car to car he found a stranger and demanded that this person show him identification. Smith had his gun drawn. This person reached into his coat pocket and produced a Secret Service I.D. It has long been established that there were no Secret Service Agents that remained at the assassination site as all traveled with the Presidential car to Parkland Hospital.

THE WILLISES   Phil and Marilyn Willis as well as Rose Willis (their daughter) were standing up towards the eastern corner of Houston and Elm. Rose Willis, the young child, had been running along side the President's vehicle as he rolled through the plaza. She said that she caught a glimpse of someone who was standing behind the wooden fence who seemed to disappear almost instantly. Phil Willis snapped a photograph just as the shots rang out which were published in the Warren Commission Report and widely circulated. The photograph shows Kennedy starting to bring his arms up towards his head. Willis has made statements to many researchers that he noticed a man in the photograph standing near the School Book Depository that looks like Jack Ruby. However, the Warren Commission cropped this photograph so the person Willis describes as Ruby would not be seen. Altough Mr. and Mrs. Willis have stated that they thought the shots came from the School Book Depository Building, their daughter thought that at least one shot had come from the grassy knoll and fence area.

GORDON ARNOLD AND THE BADGEMAN PHOTOGRAPH

Arnold was a twenty-two year old service man just out of basic training who had gone downtown to watch the presidential motorcade. He was recently interviewed by *Investigative Reports*, a cable television program that produced a four hour long documentary on the Kennedy Assassination which aired in the fall of 1991 on the Arts and Entertainment channel. According to the program, this was Arnold's first filmed interview. Arnold stated that he had parked in a downtown parking lot which was located west of the School Book Depository Building and walked through the area which was then a dirt parking lot and railroad yard behind the picket fence area. He attempted to gain access to the railroad bridge to film the motorcade by crossing over a steampipe but was stopped by a man dressed in a dark suit. This man produced government I.D. and told Arnold that he could not come up on the bridge. With his interviews with *Investigative Reports*, he stated that the I.D. that this man produced was C.I.A. Identification. In interviews with other researchers, he said the identification was Secret Service. After being denied access to the bridge area, Arnold then walked along the back side of the picket fence and found a good location to film the motorcade from the back side of the wooden fence. The same man came up to him again and told him that he could not remain behind the picket fence either. Arnold then walked around the the front side of the fence which is the grassy knoll area and positioned himself in a suitable location to film the motorcade.

Arnold stated that he was filming the motorcade as the Presidential vehicle passed in front of him when he heard a rifle shot and a bullet "whiz" by his left ear. Arnold says he fell to the ground and heard several other reports. He heard another shot and bullet go right over his head. Arnold has been unspecific on how many shots he heard but he has stated with certainty that one shot went right past his left ear before he hit the ground and another shot went right over his head after he was on the ground and he believes that these shots came from behind the picket fence.

Just after the assassination, Arnold stated in his interview with *Investigative Reports* that a man dressed as a police officer came from a direction that would indicate that this officer had been behind the wooden fence. This man had a police uniform on and kicked Arnold asking him if he was taking pictures. The man had a gun in his hand and took the film that was in Arnold's camera. Arnold related that he thought it odd that the man was dressed in a police officer's uniform but had dirty hands. The man, according to Arnold, was shaking. After confronting Arnold and obtaining his film, this man walked off in the direction of the School Book Depository Building.

Arnold's story did not surface for many years. Three days after the assassination, he was sent to Alaska for eighteen months as a member of the armed forces. Arnold was, at first, hesitant to talk about these events as they didn't go along with the official version of the Warren Commission. Years after the assassination, Arnold was interviewed by a few assassination researchers but pro-

Warren Commission spokesmen pointed to the fact that, although many photographs were taken of the area, Arnold didn't show up in any of them. It was not until Dallas researcher *Jack White* started his painstaking study of assassination photographs that he identified the shape of a man on the grassy knoll holding what looks like a camera in his hands wearing a summer military uniform that proof of Arnold's presence on the knoll was found. Because of Jack White's work on the badgeman photograph, the record finally proves that Arnold was present on the Knoll.

The badgeman photograph contains images behind the picket fence that have been enhanced by the work of Dallas photographic expert *Jack White* after decades of study. They were taken by Mary Moorman. White points out that the photograph is a small polaroid type photograph and the area in question behind the picket fence is a square area of less than one eighth of an inch by one eighth of an inch. He has worked with this photograph for years. He was called as a witness during the House Select Committee hearings and the committee determined that the photograph contains flesh tones of a human. White has developed an enhanced version of the badgeman photograph that shows what appears to be a white male behind the fence wearing a police uniform with a man standing next to him wearing what looks like a hardhat. The man in the police uniform appears to be involved in some activity and the position of his arms and face look as if he is pointing a rifle. There is what seems to be a muzzle blast (white spot) on the photograph. On the front side of the fence is the image of a man in what looks like a summer military uniform falling or leaning to his right.

During the interview with *Investigative Reports*, Arnold was shown enhanced blowups and colorized versions of the badgeman photograph. Without prompting, Arnold pointed to the men behind the fence and stated that the man with the police uniform appeared to be firing a weapon where the muzzle blast occurred. He further commented that the man with the hardhat on looked to him like he was dressed in a railroad uniform and that he had seen such a man in the area earlier. Arnold stated that the image in front of the fence was him. Upon his examination of the White photographs, Arnold became very upset stating that, if he had known in advance of the photographic evidence he was shown, he would not have done the interview. Towards the end of the video, Arnold was almost in tears.

In the course of developing *Missing Links*, I obtained a tape recording of the Arnold interviews done with *Investigative Reports* and performed deception/detection testing with his statements using the new investigative technique, Reverse Speech. I will go into Reverse Speech in later parts of this investigation but the point I want to make is that no deception is indicated in Arnold's statements and this test confirms that Arnold is telling the truth.

In November of 1991, Tom Wilson, a photographic computer image processing expert presented his analysis of the badgeman photograph to the JFK Assassination Symposium, a group of researchers, writers and experts on the subject. Being present at this historical event, I was able to see the photographic evidence Wilson presented and hear his remarks. Wilson was able to scan the badgeman photograph into a computer image and manipulate this image through various means. One of the processes he is able to conduct is to positively identify metal objects, and flesh tones. Wilson presented the following findings concerning the badgeman photograph:

> *A) HUMAN BEHIND THE FENCE: Flesh tone studies were done and Wislon concludes that the upper portion of a human is present in the photograph.*

B) BADGE ON THE HUMAN: The object thought to be a badge is indentified as a metal object and has a head of an eagle at the top.

C) THE HUMAN IS HOLDING AND FIRING A RIFLE: The object thought to be a rifle is identifed as a metal object and the flash in the photograph is smoke from the muzzle blast.

D) HUMAN IN THE FRONT PORTION OF FENCE: Wilson says that Arnold is in the photograph 27 feet away from the badgeman on the other side of the fence and that Arnold would have been in the direct line of fire if he had not hit the ground.

BILLY NEWMAN AND FAMILY: BILLY NEWMAN was a local electrician who had taken the day off and took his spouse and two small children to downtown Dallas to see the President. The NEWMANS were located on the north side of Elm Street in the eastern section of the grassy knoll which was east and south of the location of Arnold. The Newmans were standing on the curb as the Presidential motorcade went by. Both Mr. and Mrs. NEWMAN and their two small children were approached by newsmen from local television station WFAA Television as they were laying on the ground seconds after the assassination. The newsmen took the NEWMAN'S back to the television station and put them on the air about fifteen minutes after the assassination took place. BILLY NEWMAN stated on television that he and his family were on the curb as the President went by. He stated that he believed that the shots came from back up on the mall which was behind him and to the right. Mrs. NEWMAN stated that she had thought the shots came from the same direction. The NEWMANS dropped to the ground on top of their two small children. The location given by these witnesses of the location of the shots, track back to the top of the grassy knoll area and picket fence.

BEVERLY OLIVER: Oliver was standing on the other side of the roadway on the same side that Marry Moorman was on but a little more west into the plaza. Oliver is another witness that did not surface for many years. She became an unidentified witness from photographic evidence assassination researches coined as "the babushka lady". Years after the assassination, Oliver surfaced and started to talk. Her eyewitness account has been well documented in Jim Marrs' book *Crossfire*, the Groden/Livingstone work, *High Treason* and interviewed for the cable television documentary done by *Investigative Reports* and aired on the Art and Entertainment channel in the fall of 1991.

OLIVER consistently states that she was taking 8 mm movies of the presidential motorcade and continued to film as the shots rang out. She says that, although she heard loud reports, she did not think these sounds to be gunshots until she noted the top of the President's head come off. OLIVER also states that she believes the shots came from the area behind the wooden fence on top of the grassy knoll and saw a figure of a man behind the fence. She also states that she noted the white smoke and flash of light come from the area around the fence as many other witnesses related.

In an interview with assassination researcher *G. Gray Shaw*, OLIVER stated that a few days after the assassination, an FBI agent came to talk to her and took Oliver's undeveloped film stating that it would be returned within ten days. In my talks with G. Gary Shaw, now head of the *JFK Assassination Research Center* in Dallas, Texas, Shaw has stated that he is certain of OLIVER'S remarks to him. OLIVER told SHAW that the F.B.I. agent who took the film was Regis Kennedy. The film has never surfaced, but OLIVER believes that she had taken the best shots of the picket fence area during the time that the shots were being fired.

OLIVER was a stripper at a nightclub called The Colony Club which was right next door to Jack Ruby's club. She has stated that she knew Jack Ruby and that Ruby introduced her to his friend "Lee Oswald from the CIA" shortly before the assassination. OLIVER has given explanations as to why it took so long for her to come forward concerning her testimony. During the interview with *Investigative Reports,* she stated that she knew that many of the witnesses connected to the assassination were being forever silenced through strange deaths and she, "did not want to become another statistic."

Like the Arnold interviews, I conducted tests on the OLIVER statements made to *Investigative Reports* and the tests show that OLIVER is telling the truth.

JOHN TILSON   Tilson was another policeman who was off duty at the time. He happened to be on the other side of the bridge from the knoll area when he heard the first report of the assassination come over his police radio. Tilson had his daughter with him and he was on his way to pick up his other daughter who was in the downtown area to watch the motorcade. As he approached the plaza area from the south, he noted a man slipping and sliding down the railroad embankment. Tilson stated that this man put something into the back seat of a black car and then drove off. Tilson described this man as:

Stocky build, 5 '9", 185 to 195 lbs,
wearing a dark suit.

Just after sighting this man, he saw the black Presidential limo pull through the underpass. He noted that everyone was running into the plaza area, but the man he saw was running away. Tilson attempted to follow the subject but lost the tail. He did report that it had out of state tags and his daughter wrote down the tag number that was called in to the homicide division of the Dallas police. After reporting the tag number, Tilson disposed of it. No record of whom he spoke with or what became of the information he reported has ever been found. Tilson's account is corroborated through his daughter.

ED HOFFMAN   Hoffman was traveling on the Simmons Freeway on the day of the assassination. As he approached the plaza area, he noted several vehicles pulled over to the side of the highway and remembered that the Presidential motorcade was about to pass this location. He pulled over to the shoulder of the highway and exited his vehicle to watch the event. In order to obtain the best view, he started walking along the freeway. Hoffman was totally deaf so he was not aware of the sounds from the motorcade as it passed through the plaza. He reached an area that was about 200 yards from the parking lot behind the wooden fence in the plaza area. Due to the highway elevation, he was actually about one story up in the air. Hoffman noted a man running behind the fence area carrying a gun. The man was described by Hoffman:

wearing a dark suit and overcoat.

He ran from the fence area toward the railroad tracks and tossed a rifle to another man just at the end of the wooden fence and railroad tracks meet. The second person was dressed in what looked like railroad workman clothes. The railroad worker took the rifle and ducked behind a railroad switch box and then took the rifle apart placing it in what looked to Hoffman like a typical railroad worker's tool box. The railroad worker then walked at a slow rate of speed toward the railroad tower. The man in the dark suit and trench coat turned around and ran about halfway along the back side of the picket fence. He then stopped running and started walking slowly toward the corner of the fence. A moment later, the Presidential limo came into Hoffman's line of sight and he noted that the President was lying down in the back set covered with blood. The Secret Service follow-up car was right behind it. He waved his hands and started running toward the presidential cars. A Secret Service agent in the second car pulled out what appeared to be a machine gun and pointed it at Hoffman. Hoffman stopped in his tracks and watched the motorcade speed off toward the hospital at a high rate of speed.

Hoffman attempted to tell a policeman on the railroad overpass what he had witnessed but the policeman could not understand him and walked away. Hoffman got back in his vehicle and traveled around to the parking lot behind the wooden fence looking for the man in the overcoat or the railroad worker. It's hard to understand why the area was not sealed. But Hoffman was able to freely enter the parking lot, drive around and exit without being stopped. He drove to the FBI office and left his name with a secretary explaining what he saw. He was never contacted.

DESCRIPTION, COMPARISON, ANALYSIS AND CORROBORATION OF EYEWITNESS DESCRIPTIONS

You will note that several of these witnesses provided descriptions of suspect men around the picket fence. When we compare them to each other, we have several positive matches. These positive matches tend to corroborate each other.

JULIA ANN MERCER

heavy set, middle aged white male with a round face wearing a green jacket.

white male, late 20's or early 30's wearing a grey jacket, brown pants and a plaid shirt.

LEE BOWERS

middle aged-fairly heavy set and wearing a white shirt with dark pants.

The second man Bowers described as: a white male in his mid 20's with a plaid shirt.

NOTE: We have almost a complete match concerning the description of Mercer and Bowers. Both described a heavy set middle aged man and a younger male with a plaid shirt.

JESSE C. PRICE
young white male, wearing a white dress shirt, with no tie and khaki colored pants.

JOHN TILSON
(MAN RUNNING DOWN EMBANKMENT ON OTHER SIDE OF RAILROAD TRACKS RIGHT AFTER SHOOTING)

Stocky build, 5 '9", 185 to 195 lbs, wearing a dark suit.

NOTE: This description matches that description of the heavy set male reported by Mercer and Bowers.

HOFFMAN

wearing a dark suit and overcoat.

NOTE: This description matches Tilson's description.

OFFICIALS IN THE MOTORCADE: The police chief, who was riding in a lead car just in front of the presidential car made the remark on the radio "to get all men up on the grassy knoll area to see what is going on", just as the shots rang out. Governor Connally, who was riding in the presidential vehicle and was also wounded, thought that more than one person was firing. He has stated again and again that he thought the presidential vehicle had been caught in a "crossfire." He has also stated that he thought the shots came from the grassy knoll area. His last comment before losing consciousness was. *"Oh my God! They are going to kill us all!."* Mrs. Kennedy who was seated next to the President made the remark," *They have killed my husband. I have his brains in my hands."* Both Mrs. Kennedy and Connally used words that described more than one gunman firing the shots.

Two Sercret Service Agents, and one Presidential aide, all riding behind the President in the motorcade indicated shots from the grassy knoll. Secret Service Agent Paul Landis, Jr. was riding on the rear right runningboard of the third motorcade car stated to the Warren Commission that his first reaction concerning the direction of the shots were, "towards the the front right-hand side of the road," the area of the grassy knoll and picket fence. Thomas Johns, an agent riding in the rear of motorcade vehicle number five stated to the Warren Commision concerning the location of the shots, "on the right-hand side of the motorcade from the street, a grassy knoll area sloped upward to a small two or three foot concrete wall with sidewalk area." This too describes the area of the picket fence on top of the grassy knoll. Presidential aide David Powers riding in motorcade vehicle number three stated to the Warren Commission that he had a, " fleeting impression that the noise appeared to come from the front."

PUFFS OF WHITE SMOKE AND FLASHES OF LIGHT: There were no less than ten eye witnesses who stated that they saw puffs of white smoke and a flash of light come from the knoll and fence area. Over the years, a number of people have attempted to explain away the puffs of smoke and flashes of light. The first explanations stated that a steam pipe ran between the railroad and picket fen area and that the white smoke came from the steam pipe. This makes no sense for several reasons. First, the steam pipe was quite a distance from the area described and the wind conditions that day determined by studying weather reports would not in any way indicate that steam could be carried from the steam pipe in a northern direction and to the east. Secondly, no evidence has ever surfaced that a leak in the steam pipe was ever present. Third, even if the steam pipe would have had a leak, which it did not, this could not explain flashes of light. Opponents of the Warren Commission attempted to state that guns do not emit puffs of white smoke. The House Assassination Committee addressed this very question. Experts more than confirmed that guns do indeed emit smoke.

In Jim Moore's book *Conspiracy Of One*, he states that he believes and has noticed that the puffs of smoke observed by many witnesses were likely the result of someone starting a vehicle behind the picket fence. In my opinion, I find this explanation no more creditable than the "steam pipe" story or the "rifles don't give off puffs of smoke" story. I have spent many hours in the grassy knoll area in the summer, winter, fall and spring, in the morning, noontime and evening. I have watched people come and go from the parking lot behind the wooden fence and at no time did I ever observe exhaust fume from vehicles being started ever present itself at the top of the fence. As a professional investigator who has done thousands of physical surveillances in which I have observed and filmed subjects entering and starting vehicles from behind fences, I have never noticed with my eyes or observed in my films any smoke from exhaust fumes come up over the tops of a fence in a way that could be mistaken for gunshots. Even if this was true, you can not reasonably expect to account for a person starting a vehicle at the exact time the Presidential motorcade was passing through the area and during a time when shots rang out unless this vehicle had something to do with the sniper behind the fence. At no time is there any indication from any of the dozens of witnesses any information about a vehicle starting and leaving the area as Jim Moore indicates and Moore fails to even mention any explanation of the flash of light.

GENERAL WITNESS CONSENSUS OF THE DIRECTION OF THE SHOTS: Moore makes the statement in *Conspiracy Of One* indicating that people around the School Book Depository building generally thought the shots had all come from the building or nearby the building and people deeper in the plaza generally throught that the shots had come from the grasy knoll. Altough Moore provides no data to back up this statement, I relied on a detailed chart and blueprint prepared by Gregory L. Brooks. I purchased this blueprint chart at the JKF Assassination Symposium in Dallas Texas, November 16th, 1991. Before making the purchase, I spoke with dozens of experts who attended the symposium who had studied the blueprint as to it's validity and completeness. Everyone I spoke with who can be considered experts on the subject confirmed that the Brooks blueprint is very good.

I notice that Brooks identifies fourteen people standing on the sidewalk in front of the School Book Depository Building. Of those fourteen people, seven identified the shots as coming from the building and seven identifed at least one shot as coming from the knoll area. The Moore statement does qualify the location of the shots as not only from but near the building and I submit to you that the area behind the fence is near the School Book Depository Building.

Of the six witnesses standing on the sidewalk or grassy knoll area directly in front of the School Book Depository Building in the Brooks blueprint, three describe shots coming from the grassy knoll, two from the School Book Depository Building and one had no opinion. Of the five witnesses on the Brooks blueprint standing in the street in front of the building, two indicated at least one of the shots came from the knoll/fence area, one from the School Book Depository Building and one stated that shots came from both locations.

Of eleven witnesses charted on the Brooks blueprint standing to the south of the School Book Depository Building on Houston Street, seven thought the shots had come from the knoll/fence area, two from the School Book Depository Building and one indicated that shots came from both locations.

Of twenty-four witnesses standing on the north side of Elm Street just east of the Stemmons highway sign on the Brooks chart, eleven stated that the shots came from the picket fence knoll area, four thought the shots had come from the School Book Depository Building, one from both locations, and seven either could not make a judgment or their opinion is not known.

Of the ten witnesses charted on the blueprint located west of the Simmons Highway Sign on the north side of Elm Street, seven indicate that the shots came from the grassy knoll/fence area, three either gave no opinion or their opinion is not known and none indicted shots from the School Book Depository Building.

Of the ten witnesses charted on the Brooks blueprint standing in the grassy knoll area on the south side of Elm Street and past the general frontage of the School Book Depository Building, six stated that the shots came from the knoll/picket fence area, three from the School Book Depository Building and the opinion of one is not known.

Of the fifteen witnesses documented on the Brooks blueprint located on the Triple Overpass, twelve gave statements that the shots came from the knoll/fence area and only one stated that they came from the School Book Depository Building. The other witness either did not have an opinion of the direction of the shots or his opinion was not known.

In every location documented above, the majority opinion of the witnesses are shots from the grassy knoll/picket fence area except in front of the School Book Depository Building in which the opinion is split 50/50. Therefore, the statement that people deep in the plaza tended to feel the shots came from the School Book Depository Building and the people who were located deeper in the plaza thought the shots came from the knoll/fence area is not exactly correct from my analysis. My analysis is that the overall general opinion based on two hundred and sixty-six witnesses charted on the Brooks blueprint is that the shots came from the picket fence/knoll area although a minority thought the shots had come totally from the School Book Depository Building. Here is the total breakdown of people in the plaza watching the motorcade:

96 SHOTS FROM THE KNOLL
45 SHOTS FROM THE SCHOOL BOOK DEPOSITORY BUILDING
 5 FROM BOTH THE KNOLL AND BUILDING
32 UNKNOWN

ABRAHAM ZAPRUDER AND THE ZAPRUDER FILM: Zapruder was standing on the north side of the plaza from Elm Street on top of a cement wall taking 8 mm homes movies. His movie became one of the most famous pieces of evidence in the Kennedy Assassination. What the Zapruder Film shows and the way in which the film was handled is puzzling at best.

In conducting the work found for Missing Links, I had purchased a complete set of video news reels on the entire television coverage of local Dallas television station WFAA. On the afternoon after the assassination, WFAA located Abraham Zapruder who had taken the famous 8 mm footage and interviewed him on the air. The announcer stated, after they had interviewed Zapruder, that they would develop the film and show it later. That never happened. The television station states that they found out after the announcement that they would air the film that they were not in the possession and did not have the equipment to develop 8 mm film. Zapruder eventually sold the film to Life Magazine and the footage was kept from the public for years.

The film shows details of Kennedy being struck at least two times. First, he starts to bring his hands up to his throat after he is apparently hit either in the back or in the front in the throat. In a later chapter we will examine evidence that would indicate that the first shot was a front wound which would mean that the first shot didn't come from the rear. A few seconds after the first shot, the front right section of Kennedy's head explodes. At no time is there any indication that this bullet first struck Kennedy in the rear. A mass of blood and brain tissue can clearly be seen in the right front of his head in the blow-ups but no indication of any wound is present towards the rear of the head. Kennedy's body is thrown backwards and to the right and his head snaps violently backwards. Matter resulting from the headshot is clearly seen to travel backwards and to the left. This can be confirmed by motorcycle patrolman Bobby Hargis riding on the south side of the President's vehicle and to the rear who was splattered in the face with a fine mist of blood and brain tissue from the headshot. In fact, he was hit so hard that he, at first, thought he was hit. It can also be confirmed by Mrs. Kennedy's reaction when she jumped up out of her seat, turned around and attempted to pick up a piece of the President's skull that had gone towards the rear. At no time during the headshot is there any evidence in the film that would indicate that this fatal shot hit Kennedy from the rear. All photographic evidence and body movement would indicate that the shot came from the right front of Kennedy's position.

The important point about all this is that if the President's head and body moved backwards and to the left and if matter from the headshot traveled backwards and to the left, this shot did not come from the rear but from the right front unless, for some reason, God decided to suspend the laws of physics for this split second. Sight observation of the President's head wound reveals no wound towards the rear of the head and, again, unless God suspended known scientific law, the President was hit from the front. When you look at the area of the assassination site, a six year old can determine that a shot from the front right section of the President would track back to the area of the grassy knoll and picket fence.

Pro-Warren Commission spokespersons have always explained these things away by saying that this was a common trauma spasm reaction but experts in these matters say otherwise. We have to remember that these same spokespersons were the same people who explained away all the witnesses who saw a puff of white smoke state that rifles don't admit puffs of white smoke. Evidently, these people failed to watch the film of the Warren Commission's reenactment of the shooting from the sixth floor window in the School Book Depository Building where "white smoke" is evident when the shots were fired and have failed to listen to all the rifle and ballistics experts who state the opposite.

For years, few people were permitted to view the Zapruder film and any information that came out about it seemed to be a white wash. Life magazine wrote an article about the film but the article stated that Kennedy had jumped up in his seat, turned around towards the rear of the vehicle and that is how the shooting occurred but this was a bold face lie. Kennedy never jumped up in his seat and turned around towards the rear. In dealing with the Warren Commission, the FBI inverted two stills of the Zapruder film making it look as if the President's body moved forward instead of backwards after the fatal head shot. The Warren Commission did not publish any significant frames from the Zapruder film stating that it was in the best interest of the Kennedy family not to do so.

The Zapruder Film was first made public during the Clay Shaw Conspiracy Trial in New Orleans through the efforts of District Attorney Jim Garrision which we will go into later but I believe that it is important to point out that Life Magazine and the Federal Government attempted to fight it's release. My observations are that both the federal government and Life Magazine did not want the Zapruder Film made public for two reasons. First, they didn't want any evidence to surface that would indicate a shot came from the grassy knoll. Secondly, both the FBI and Life magazine had already attempted to cover-up what the film revealed.

I was finally able to obtain a copy of the Zapruder Film on video which is the enhanced version made for the House Select Committee on Assassinations which contains slow motion frames, blow-up frames and so forth. It's important to note that the video equipment common in the average American's home today was not common equipment at the time of or years after the assassination occurred. You really could not take 8 mm motion picture film with standard equipment and freeze frames like you can now do with standard video equipment. Thus, I was able to do some interesting studies with the Zapruder Film with standard video equipment that could not have been conducted in the 1960's unless one had access to expensive state of the art equipment. Aside from the fact that the Zapruder Film reveals that the fatal headshot came from the President's right front (the grassy knoll and picket fence area), I found several other revealing things in the film.

Zapruder was filming the motorcade as it turned onto Elm Street from Houston Street. Right before the presidential vehicle comes into view, two motorcycle officers are observed. As they approached the turn onto Elm Street from Houston, one motorcycle did not turn onto Elm and traveled out of the line of view of Zapruder's camera. As this patrolman was going out of view of the Zapruder camera, the second patrolman made the turn but continued to look at the first motorcycle patrolman that didn't turn. It appears to me that the motorcycle patrolman that did turn is looking at the one that didn't wondering what he was doing. At first, I was puzzled until I studied other photographs of the Plaza. I found that Houston Street runs East and West right by the School Book Depository Building but that there was a road block and crowd of people blocking Houston Street that was about in line with the front of the School Book Depository Building. There was also blockage of people in the street that would not permit anyone from turning east onto Elm instead of west into the assassination site. This leaves only one place for the patrolman to have gone and that is up a side street just past Elm which is a little road that travels in front of the School Book Depository Building and ends up behind the picket fence area on top of the grassy knoll. To this date, I have been unable to locate any witness testimony that was paying any attention to the motorcycle patrolman who didn't turn South onto Elm Street as everyone's attention was drawn to the Presidential car. However, I suspect that the motorcycle patrolman who didn't turn could have been the man in the photograph known as the badgeman photograph although no other information could be located that would point to this.

The second funny thing about the Zapruder Film I noted was found shortly after the Presidential Motorcade made the turn onto Elm Street. A splice in the film is present. Documented evidence reveals that Life Magazine spokespersons have stated that this splice resulted from normal wear and the film had broken from extended viewing. I would wonder, however, who was seeing this extended viewing.

Although the first splice in the film is understandable and explanation given believable, the second splice I found in the film is not. There has always been this rumor that bullets hit a highway sign that was on the right side of the highway on Elm Street just as the President's vehicle passed in front of it. This story has several footnotes about it in many of the assassination works that have been published. The story goes that the day after the assassination, the sign was removed and had never seen the light of day or every explained. On the back cover of Forgive My Grief by Penn Jones, an overhead photograph of Dealey Plaza was published which was taken from an airplane on November 23rd, 1961, the day after the assassination. The sign is not present in this photograph. But the Zapruder Film throws a great deal of light on this story.

Zapruder was positioned behind the sign and as he panned his camera down the street as the President's vehicle went by, the vehicle disappears for a few seconds behind the highway sign. It's evident in the film that the President is not wounded before he disappears under the sign. It's obvious that he has been hit by the time he reappears on the other side of the sign. But the curious point is that another splice and ablation in the film occurs just after the President disappears behind the highway sign and some unusual activity concerning the sign is taking place. Hours of viewing this section of the Zapruder Film frame by frame and in slow motion of the blow-up shots reveal to me that the sign starts to buckle right before and just after the splice. What is even more puzzling is that this ablation is very different from the first one. The first splice contains a small black line but the second splice contains a much wider ablation that doesn't seem to be a black line at all but more of an ablation that appears to be done on purpose. In frames directly after the splice, you can clearly see what looks like debris coming off the back of the sign with these little white lines traveling around just as if something had smashed into the back of the sign. Of course, if the back of the sign was hit by a bullet that missed the president, the shot would have had to come from the grassy knoll and picket fence area and could, in no way, have come from the School Book Depository Building.

If the first splice was a legitimate break, I find it hard to believe that the same thing could have happened a few frames later at the exact frame in which questions need to be answered but that seems to happen a great deal in the Kennedy Assassination. In watching a less revealing film called the Bronson Film taken from the other side of the plaza, I find that there is a splice in this film at an exact frame in which the President was supposed to have been hit in the head.

In November of 1991, Tom Wilson, a computer image processing expert, presented his study of the Zapruder film at the JFK Assassination Symposium in Dallas Texas. Wilson conducted gray scale stripping which involves stripping away different shades of gray. This process can strip a photograph down to it's grain. What Wilson found through this process is a large section of the grassy knoll behind the presidential vehicle that has been touched up.

Wilson was also able to conduct a test of bone fragment and tissue movement of the fatal headshot.

This image analysis revealed that the tissue and bone fragment particals at the second of impact occured in the right frontal portion of the president's head. At no time is there any indication of anything happening at the back or rear of the President's head.

Through computer analysis of individual frames of the Zapruder film, Wilson was also able to conduct color matching of blood. This was done for both the headshot and the throat wound. Wilson concluded that both the head wound and that wound were likely intrace wounds.

The fourth thing I noted about the Zapruder Film was further touching up of the Connally wound that I will go into in the chapter on the Magic Bullet Theory.

CORROBORATION OF THE SHOTS FIRED FROM THE PICKET FENCE

Based on the above nineteen eyewitness accounts, and the photographic evidence examined I conclude that there was a man behind the picket fence with a rifle who fired the fatal shot that killed the President. In order to put the puzzle together correctly however, we will not rely solely on just one person's testimony or one photograph. That is, let us corroborate the evidence with other pieces of information so our conclusion will not be drawn from just one piece of evidence or one statement. Although other researchers have done this and many of the government investigations have done this, I wanted to firm up any piece of evidence or statement so it would fit correctly into the puzzle and be rock solid which is the way in which evidence is supposed to be looked at. Putting the complete piece of the puzzle together in this manner, let us review and see what we have.

A) The House Assassinations Committee concluded that there is a ninety-five percent chance that a shot was fired from the picket fence. This corroborates the other evidence, both photographic and eyewitness accounts presented here.

B) MERCER saw two man at the edge of the grassy knoll carrying what looked like a rifle case towards the wooden fence area one and one half hours before the assassination. She was interviewed by FBI agents who permitted her to view photographs in which she identified one of the men as RUBY and the other man as OSWALD. Two Dallas police officers corroborates the story about the two men and the panel truck. MERCER'S statement about RUBY is corroborated by the HILL statement as both witnesses place Ruby at the assassination site.

C) Three witnesses, JULIUS HARDIE, PHILLIP HATHAWAY and ERNEST JAY OWENS witnessed men other than OSWALD carrying rifles into the assassination site. Their stories tend to corroborate each others and tend to corroborate the eyewitness accounts of the other witnesses as well as the photographic evidence.

D) BOWERS who was in a railroad tower behind the picket fence witnessed suspicious activity of men in vehicles combing the area behind the fence right before the assassination and noted men behind the fence moments before the motorcade passed. He also stated that, as the shots rang out, his eyes were drawn to this area due to a flash of light or smoke. This data corroborates the statements of HILL, OLIVER AND ARNOLD.

E) Men positioned on the railroad bridge, including but not limited to SAM HOLLAND and JAMES SIMMONS thought that shots had come from behind the picket fence area and saw a puff of white smoke come form out from some bushes just in front of the picket fence. Their statements corroborates the other statements and photographic evidence.

F) Several witnesses, including BEVERLY OLIVER and ROSE WILLIS saw an image of a man behind the picket fence and OLIVER reported that she thought she had seen him fire the last shot. Their statements tend to corroborate each other correctly and that of the others witnesses and photographic evidence.

G) One witness, GORDON ARNOLD, heard and felt bullets "wizz" by his head that would have had to come from the picket fence area. His statements about hearing the bullets wizz by corroborates the other statements that used the sense of sight and corroborates the photographic evidence. Two other witnesses, Mr. and Mrs. BILLY NEWMAN thought that the shots had come from behind them and to the right which corroborates the ARNOLD statements and the photographic evidence in the ZAPRUDER film and BADGEMAN photograph.

H) Witnesses JESSE C. PRICE and ED HOFFMAN saw men behind the fence after the assassination with rifles and their stories corroborates each other.

G) The badgeman photograph was studied by photographic expert JACK WHITE and TOM WILSON. After years of study, WHITE located an area within the photograph behind the picket fence area and enhanced it. The photograph corroborates eyewitness testimony of a man dressed in a police uniform firing a shot with a man dressed in what appears to be a railroad uniform with a hardhat standing next to him. The BADGEMAN photograph is also corroborated by the ZAPRUDER FILM as to where the shots came from. ARNOLD, dressed in his summer military uniform, is standing in the photograph pointing his camera and starting to fall to his right. This portion of the photograph corroborates his statement about him being in that location. WILSON'S computer image analysis confirm and corrobrate WHITE'S orginal findings.

H) I conclude that a man dressed in a police uniform was the gunman behind the picket fence and that this gunman fired the shot that took off a portion of Kennedy's head. I also believe that the motorcycle patrolman who did not turn on Elm street found in the ZAPRUDER FILM somewhat corroborates the BADGEMAN PHOTOGRAPH. The evidence presented from viewing the long suppressed ZAPRUDER FILM clearly indicates that the fatal headshot came from the right front of the President, the area of the grassy knoll and picket fence. The ZAPRUDER FILM corroborates the BADGEMAN PHOTOGRAPH and all of the witness testimony presented here.

F) Several witnesses encountered men posing as federal government agents, especially Secret Service agents who, it had been conclusively determined, were not in the area. Eyewitness accounts from HILL, SMITH and ARNOLD all report being confronted by men in dark suits with these Federal Identifications and each person's testimony tends to corroborate the other. I conclude that there were men in the area with false federal agent identification cards.

F) It looks as if men were around to quickly remove the rifle from the area which appears to be corroborated with the witness testimony. HILL noted a man in motion in the area of the School Book Depository Building running towards the area behind the wooden fence who meets the description of MERCER who had seen the man an hour and one half earlier. Both HILL and MERCER identify this man as JACK RUBY. Police officer TILSON describes a man that meets about the same description of HILL and MERCER slipping down the other side of the bridge and putting something into the back of a vehicle. HOFFMAN also describes a man behind the fence handing a rifle to a railroad worker and PRICE describes a man running from the picket fence area carrying what appeared to be a rifle.

G) The HOFFMAN and ARNOLD accounts corroborates each other about a man dressed in a railroad uniform being someway involved in the shots from behind the fence.

H) I find conclusive evidence that photographic evidence was being covered up by someone. Both the OLIVER film and the ARNOLD film were taken before they were developed and apparently never saw the light of day. The Zapruder film appears to have been doctored and I suspect that the Bronson film has had a workover before being released to the public.

I) Of 178 witnesses to the assassination watching the motorcade, 96 of them indicate that the shots came from the knoll and picket fence area, 45 from the School Book Depository Building, 5 stated the shots came from both locations and 32 of the witnesses either expressed no opinion or their opinion is unknown. Even if we assume that the 32 unknowns would place all of the shots from the School Book Depository Building the total number placing shots from that location would only be 83 and the majority would still place all or some of the shots from the grassy knoll which would total 101.

NOTE: I have spent some time attempting to obtain a photographic enhancement of the Mooreman Photograph done by Jack White for this investigation. I have talked with both White and Jean Hill about this and neither said that the photograph could be published until further work is done and studied. The badgeman photograph I was able to observe came from freeze frames from the documentary on the assassination conducted by Investigative Reports. I was also able to view the badgeman photograph in a slide presentation done by Tom Wilson as the 1991 Assassination Symposium in Dallas, Texas in November. Due to copyright problems, I am unable to publish a copy of Jack White's work in this section.

1) CASTRO & CUBA: Ruby made several unexplained trips to Cuba. Oswald was involved in attempts to travel to Cuba. The CIA was involved in covert activities in Cuba and assassination attempts on Castro.

2) ORGANIZED CRIME: Ruby was a member of organized crime. The CIA was in bed with organized crime in attempts to assassinate Castro. Organized crime was attempting to monitor Kennedy by placing females in his company. Kennedy was attempting to destroy organized crime.

3) OIL INDUSTRY: A letter has surfaced from Oswald to H.L. Hunt. Ruby visted the Hunt office the day before the assassination. The CIA was covertly involved with the oil industry. Kennedy threatened the oil depletion allowance.

4) THE F.B.I.: Oswald was likely an FBI informer. Ruby was a one-time FBI informer. The FBI is linked to the CIA as part of the overall American intelligence establishment. Hoover was going to be retired and hated the Kennedys.

5) CUBAN REFUGEES: Oswald was involved with this group which was covertly sponsored by the CIA. The Cubans were outraged for Kennedy's actions concerning the Bay Of Pigs. The FBI was monitoring Cuban Refugee activity using undercover methods.

6) VIETNAM WAR: The CIA was covertly involved in the Vietnam war and likely had something to do with the Diem assassination. Kennedy was withdrawing from Vietnam. The CIA forged cables that would point to Kennedy involvement in the Diem murder.

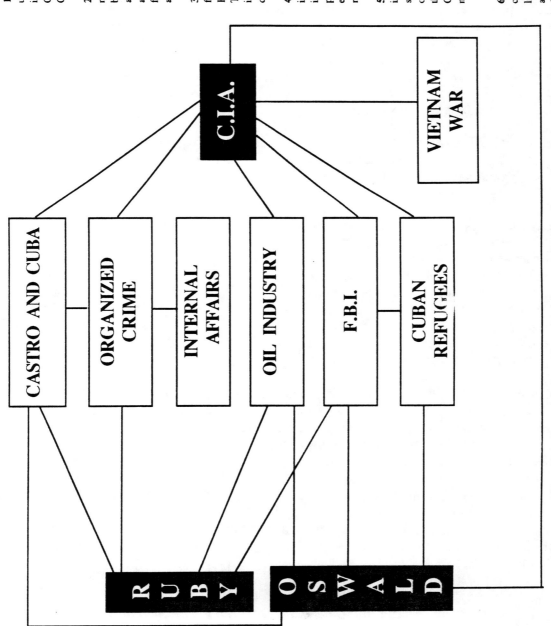

THE LINKAGE THAT TRACES BACK TO THE CIA

COPYRIGHT: 1991, National Association Of Investigative Specialists, Inc.

CONFLICTING EVIDENCE AT THE
SCHOOL BOOK DEPOSITORY BUILDING

If Oswald was the assassin in the sixth floor window of the School Book Depository, he would have to have been there some time before the Presidential motorcade arrived in the Plaza. The assassination occurred at 12:30. Kennedy delayed the start of the motorcade at Love Field when he broke away from the official welcoming party to meet and shake hands with citizens who had come to greet him. By the time the motorcade reached Dealey Plaza, it was running another five minutes behind due to two unplanned stops requested by President Kennedy to shake hands with the crowds. The assassin on the 6th floor would have had to have been in place sometime before the motorcade arrived to arrange the boxes in the window and certainly would not have known that the motorcade was running at least nine minutes behind. Yet, several witnesses place Oswald on the first and second floors of the building just before and just after the assassination.

> *BILL SHELLEY:* Shelley was Oswald's supervisor. He has stated before the Warren Commission that he saw Oswald on the second floor by a telephone at 11:40.

> *CAROLYN ARNOLD:* Arnold was an executive secretary in the building. She said that she saw Oswald in the lunch room at 12:15 (and says it could have been later) on the second floor eating lunch by himself.

If the assassination occurred at 12:30, why was Oswald eating his lunch on the second floor of the building at 12:15. He would have had to have had time to build his sniper's nest with boxes and be in position as no one was sure of the exact minute the motorcade would pass the building. The Shelley statement that OSWALD was positioned near a telephone at 11:40 seems suspicious to me. If OSWALD was standing near the telephone forty minutes before the assassination, was he awaiting a call or did he use the telephone? If he did, this would certainly provide circumstantial evidence of something more than the lone gunman theory. It would tend to point to a conspiracy. Unanswered questions remain because the Warren Commission failed to ask any relevant questions concerning this incident.

PATROLMAN MARRION BAKER: Baker was a motorcycle patrolman in the motorcade. Upon hearing the shoots, he thought that they had come from the School Book Depository. It's been established by Baker himself that this was not after the last shot but was just after the first shot. Baker said that he heard the first shot and saw pigeons fly off the top of the building. It was at this point that he rode his motorcycle to the steps of the School Book Depository Building and ran up the front steps. Ninety seconds later, he ran into Oswald in the lunch room drinking a coke and asked Oswald if he worked here. Oswald's supervisor explained to the police officer that Oswald worked in the building and was ok. Baker stated that the two elevators were stuck on the fifth floor so he started running up the back stairs. In a reenactment during the Warren Commission, it only took Baker fifteen seconds to enter the building. Here is his testimony before the Warren Commission:

I had it in mind that the shots came from the top of the building. As

36

I entered this lobby there were people going in as I entered and I asked...where the stairs or elevator was, this man, Mr. Truly, spoke up and says to me...I'm the building manager...follow me officer, and I will show you. So we immediately went through the second set of doors, and we ran into the swinging door.

The elevators had been stuck on the 5th floor. This was established by Warren Commission testimony given by Mr. Roy Truly. He said:

Those elevators were both on the fifth floor, they were both even. And I tried to get one of them..it would have been impossible for Oswald to have come down either one of the elevators after the assassination. He had to use the stairway as his only way of getting down since we did see the elevators were in those positions.

Officer Baker and Truly then took the stairs but just before, Officer Baker saw a white male through a glass window by the second floor landing. Baker had his gun out and yelled out an order for this man to come to him. Baker gave the FBI a statement that said:

"On the second floor where the lunch room is located, I saw a man standing in the lunchroom drinking a coke."

What is curious about this statement is that the words, "drinking a coke" are scratched out in the F.B.I. report. When Baker testified before the Warren Commission, he gave no mention of any coke. It appears that this evidence too was "cloaked". I would have wanted to know how full the coke bottle was which would provide some evidence of OSWALD'S time in the lunch room but by the time Baker's statement was made to the Warren Commission, no mention of the coke was made.

Baker asked Truly if this man was an employee of the building and Truly replied positively. Baker then continued his climb up the stairs.

Other witnesses were around the stairwell within seconds after the shots were fired but none of them saw Oswald come down the stairwell. Both Billy Lovelady and William Shelley were around the bottom of the stairwell right after the motorcade passed the building but neither saw nor heard anyone coming down the stairs. Victoria Adams and Sandra Styles had gone up to the fourth floor of the building to watch the motorcade. Within seconds after the shots rang out, both had ran down the stairs. Neither of these witnesses saw Oswald around the stairwell or heard any other footsteps.

What is important here is that when you look at the time, it is almost impossible for Oswald to have been at the 6th floor window of the building firing the last shots 90 seconds earlier. The elevators were not operational as both were stuck on the 5th floor. Oswald would have had to fire two more shots, wipe his fingerprints off the weapon, run to the other corner of the building, hide his rifle, run over to the stairs, run down four flights of stairs, enter the lunch room, obtain correct change from his pocket, purchase a soft drink from the soft drink machine and causally be standing there when officer Baker arrived all in 90 seconds. Let us go over these steps in a little more detail:

> A) *Fire two more shots*
>   *(Baker said he started to the building upon hearing the first shot)*
> B) *Wipe off the fingerprints on the rifle*
>   *(no fingerprints on the exterior were found)*
> C) *Run over to the other corner of the building*
>   *(the distance of several large living rooms)*
> D) *Reach down and hide the rifle between two cartons*
>   *(this is the location the rifle was found)*
> E) *Run over to the stairwell*
> F) *Run down four flights of stairs*
> G) *Enter the lunch room*
> H) *Go through his pockets for change*
> I) *Insert the correct amount of change in the soda machine*
> J) *Hit his selection*
> K) *Take his selection out of the dispenser tray*
> L) *Open the soft drink*

Recently Jim Moore attempted to focus away from this issue in his book _Conspiracy Of One_ by showing that Oswald didn't drink Coke but, instead, drank Dr. Pepper. Moore, an Oklahoma researcher who claims to have spent more time in Dealey Plaza than any researcher who has written about the subject but failed to back up that statement with any data, fails to point out the common expression used in Texas when one makes a statement about drinking a soft drink. We almost always call any soft drink a coke. Moore's focus on the brand name of the soft drink is not relevant anyway. What is relevant is the time study of Oswald getting from the sixth floor to the second floor lunch room. During the 1991 assassination symposium in November of 1991, I looked at the panel of speakers and noted that Moore was going to be speaking in two panels. I had planned to question him about his statement about being in Dealey Plaza more than any other researcher and what in the world was the relevancy about the brand of soft drink Oswald had in his hand but Moore failed to show up for the second panel.

The Warren Commission concluded that a person could run down the flight of stairs and be in the lunch room in the time allowed but one could just barely do it in that amount of time. More than that, the Warren Commission failed to take into account the fact that Oswald would have had to wipe fingerprints off his gun (as none where found on it's exterior) run to the other corner of the sixth floor (where the rifle was found) and purchase a soft drink from the drink machine. It would be an impossibility. Either Oswald was not on the sixth floor at the time of the shooting or he was there with someone else who wiped off the prints and hid the gun as Oswald quickly ran down the stairs and we still have not accounted for the time it took to purchase a soft drink.

Instead of a pointed investigation that would have attempted to obtain the coins in the soft drink machine, check the empty pop bottles for fingerprints, and attempt to determine how full or how empty the soft drink bottle was when Oswald was observed drinking it, the official investigation pretended that the soft drink evidence didn't exist simply by crossing out the reference to it on the police statement. I believe that this was done because those who did it knew full well that if a time study was done, it would present evidence that would show that Oswald could not have fired the shots. In my investigation, I found another witness who observed Oswald drinking a coke:

ROBERTA REID: Reid is another secretary who worked in the building and noted Oswald on the second floor about two minutes after the assassination drinking a coke.

A study of Oswald's activity just before the assassination is also very puzzling. At about 11:45, Oswald was working with two other males on the 5th floor. The two other workers went downstairs for lunch leaving Oswald on the 5th floor by himself. He asked the other employees to send the elevator back up.

Ray Williams, another employee, went to the 6th floor at about 12 noon to eat his lunch alone. Garbage from his lunch was later found by police. Williams testified that he remained on the 6th floor until about 12:20 P.M., ten minutes before the assassination. Williams saw no one and nothing unusual on the 6th floor as he ate his lunch. An empty soda bottle and chicken bones from Williams' lunch were left on the sixth floor which were incorrectly identified in the news media as belonging to the sniper. Surely fingerprints were found on the soda bottle found on the sixth floor on the afternoon after the assassination that were not OSWALD'S but no information concerning this negative was ever made.

The weight of the evidence of Oswald's location before and after the assassination shows that Oswald was not in the sixth floor window. The weight of the evidence of Oswald's location right before the assassination would tend to indicate that Oswald was not on the sixth floor. If Oswald was observed on the second floor lunch room at 12:15 by Carolyn Arnold and Ray Williams was on the sixth floor between noon and 12:20, this only leaves ten minutes for Oswald to have traveled from the second floor lunch room to the sixth floor to be in the sniper's window. Considering the fact that the motorcade was running five minutes behind, Oswald would have surely wanted to be in the window by at least 12:25. This leaves a five minute period of time for Oswald to be in the sniper's window ready to fire the shots. It's hardly likely. The weight of the evidence of Oswald's location right after the assassination would tend to indicate that Oswald was not on the sixth floor at the sniper's nest as he was found in the lunch room on the second floor drinking a coke (or Dr. Pepper as Moore expounds) 90 seconds after the first shot.

THE LONE WITNESS OF THE LONE GUNMAN

There was only one witness who identified Oswald as the assassin in the 6th floor window and this one witness account is shakey. The witness's name was Howard Brennan who was standing on Elm Street about 120 feet from the 6th floor window. Brennan claimed to have been facing the Book Depository Building as the shooting started and saw a man in the 6th floor window. He described the man with a general description as a white male in his thirties with dark hair. This could have described half the males that worked in the building. The night of the assassination, Brennan was given a police lineup with Oswald in it and he failed to ID Oswald as the man in the window despite the fact that the other men in the line-up appeared to be stacked with other men who bore a descriptive contrast from OSWALD. Later, Brennan claimed he had changed his mind and that Oswald was the man he saw in the window. Later, he switched his thinking again and said that he couldn't identify Oswald. By the time Brennan was called as a witness before the Warren Commission, he had once again changed his mind and told the commission that he was able to identify the man in the window as Oswald. But Brennan told the commission that he saw Oswald standing in the window when he would have had to have been squatting or sitting. Brennan was not able to say he witnessed the man in the window fire any shots. The Warren Commission or the Select Committee nor anyone else was able to produce any other witnesses that either place Oswald in the 6th floor window or place him any place around the sixth floor firing any rifles.

Not only has the Brennan account of Oswald in the sixth floor window been completely inconsistent, a Psychological Stress Examination by George O'Toole conducted in 1974 indicated that he was not telling the truth. A Psychological Stress Examination, commonly called PSE, is one of the newest forms of deception/detection testing that utilizes audio tape recordings . Although I do not like to use the term "lie detector", it's a term commonly applied to both polygraph and PSE tests. As a former PSE examiner myself, I can attest to the fact that PSE technology is superior to polygraph technology. In 1974, O'Toole located a news video of Brennan and conducted his tests and specifically tested Brennan on the following comment:

> *BRENNAN: "This man-the same man I had saw prior to the President's arrival- was in the window and taking aim for his last shot." (referring to Oswald)*

O'Tool's tests were published in his book, _The Assassination Tapes_, published by Penthouse Press in 1975. The above comment reveals hard stress which is a strong indicator of deception. As a former PSE tester, I reviewed O'Toole's results and found them to be correct. I believe that it is worth pointing out that O'Toole is a respected member of the investigative/intelligence community. He is a former CIA computer specialist who was certified in PSE technology through Dektor, the developers of the PSE equipment and the most respected name in the technology.

SUMMARY OF THE BRENNAN ACCOUNT

> *1) Brennan's account is inconsistent and he kept changing his story concerning rather or not he could identify Oswald in the sixth floor window.*

> *2) Brennan failed to positively identify Oswald in a police line up on the night of the assassination.*

> *3) The description given to police by Brennan was general in nature and could have described a number of persons.*

> *4) Brennan stated that he saw Oswald standing in the window when he would have had to have been squatting.*

> *5) PSE testing indicates that Brennan was not telling the truth about Oswald in tests conducted by George O'Toole and verified by myself.*

Although no one else could state that they saw Oswald on the sixth floor, several witnesses indicate that other people were there.

PHILLIP HATHAWAY/JOHN LAWRENCE: About noon time (one half hour before the assassination) these two men were walking on Akard Street near Main Street a few blocks from the assassination site and saw a man carrying what appeared to be a rifle in a brown leather rife case. This man was described by the two as:

HATHAWAY/LAWRENCE DESCRIPTION
White male, 6' 5", 250 lbs., early to mid 30, blond hair,
short crewcut wearing a gray suit.

ERNEST OWENS: Owens also noted a white heavy set male carrying a rifle out of a parking lot area on Wood Street a few blocks from the assassination site a little before noon. This person was wearing a dark suit.

OWENS DESCRIPTION
White, heavy set male
wearing a dark suit.

ARNOLD ROWLAND: Arnold Rowland was with his spouse on a street directly across from the Depository Building. Right after the assassination took place, he told a police officer that he saw a light Latin standing in the far left window with a rifle right before the motorcade came into view and that he thought this man was a Secret Service agent. He was referring to the opposite corner of where Oswald was supposed to have been. The time frame for this stated by Rowland was 12:15, the same time other witnesses place Oswald on the second floor.

ROWLAND DESCRIPTION
Light Latin with rifle

CAROLYN WALTHER: Walther gave a statement to the FBI that she saw two men in the 6th floor just before the assassination. One man had a rifle in his hand and had "lightish" hair. The person was wearing a white shirt. She also stated that the second person was a white male wearing a brown suit.

WALTHER DESCRIPTION
Lightish hair wearing a white shirt.
White male wearing a brown suit

RUBY HENDERSON: Henderson gave a statement to the FBI in 1963 that revealed she also saw two men in the upper floor windows of the School Book Depository Building. She didn't see any guns but said these men where standing back away from the windows and appeared to be watching for the motorcade. Henderson said that the first suspect she saw was a taller black male wearing a white shirt. The second suspect was a shorter white male with a dark suit.

HENDERSON DESCRIPTION
Taller black male, white shirt
Shorter white male, dark suit

JOHN POWELL: Powell was a white male who was in jail at the time of the assassination but had a view of the sixth floor window. The Dallas County Jail is directly across from the School

Book Depository Building. This inmate said he and several other inmates were looking out the window about five or six minutes before the shots rang out and they saw two men in the 6th floor window. Both had dark complexions and one was adjusting the sight on a rifle.

POWELL DESCRIPTION
Two men with dark complexions

CORROBORATION OF DESCRIPTIVE WITNESS STATEMENTS: Although only one witness was ever produced that kept changing his story concerning OSWALD being in the 6th floor window who failed PSE testing, at least four other witnesses stated that they saw men other than OSWALD in the window. Their statements tend to corroborate each other. Both OWENS and WALTHER describe a white male wearing a suit. Both POWELL and ROWLAND describe a man with a dark complexion. WALTHER, HATHAWAY and LAWRENCE describe a man with lightish hair color.

PHOTOGRAPHIC EVIDENCE CORROBORATES WITNESS STATEMENTS: Of the witnesses listed, WALTHER, HENDERSON and POWELL describe two men on in the sixth floor windows. The below photographic evidence tends to go along with the witness statements that reveal more than one person in the windows of the sixth floor of the School Book Depository Building.

THE DILLARD PHOTO: Tom Dillard was a newspaper photographer riding in the motorcade. Dillard snapped a photo of the School Book Depository Building about 30 seconds after the final shot which gives a good view of the so called sniper's nest on the sixth floor. Photographic experts of the House Assassination Select Committee studied these photographs and compared them to photographs taken just prior to the shots. The committee concluded that someone had apparently rearranged the configuration of the boxes in the sixth floor window between the two photographs. If Oswald was on the second floor just a minute or two minutes after the last shot, how could he have been on the sixth floor rearranging the boxes.

THE BRONSON FILM: Charles Bronson had taken movie film several minutes up until a few seconds before the shots rang out. The Bronson film has views of the School Book Depository Building and the famous sixth floor window as it's backdrop. The film revealed what appeared to be two persons walking around on the 6th floor minutes before the assassination. During the House Select Committee hearings, Robert Gorden was hired to study the film which surfaced right before the close of the hearings. Groden's findings in writing to the committee state:

Close inspection and optical enhancement reveals definite movement in at least two and probably three of the windows in question....the man in the window number one is moving rapidly back and forth, the man in number two seems to be crouched down at the window and rocking his toes in much the manner of a baseball catcher.

The shape in window number two is slightly less distinct than the other one. I originally felt that this man was actually the man in window number one leaning back and forth, probably moving

*boxes around to construct what would be called the sniper's nest. I
now feel that this is a distinctly different person who is probably
handing boxes to man number one.*

SUMMARY

1) Oswald was not on the 6th floor minutes before and ninety seconds after the first shot.

*2) Evidence shows that Oswald could not have been in the second floor lunch room drinking a
soda if he was at the sixth floor window to fire the last two shots.*

*3) The only witness who was ever found that stated that Oswald was in the sixth floor window
could not identify him in a police lineup, continued to change his story, and failed PSE testing.*

*4) At least seven other witnesses saw people other than Oswald on the sixth floor, some with
rifles.*

5) Photographic evidence shows at least two people in the sixth floor window.

*6) Photographic evidence shows that someone had rearranged the boxes in the window right after
the shots were fired at a time that Oswald was observed on the second floor.*

CONCLUSION: The weight of the evidence tends to prove that at least two men were in the sixth
floor window and neither of these men were Oswald. This conclusion is drawn from eyewitness
accounts, photographic evidence and PSE testing all of which tends to corroborate each other.

THE MAGIC BULLET AND THE LONE ASSASSIN THEORY

The magic bullet theory was developed by the Warren Commission to explain how all the wounds in the Presidential vehicle were caused by three shots (including one shot that missed). The commission had evidence before it that revealed that all shots had to be fired within 5.9 seconds with the Zapruder film. The Zapruder film was taken from the side of the road up on the grassy knoll with an 8mm movie camera. By determining the length of time it took the film to go through the camera and by studying each frame and comparing it to when Oswald could have fired, it was determined that the shots from the sixth floor window of the School Book Depository Building had to be fired within 5.8 seconds. The F.B.I., even before the Warren Commission was set up, determined that three shots were fired and recovered one of the bullets found on a stretcher at Parkland Hospital.

There were nine wounds found on Kennedy and Connally. They can be summarized as follows:

KENNEDY:
A)Upper back wound slightly to the right
B) Neck wound just about at the adam's apple
C) Rear head wound on the right hand side.
D) Frontal head wound on the right hand side

CONNALLY
A) Back wound at shoulder blade just above armpit
B) Chest wound just above right nipple
C) Entrance wound in wrist
D) Exit wound in wrist
E) Left thigh wound

After the Warren Commission started it's investigation, a witness surfaced that was standing at the southeastern end of Dealey Plaza that had been hit in the face by a piece of flying cement. The flying cement was caused when a bullet hit the curb near the witness. This means that out of the three bullets, one bullet missed. Since the third bullet (the last bullet) was clearly the one that caused the President's head explosion, the investigative staff was left with explaining how one bullet could have caused the neck and back wound of President Kennedy, as well as the chest wound, wrist wound and left thigh wound of Connally. If they could not explain how all these wounds where caused by one shot, then at least four shots were fired. If four or more shots were fired then more than one gunman had to have done the shooting because no human could have fired more than three shoots in 5.8 seconds and it is questionable if three shots could have been fired by one person accurately. The commission came up with the theory that the first shot did all the damage but the weight of the evidence, as you will see, does not support this theory. Here is a summary of the official findings of the Warren Commission:

FIRST SHOT:
The first shot was fired from the School Book Depository building and caused the following wounds:

A) Entered the back of the President.
B) Exited the throat of the President.

C) *Entered Connally's back.*
D) *Shattered Connally's fifth rib.*
E) *Exited Connally's chest just under the right nipple.*
F) *Entered Connally's right wrist.*
G) *Shattered Connally's right wrist bone.*
H) *Exited the wrist.*
J) *Entered Connally's left thigh and came to a halt at the thigh bone.*

The Warren Commission said that this bullet fell out of Connally's wound at Parkland hospital onto his stretcher and was later recovered.

SECOND SHOT:

The second shot missed the Presidential car altogether and struck a concrete curb near the triple underpass. Flying cement from the impact hit James Tague on the face causing a very minor wound.

THIRD SHOT:

The third shot hit the President in the rear right side of his head and came out the right front of his head causing a massive head explosion.

All shots were fired from the sixth floor window by Lee H. Oswald who was acting alone in the assassination attempt.

PROBLEMS WITH THE MAGIC BULLET THEORY

The lone assassin theory seems to make sense. But, the physical evidence, witness testimony, photographic evidence and other statements made before the Warren Commission's findings does not support the lone assassin theory at all.

FBI REPORT ABOUT THE PRESIDENT'S BACK WOUND: An FBI report dated December 9th, 1963 by agents who observed the official autopsy stated that the back wound of the President lacked any point of exit. If the back wound had no point of exit and it was the first shot fired, it could not have come out Kennedy's throat and it could not have caused all the wounds to Connally. If this is this case, more than three shots were fired. If more than three shots were fired, then, at least two gunmen did the shooting. If two gunmen did the shooting, then Oswald was not the lone assassin. The FBI report in question was first published in assassination researcher Mark Lane's book *Rush To Judgment* in the appendix.

TAGUE INCIDENT CLOAKING ATTEMPT: If it would not have been for the Tague incident, the Warren Commission could have had an extra bullet to work with that explained all the wounds. Although James Tague's nick in the face had already been reported in the press, it seems that the FBI attempted to "cloak" this evidence. The Warren Commission asked the FBI to look into this matter. Their first report stated that they could find no evidence that a bullet hit the curb although they had examined the curb area. Finally, a photograph taken by Tom Dillard of the *Dallas Morning News* just after the assassination was put in the hands of the Warren Commission. Tague himself has stated that he called the FBI Dallas office after the assassination to report the bullet hitting the curb and his nick on the face but they apparently did not want to know about it. The Warren Commission relied upon the FBI as it's investigative body but the FBI had reported to them that no evidence of a nick in the curb existed. The commission then had Tauge's statement taken in Dallas. After the statement was taken, the FBI was again asked to look into this matter. This time, they removed a portion of the curb and had it analyzed. Confronted with the Tague statement in the official record, the FBI finally reported to the commission that the bullet did strike the curb which apparently retracted their first statements and their interest in Tague as a witness when he had contacted the FBI on the day of the assassination.

JOHN CONNALLY TESTIMONY: Connally is perhaps one of the most important witnesses of the entire assassination. Other than Mrs. Kennedy, he was the closest witness to the President. Connally stated that he heard the first shot and the effects of the first shot hitting the President. He said that he started to turn to his right to turn around and see if the President was okay. He said that he didn't catch the President out of the corner of his right eye so he started to turn around to the left to see if he could see the President. At this point, Connally said he felt the bullet hit his back. He stated that he didn't hear the second bullet that hit him which is consistent with proven facts that the bullet would have hit him before he heard it as bullets travel faster than the speed of sound. Connally says that after he was hit, he couldn't recall hearing any other shots. Connally states that he is sure that he was hit by a different shot than the first shot that hit the President. The Warren Commission concluded that he was mistaken.

CONNALLY ABRIDGED TESTIMONY BEFORE THE WARREN COMMISSION:

> " It is not conceivable to me that I could have been hit by the first bullet. When I heard what I thought was a shot..I turned to look back over my right shoulder and I saw nothing unusual except just the people in the crowd, but I did not catch the President in the corner of my eye, and I was interested, because once I heard the shot in my own mind I identified it as a rifle shot, and I immediately...the only thought that crossed my mind was that this is an assassination attempt."

Failing to see the President, Connally went on to tell the commission, "I was turning to look back over my left shoulder into the back seat." At this point Connally said he concluded, "there were either two or three people involved or more in this or someone was shooting with an automatic rifle. These were just thoughts that went through my mind because of the rapidity of these two, of the first shot plus the blow that I took." Connally then stated that he was hit by the second bullet and the Warren Commission then asked him what reasoning he used to make that conclusion. He said:

> "Well, in my judgment it just couldn't conceivably have been the first one because I heard the sound of the shot. In the first place, I don't know anything about the velocity of this particular bullet, but any rifle has a velocity that exceeds the speed of sound, and when I heard the sound of that first shot, that bullet had already reached where I was, or it had reached that far, and after I heard that shot, I had time to turn to my right, and start to turn to my left before I felt anything."

If Connally was hit by a different shot than the first shot that hit the President, then, at least two rifles had to have fired at the Presidential limo as there was not enough time for more than three shots to have been fired from the sixth floor.

Jim Moore, in his work, <u>Conspiracy Of One</u>, attempts to explain this discrepancy away by saying that it was the first shot, not the second shot, that missed the target and it was this first shot that hit the curb. Moore states that this first shot that missed both Kennedy and Connally, was the shot that

Connally heard. However, the President can clearly be seen to be reacting to the first shot in the Zapruder film as he brings his hands up towards his neck. Moore states that this was a reflex reaction caused by Kennedy hearing the first shot that missed. However, witness testimony does not support this Moore theory and neither does the computer image processing work of Tom Wilson. Witnesses state that Kennedy was hit with the first shot and the Wilson computer study of Zapruder frames during this period reveal blood in Kennedy's throat area.

MRS. CONNALLY TESTIMONY: Mrs. Connally, the second closest witness to Kennedy (other than Mrs. Kennedy) and the closest witness to Connally also thought that Connally was hit by a different shot than the first shot that hit the president. Mrs. Connally was sitting right next to John Connally in the jump seat of the limo. Before the Warren Commission she testified:

> *"I heard a noise, and not being an expert rifleman, I was not aware that it was a rifle. It was just a frightening noise, and it came from the right. I turned over my right shoulder and looked back, and saw the President as he had both hands at his neck....and it seemed to me there was...he made no utterance or cry. I saw no blood, no anything. It was just sort of nothing, the expression on his face, and he just sort of slumped down. Then very soon there was a second shot that hit John. As the first shot was hit, and I turned to look at the same time, I recall John saying, Oh no, no, no, then there was a second shot and it hit John, and as he recoiled to the right, just crumpled like a wounded animal to the right, he said, My God, they are going to kill us all."*

OTHER WITNESS TESTIMONY: We have documented in another chapter the fact that others stated someone had fired from the grassy knoll. Holland, a key witness, says that Kennedy and Connally were hit by separate shots. All the other witnesses who had a comment on this stated that they thought Connally and Kennedy were hit by two separate bullets. Not one witness has stated that they thought both Connally and Kennedy were hit by the same bullet.

TRAJECTORY OF THE BULLET: The tracking of the bullet just doesn't line up to prove the magic bullet theory. First off, the bullet hole in the President's back has been moved between the Warren Commission and the House Select Committee. We will get into the details of the wounds in another section but even the location of the wounds by the Warren Commission will not traject out in the right manner. If the shot came from the sixth floor of the Texas School Book Depository Building when it hit Kennedy's back, it had to have been traveling at a slightly downward angle and slightly to the left. The official version is that the bullet that went through Kennedy's back and throat didn't hit any bone. That doesn't make much sense as it came out his adam's apple. Moreover, the bullet that pierced Kennedy's back had to have traveled upwards at a forty five degree angle to have come out his throat. The question remains unanswered as to how a bullet traveling at a downward angle could have hit the President in the back and then traveled upward at a forty five degree angle. When the bullet came out of Kennedy's throat, the trajectory was to the left and now upwards but the bullet had to have changed direction to slightly downward and to the right to have hit Connally in the right section of his back near the armpit. Could the bullet have changed direction in mid air? After the bullet had passed through Connally's chest and wrist, it would have had to change direction again, this time turning back to the left and down to have hit him in the left thigh. Dr. Cyril Wecht was hired by the Select Committee on it's forensic pathology panel. Based on the trajectory, he didn't see how this bullet could have hit both Kennedy and Connally. He said, "The vertical and horizontal trajectory of this bullet under the single bullet theory is absolutely unfathomable, indefensible and incredible."

THE ZAPRUDER FILM (AGAIN): Pro-Warren Commission people have always stated that there is no photographic evidence of the exact position of Kennedy and Connally at the time of the shot in question because the Zapruder film has the incident blocked by a highway sign at the time of the shots. However, this period of time is only a few seconds. Kennedy and Connally were not in alignment before they went out of view and were not in alignment after they came back into view and these spokespersons are asking one to believe that Connally somehow moved to his left right after he went out of view behind the sign just to put himself in proper alignment and then move back to his original position right before he came back into view all in the time span of a one or two seconds. I don't see how this would likely be the case. Besides, as Connally came back into view, it is obvious to me that he is not hit. But these Pro-Warren Commission spokespersons want us to believe that, somehow, Connally moved to his right to get in alignment and then moved back to his left during the second or so he was out of view behind the highway sign in the Zapruder film.

As covered earlier you will recall Mr. Zapruder was an amateur photographer who recorded the motorcade with an 8 mm home movie camera. This investigator has watched this film over and over again and again. It appears from the film that Kennedy is hit on the right front of the head indicating a shot fired from the right front of the president, not the right rear. Skull fragments can clearly be seen traveling to the left and to the rear of the limo. Mrs. Kennedy jumps up from her seat and crawls out onto the trunk of the limo reaching for what appears to be a skull fragment. After the head explosion, Kennedy's body is clearly thrust backward and to the left, again consistent with a shot fired from the right front, the area of the grassy knoll. When the first shot hit the President in the back and went through his throat, it's clear that Connally was not hit by that shot. As Connally has stated, he started to turn to his right in the film and his head starts to move around. The film looks like Connally has turned all the way around and is looking directly at Kennedy when he appears to be hit. Connally's body falls to the left into the limo into the lap of his wife. At the time that the Warren Commission says that Connally was hit, he is still holding on to his stetson hat and I fail to see how someone could continue to hold such an item when the wrist of that same hand has just been shattered.

The version I have of the Zapruder film is an enhanced video version that was prepared with blow-ups and slow motion for the House Select Committee. During the time in question that Connally is holding his hat, a black mark runs through the film covering his hand and wrist. Evidently, in earlier versions, this line was not present as dozens of assassination researchers who have seen earlier versions of the film indicate that Connally was holding his hat at the time the Warren Commission says that his wrist was shattered. My version has the frames start further up from the bottom of each frame which would indicate that the bottom portion of the film has been blacked out enough so you cannot see Connally holding his hat. I believe that this is another puzzle that would indicate that the evidence was "cloaked".

OSWALD COULDN'T HAVE FIRED ALL THREE SHOTS: Although the Warren Commission knew that four shots would mean more than one gunman fired, they appear to be stretching it to have three shots fired from a sixth floor window at a target 100 yards away and moving in 5.8 seconds and hit the target twice. No one has ever been able to duplicate this feat, especially with such an inferior weapon as the rifle that Oswald was supposed to have fired with. Just think about the steps involved accordingly. Let us put ourselves in what the Warren Commission calls the assassination window:

You are six floors up looking out of a window that is half opened. You aim your first shot and fire at a moving target 100 yards away and hit the back of Kennedy. You pull back the bolt action that discharges the spent shell letting the second round into the chamber. You push the bolt forward again that places the second round into the barrel. You take aim for the second shot and pull the trigger. This shot misses. You pull back the bolt again to eject the shell from the second shot and the third round pops up into position. You pull back the bolt that pushes the third round into the barrel. You aim for the third shot and pull the trigger this time hitting the President in the head. All this is done in 5.8 seconds. I have tried this feat with a like weapon and could hardly pull the bolt action back and up twice in the allotted time and we are not even allowing enough time for aim and pulling the trigger. If you have a bolt action rifle, you can try this yourself and you'll find it almost impossible to have fired all three shots in such a manner in 5.8 seconds.

Experts attempted to duplicate this feat for the Warren Commission but they were unable to do so. Top marksman from both the FBI and the National Rifle Association had been given the rifle after it had been overhauled. All of these expert marksmen had a very hard time getting the shots off in 5.8 seconds let alone doing so with any accuracy.

Key witnesses including Holland, Hill, Oliver, Bowers, Mooreman, the Newmans and Arnold all state that the shots were not evenly spaced and that some of the shots were right on top of each other. If the spacing of the shots were not even, Oswald could not have fired all of the shots. Many of these witnesses stated that more than three shots were fired and, from the witness accounts I have studied, the weight of the evidence would suggest that between four and six shots were fired.

CONDITION OF THE MAGIC BULLET: The magic bullet (the bullet recovered on a stretcher at Parkland Hospital) is called the magic bullet because it's in almost pristine condition. It's almost unscratched as if he had been test fired into water or cotton. The bullet has it's general shape, grooves and jacket intact. Tests show that the amount of lead lost from the bullet is very small that cannot even be seen with the naked eye. There is more bullet fragments in John Connally today than what is missing from the magic bullet and we aren't even counting the fragments taken out of Connally during surgery.

Audrey Bell was one of the surgical nurses that helped with the surgery of John Connally. She has stated that she placed bullet fragments that had been taken from Connally's wrist into an envelope. She had stated officially that she placed four or five fragments into the envelope the smallest being about the "size of the striking end of a match" and the largest " twice that big." Mark Lane, in _Rush To Judgment_ points out that three grains of metal are found in the wrist alone but only 1.4 to 2.4 grains are missing from the bullet.

Dr. Humes, one of the Kennedy autopsist said that he felt it was " extremely unlikely" that the bullet found at Parkland was the same bullet that went through Connally. Dr. J. Thornton Boswell assisted Dr. Humes with the autopsy and stated that Humes is correct about the bullet found at Parkland. Dr. Pierre Finck, another doctor involved in the Kennedy autopsy said that he didn't see how the bullet found at Parkland could have been the bullet that went through Connally because "there were too many fragments described in the wrist." Dr. Shaw, another involved physician, also stated that he didn't see how this bullet could have been the bullet that caused the wounds.

Dr. Milton H. Helpren is one of the foremost authorities on gunshot wounds in the United States. He has been in charge of over 10,000 gunshot autopsies in his career that has spanned over four decades in New York. In assassination researcher Henry Hurt's book, _Reasonable Doubt_, Dr. Helpren is quoted on page 69:

> "This bullet wasn't distorted in any way. I cannot accept the premise that this bullet thrashed around in all that bony tissue and lost only 1.4 to 2.4 grains....I cannot believe either that this bullet is going to emerge miraculously unscathed, without any deformity......

The energy of the bullet is sometimes so spent that it can't quite get out through the final layer of skin, (Dr. Helpren talking about going through just one body), and it comes to rest just beneath the outside layer of skin. If it does get through the skin, it may not have enough energy to penetrate even an undershirt or a light cotton blouse. It has exhausted itself, and just more or less plops to a stop."

The Warren Commission hired a wound ballistics expert to attempt to duplicate the firing. Using the actual alleged rifle found on the 6th floor Depository Building, the ballistics expert fired through both a carcass of a goat and through the wrist of human body. In both cases, the bullet recovered was completely flattened. The commission never attempted to test a bullet through seven layers of skin as the magic bullet was supposed to have done but large deformity was found with the bullet when a mere fraction of the duplication was found.

The Select Committee did the same thing. Some of the official testing for the Select Committee was done by Dr. Wecht. His presentation before the committee went like this:

Using the same type ammo as that of the magic bullet, he shows one bullet that has not been fired that looks almost perfect. He then shows two bullets that have marked deformity that have been fired into cotton that actually never hit anything. However, the deformity to one of these bullets to the naked eye is greater than that of the actual magic bullet. The next bullet displayed is a bullet that was shot though the carcass of a goat going through one of the goat's ribs. On this bullet, there is a very significant loss of lead from the jacket and the deformity appears much greater than that of the magic bullet. The final bullet displayed is one fired though the wrist of a human body at the radius bone. This bullet has a completely flattened head.

At the end of his presentation, Dr. Wecht is quoted stating the following:

"I have repeatedly...implored, beseeched, urged, in writing, orally, privately, collectively, my colleagues, to come up with one bullet that has done all this. I am not talking about fifty percent of the time plus one or five percent or one percent....just one bullet that has done this. ....I can only say to you as a member of the panel, at no time did any of my colleagues ever bring in a bullet....and say here is a bullet in a documented case that broke two bones in some human being, and look at its condition, it is pristine."

Besides the condition of the bullet itself, when it was found it had no blood and no flesh tissue on it. The bullet had gone through seven layers of skin causing bleeding and gaping wounds and broken several bones but was, itself, quite clean when found.

Thus it's highly unlikely that the bullet found on a stretcher at Parkland Hospital could have been the bullet that did all the damage as the Warren Commission claimed. If it was not, what was it? It if was not, how did the bullet get there?

HOW THE BULLET WAS FOUND: The recovered magic bullet was found on a stretcher at Parkland Hospital by a hospital employee who was working the elevator, Darrell C. Tomlinson. Tomlinson told the Warren Commission that he discovered the bullet on a stretcher parked near the doorway to the elevator that had bloody sheets rolled-up, some surgical instruments and some compression packs on it. At first the experts assumed that this was Connally's stretcher. Connally's stretcher had carried him up the elevator to the second floor for surgery and the stretcher might have been brought back down to the hallway but no evidence was ever brought out that indicated that Connally's stretcher would have contained rolled up sheets with blood on them, surgical instruments and compression packs which Tomlison has testified that the stretcher contained. Many later day researchers have indicated that the stretcher Tomlison found the bullet on might have been the stretcher that Kennedy was on but it's been established that Kennedy's original stretcher was never placed in the hallway. There was another stretcher that was placed in the hallway that was used to treat Ronald Fuller who entered Parkland Hospital at 12:54. Fuller was treated for a minor cut on his chin. He was briefly treated on a stretcher that contained surgical instruments and compression packs and it's likely that this is the stretcher that the magic bullet was found on. Thus, there is a question as to whether or not the stretcher the bullet was found on had anything at all to do with Kennedy or Connally.

After Tomlison found the bullet, he turned it over to the chief of security at Parkland Hospital, O. P. Wright. Mr. Wright is the father-in-law of Patrick T. Dean, a Dallas police officer who the Warren Commission says was the officer responsible for letting Jack Ruby into the basement of the Dallas Police garage where Ruby shot Oswald. What makes this even more suspicious is that Jack Ruby was spotted at Parkland Hospital by three witnesses, newsman Seth Kantor, Mrs. Wilma Tice and a radio newsperson Roy Stamps. Ruby, in official testimony has denied that he was ever at Parkland. After Mrs. Tice made comments concerning her sighting of Jack Ruby at Parkland, she got a telephone call from a man who told her not to talk about the incident. A few days later she received another telephone call after she received a notice to testify before the Warren Commission from a man who told her, "It would pay you to keep your mouth shut."

Penn Jones, Jr., a Texas newsman who owned the *Midlothian Mirror* in Midlothian, Texas took dozens of photographs of Parkland Hospital during the time in question concerning the statements that Jack Ruby was at the hospital. In the 1960's Jones became a major researcher on the Kennedy Assassination and found among his photographs, a photo taken at Parkland Hospital that reveals the back of a man meeting the description of JACK RUBY. This photograph was published on the back cover of Jone's book, *Forgive My Grief III*. The man is walking away from the camera with one hand in his pocket which RUBY was known to do. The clothing, consisting of a dark sports coat and dark but lighter colored pants and a light colored hat fits the description of RUBY. The height, weight, build and complexion fit that of RUBY. The hair color and back hairline as well as the right ear all meet the description of RUBY. I would conclude that it is him.

So we have three witnesses and a photograph that corroborate each other concerning RUBY's presence at Parkland Hospital. But if RUBY was present, what reason would he have for his deception and saying that he was not present unless, of course, he was the person who planted the bullet on the stretcher. However, since no one can state for certain that RUBY was in the lobby near the stretchers, the questions concerning RUBY'S planting of the bullet remain unanswered although the weight of the evidence would tend to incriminate him.

Forensic scientist Charles G. Wilber speculates in his work, *Mediolegal Investigation Of The President John F. Kennedy Murder*, that an attendant might have found the bullet on the Kennedy stretcher and picked it up. Upon observation of the demanding behavior of the Secret Service that included knocking to the floor a local FBI agent, the attendant might have gotten scared and simply placed the bullet on the stretcher in the hallway. Dr. Wilber's speculation could have happened as the magic bullet might have fallen out of the back wound of the President. This back wound was probed at the Bethesda Autopsy by Dr. Humes and an FBI report shows it to have no point of exit.

If Kennedy's back wound lacked any point of exit and did not track to the throat wound, then the throat wound and the back wound were caused by different shots. If that is the case, the throat wound would have had to have been a shot fired from the front and could not have come from the sixth floor window. Moreover, if the back wound didn't come out the throat, then it could not have caused all the wounds to Connally. This would mean that more shots were fired and some were fired from the front. Oswald could not have fired more than three shots and certainly couldn't have caused front wounds when he was firing from the back. The whole idea of both a lone assassin theory and the magic bullet theory collapses with the evidence that the back wound didn't track out.

EVIDENCE OF OTHER BULLETS: Remember that the official version says that one bullet missed the limo altogether and another bullet was recovered at Parkland Hospital. A physical inspection of the limo revealed two other places where a bullet hit. Photo evidence revealed that a bullet struck a chrome frame that went around the windshield of the Presidential limo. Another bullet revealed a crack in the limousine's windshield. Several other photos in assassination researchers Robert Groden's and Harrison Livingston's book *High Treason*, show police officers examining other bullets in and around the assassination site. Evidence of one bullet was found near a manhole that traces back to a building across the street from the School Book Depository Building. Another photo reveals a man picking up a bullet and placing it in his pocket near the grassy area to the east of the roadway.The photograph was first published in Penn Jones *Forgive My Grief* series on the front cover. Penn's caption of this photograph stated that the person dressed in a suit putting the bullet into his pocket is identified as an unknown FBI agent. According to Penn, the bullet was discovered by Deputy Sheriff Buddy Walthers and that Walthers stated that the bullet was a .45 caliber and was embedded with brain matter. Photos in the book, *High Treason*, reveal another mark on the sidewalk just right of where the limo went by and several other photographs reveal other bullet evidence. If other bullets were found, then this certainly flattens the magic bullet/lone gunman theory. However, none of this was reported or investigated by the Warren Commission.

SUMMARY OF THE MAGIC BULLET THEORY

1) No witness that had an opinion stated that Connally and Kennedy were hit by the same bullet. All witnesses that had an opinion thought they were hit by separate bullets.

2) Connally, to this day, does not believe that he was hit by the same bullet.

3) Mrs. Connally, to this day, believes that her husband was hit by a separate bullet.

4) Both Connally and Mrs. Kennedy made statements seconds after the first shot rang out that would indicate that their very first thoughts were of more than one gunman.

5)The Zapruder film clearly indicates that Connally and Kennedy were not hit by the same bullet.

6) The trajectory of the bullets doesn't line up.

7) The recovered bullet is in pristine condition.

8) The recovered bullet does not have enough loss of weight to account for the bullet fragments left behind.

9) The recovered bullet probably did not come off of either Connally's stretcher or Kennedy's stretcher.

10) If the bullet was not discovered on either Connally's or Kennedy's stretcher, someone must have planted it and three witnesses indicate Oswald's assassin, Jack Ruby was present at Parkland Hospital although Ruby had denied this.

11) The Director of Security was the father-in-law of the police officer who let Jack Ruby into the police garage were he murdered Oswald.

12) There is a great deal of facts that reveal that evidence of other bullets being fired other than the three fired as claimed by the Warren Commission which, because of time restraints established by the Zapruder film, would prove that more than one gunman was firing.

EVIDENCE THAT DOESN'T ADD UP &
EVIDENCE THAT WAS TAMPERED WITH

THE PARAFFIN TEST OF OSWALD

A paraffin test is a test conducted to see if a suspect has recently fired a weapon. When a weapon is fired, elements containing nitrates escape from the weapon and become imbedded in the skin. But, many substances such as cigarette ash, toothpaste, paint, food and other items can place nitrates upon the hands. A paraffin test is conducted by placing hot wax on the hands and face. The wax is then peeled off the skin and nitrates show up on the wax. Police Chief Curry and District Attorney Wade had been asked about the paraffin tests and both said that the tests were positive indicating that Oswald had fired a gun. Wade had been asked if the test indicated that Oswald had fired a rifle and he answered that it was a gun.

The reason both the police chief and the district attorney would not state that it was a rifle but only went as far as to call it a gun was not completely clear until assassination researcher Mark Lane conducted his own investigation part of which involved obtaining copies of the paraffin tests. The test reveals a positive on the hands and a negative on the face. If the face revealed a negative test, then Oswald could not have fired a rifle, he could have only fired a pistol. So both the police chief and the district attorney's statements about Oswald firing a "gun" instead of "a rifle" are correct. But if Oswald didn't fire a rifle, then he didn't shoot the President and he didn't shoot Connally.

Mark Lane, in his book, _Rush To Judgment_, points out that Oswald likely handled painted plywood the day of the assassination. This would have caused the positive tests on his hands. Freshly painted plywood was being put down on the sixth floor of the School Book Depository Building on the day of the assassination. Lane also pointed out that in cases of people who had recently fired a rifle, one hand would be positive, one negative and the face would be positive.

Thus, the paraffin test shows that Oswald had not fired a rifle on the day of the assassination. He could have fired a side arm but Mark Lane points out that even if he had fired a side arm, the paraffin test would show one hand positive (for the hand that fired the gun) and the other hand negative (the hand that did not fire the gun). Lane contends that the evidence of the nitrates found on the hands likely came from the freshly painted plywood. The Warren Commission simply sidestepped the questions by calling the paraffin tests unreliable.

SUMMARY

1) _The paraffin test was positive on the hands and negative on the face._

2) _This test clearly shows that Oswald did not fire a rifle on the day of the assassination._

3) _The positive test on the hands was likely caused by freshly painted plywood in the building on the day of the assassination._

4) _Both the police chief and the district attorney did not tell the press the complete story about the tests._

THE RIFLE

The alleged murder weapon was found on the sixth floor in the NW corner of the School Book Depository Building at 1:22 PM by police officer E. L. Boone. Officers Weitzman and Sheriff Deputy Craig were also present. The rifle was reported to be a 7.6 mm German Mauser by officer Boone. Officer Weitzman also identified the rifle as a German Mauser. Deputy Craig stated publicly that the word "Mauser" was stamped on the weapon and he too identified the rifle as a Mauser. During a press conference, District Attorney Wade also identified the rifle as a Mauser. When the news media asked the district attorney what kind of rifle was found, Wade responded, "It's a Mauser I believe." Late Friday night, the rifle started being identified as a 6.5 mm Italian Mannlicher-Carcano which is the weapon that the Warren Commission identified as the murder weapon. But we have witnesses calling the rifle found a Mauser:

> A) DALLAS POLICE OFFICER E. L. BOONE:
> " 7.6 German Mauser"
>
> B) OFFICER WEITZMAN:
> "A German Mauser."
>
> C) DEPUTY SHERIFF CRAIG:
> "Mauser stamped on the gun."
>
> D) DISTRICT ATTORNEY WADE:
> "It's a Mauser I believe."

It is very doubtful that established police officers could have made such a mistake. It is even more doubtful that three such police officers could make such a mistake. Could the rifle have been switched? No other evidence has ever come to light that this is what happened but in 1976, for an interview for a newspaper, Chief Curry responded to that question by remarking, "It's more than possible."

According to Warren Commission exhibit 3048 the rifle was shown on local television station KBOX and described as a 7.65 Mauser.

Another rifle was found in the School Book Depository on the sixth floor and brought down the back fire escape of the building. This rifle was filmed by an independent film business called Dallas Cinema Associates. The rifle was filmed as it was brought from the sixth floor down to the ground by the Dallas police. A closeup of the rifle shows that it did not have a rifle scope.

Author Priscilla McMillan exposed in her book _Marina And Lee_ that on November 20th, two days before the assassination, The School Book Depository's supervisor, Roy Truly and several other employees recall seeing a Mauser being taken out of a carton and being shown around in Mr. Truly's office. The Mauser was shown along with another rifle, a Remington by an employee by the name of Warren Caster. No one has ever explained what happened to these rifles. Neither the Warren Commission or the Select Committee mentioned them in their published findings.

Could the police officers who described the rifle as a Mauser have been describing the second rifle that was found and taken out the rear fire escape? It is apparent that the rifle filmed by Dallas Cinema Associates was neither a Mauser nor the Carcano as this gun did not have a scope. From the evidence, it appears that at least two and more likely three guns were found on the sixth floor of the School Book Depository Building. Yet, neither the Dallas Police, the Warren Commission, the F.B.I., the Secret Service or the Select Committee revealed any other information concerning these other guns. The Warren Commission sidestepped the issue simply by stating that the police officers who described the rifle as a Mauser were mistaken.

In order to establish linkage of the Mannlicher-Carcano rifle to Oswald, the Warren Commission published a duplicated copy of an ad they said Oswald had used to order the rifle. The rifle itself was purchased from Klein's Sporting Goods in Chicago, Illinois from an ad that appeared in the February 1963 issue of *American Rifleman Magazine*. According to Klein's documentation, the order came in by mail on March 13, 1963. A 6.5 mm Italian Mannlicher-Carcano serial number C2766 was shipped to:

A. Hidell
P O Box 2915
Dallas Texas

on March 30th, 1963. It has been established and well documented that Oswald used the name A. Hidell and he had a selective service card on him with that name at the time of his arrest. The post office box was in the name of Oswald. The problem is that the ad in the magazine reveals that the rifle had an overall length of 36" but the rifle in police custody was 40" overall rifle. What the Warren Commission did was come up with a "duplicate" ad that revealed a rifle with the correct length.

Another suspicious point about the mail order is that the post office was unable to locate a form in which Oswald or anyone else signed for the rifle. Postal regulations call for this to be done and the record to be kept on file for a period of two years but officials at the post office said that the form must have been thrown away. From a standpoint of solid evidence then, nothing could determine that OSWALD picked up the mail ordered rifle at the post office as the form mysteriously disappeared.

The apparent alteration of the mail order ad that ended up as evidence in the Warren Commission is even more puzzling when you look at the details concerning the manufacturer of the weapon. The problem is with the serial number on the gun but it wasn't until I restudied forensic scientist Charles Wilber's published work, *Mediolegal Investigation Of The President John F. Kennedy Murder*, that this became quite clear. The weapon was manufactured in a small Italian factory in Terni in the 1940s. At the time, the Italian government had ordered just about all small gun manufactures to make this weapon. The weapons factories were very lax when they assigned serial numbers to the rifles and some factories would use the same serial number more than once. To make it even worse, the different factories did not share assigned serial number information with each other so it's possible that two different factories could manufacture the same make of rifle both with the same number. As far as evidence goes then, the matching of the serial number to the alleged murder weapon is of little use.

The Warren Commission and the Select Committee looked into how Oswald got the rifle into the School Book Depository Building and onto the sixth floor. The Dallas Police found a brown paper bag on the sixth floor near the corner window that was thirty-eight inches in length. The Warren Commission determined that the rifle was brought into the building in this bag. Investigators determined that the bag had Oswald's fingerprints on it. However, the rifle was described when it was found as being very well oiled and no traces of oil were found on the bag by either the Dallas Police or by the FBI.

Wesley Frazier was a co-worker of Lee Oswald at the School Book Depository and had driven Oswald to work on the morning of the assassination from Irving, Texas. Frazier stated that

Oswald was carrying a long brown paper bag when he was picked up and Oswald indicated to Frazier that it contained curtain rods for his apartment. The Warren Commission determined that this brown paper bag contained the rifle. However, Frazier stated that when Oswald got out of the vehicle in the downtown parking lot, he carried the bag by cupping it with his palm and holding it under his armpit. It's been determined that, even when the rifle is broken down, it would have been too long to be carried in this fashion. Before the Warren Commission, Frazier's testimony went as followings. (He had previously been shown the brown paper bag)

> *Question: When you were shown this bag, do you recall whether or not you told the officers who showed you the bag....did you tell them whether you thought it was or was not about the same length as the bag you saw on the back seat?*

> *Answer: I told them that as far as the length there, I told them that was entirely too long.*

One of the Commission members then asked Frazier to stand up and hold the rifle just as he had seen Oswald hold the rifle and he could not do it as the bag was too long.

Jack Dority acted as a security person during the morning hours when School Book Depository employees would arrive for work. His job was to sit at a desk near the employee entrance as each employee arrived. Dority has stated that Oswald arrived at the employee entrance empty handed and checked in. A few minutes later, manager Roy Truely stated that he saw Oswald near a book bin and noted he was empty handed.

RIFLE SUMMARY

> *1) If the rifle was in the brown paper bag, it could not be carried under the armpit as described.*

> *2) The security desk reported that Oswald entered the building the day of the assassination empty handed.*

> *3) The building manager Roy Truely stated that Oswald was empty handed just a few minutes after he entered the building.*

> *4) When the rifle was found, it was well oiled but no oil or traces of gun oil was found on the brown bag.*

> *5) The rifle was first identified as a Mauser by three Dallas police but was later changed to a Mannlicher-Carcano.*

> *6) Several witnesses were shown a Mauser rifle in the School Book Depository Building two days before the assassination.*

> *7) The Warren Commission published a mail order ad that it stated was the ad Oswald used to order the Mannlicher Carano rifle but the ad had been changed to conform to the correct length of the rifle.*

> *8) Although postal regulations state such records must be*

*maintained for two years, the post office was unable to produce a
signed release for the mail order rifle.*

*9) There was likely more than one serial number for the Mannlicher
Carcano rifle.*

*10) Another rifle was filmed being brought down the back fire
escape of the School Book Depository which was not a Carano
and not a Mauser rifle. This rifle lacked a telescopic scope.*

*11) The weight of the evidence suggests that at least two and more
likely three rifles were found on the sixth floor.*

THE EMPTY SHELLS

According to the Warren Commission, three empty shells where found on the sixth floor of the
Texas School Book Depository Building near the corner window. But, there is evidence that only
two shells were turned in and the shells had been tampered with prior to the crime scene officers
recording the position of the shells.

Tom Alger was a reporter for a local television station and was able to walk right into the
Depository Building right as it was being sealed off. Alger knew many of the police officers
working the scene and used his friendship with them to get to the sixth floor. Alger noted three
shells behind a box but he could not photograph them as the box was in the way. Captain Will
Fritz picked up the shells so Alger could photograph them and then threw them back down on the
floor. This was during a period of time before the crime scene technicians arrived which means that
the shells where not in their original position when they where photographed by the Dallas Police.

Deputy Sheriff Roger Craig and Luke Monney both stated publicly that they saw the shells at an
earlier time.They stated that there were three of them and the shells were neatly placed one next to
the other all pointing in the same direction about one inch apart as if someone had carefully
arranged them that way. One of the suspicious points about the shells is that the rifle is known to
fling them quite a way when they are ejected.

The Warren Commission states that three shells were found which is confirmed by all witness
testimony. Yet, a Texas Department Of Safety police report shows that only two shells were
found. The transfer of evidence by the Dallas Police to the F.B.I. show a transfer sheet for just
two of these shells. It's assumed that Fritz held on to one of the shells for some reason and it was
later revealed that there was a dent in this third shell. Because of the dent, the shell could not have
been fired out of the rifle. Tests were conducted by the FBI that show markings indicating that the
first two shells had been in the rifle but the third shell was never tested.

In the 1970's the FBI released an investigative document that revealed that the shells found of the
sixth floor window had been traced to an ammo manufacturer in Philadelphia. It was determined
that these particular rounds had been sold to the U.S. Marines in a lot that included four million.
Without looking any further, this appears to make sense as Oswald was in the Marines. But, the
Marines never had any use for such ammo as they didn't have or stock the type of rifles that
would fire them. Many researchers have speculated that the four million rounds must have been
for some sort of covert operation that Oswald certainly seems to be linked into as described in

another chapter. This certainly seems to fit as it was standard practice for covert action supplies to be laundered through various military purchases. No other explanation has ever surfaced and all the official investigations are strangely silent on the subject.

Finally, it's a known fact that any type of ammo could not be purchased (even from military surplus) except in boxes of twenty or fifty. Other than the empty shells found on the floor and the round found still in the rifle, no additional ammo was located either in the School Book Depository Building or among Oswald's possessions.

In the 1970's the House Select Committee On Assassinations had both the rifle and the shell cases pulled from the National Archives. They determined that the shell markings didn't match the rifle barrel markings. This fact was explained away simply by stating that the rifle had been test fired so many times that the barrel markings in the rifle had changed.

EMPTY SHELL SUMMARY

1) Fritz picked up the empty shells and then threw them back down on the floor before they could be photographed, altering their location.

2) Other witnesses said that the empty shells were neatly arranged on the floor as if they had been carefully placed there.

3) The shells could not be commercially purchased.

4) The shells had to be obtained by a box of at least twenty and no other shells had ever been found among Oswald's possessions except the three spent shells and the one live round in the rifle.

5) One spent shell that was found was bent.

6) Only two shells were first turned over to the FBI by the Dallas police.

7) The House Select Committee determined that the spent shells in the archives didn't match the rifle.

8) The rifle was known to fling the shells quite a ways upon being ejected but the shells were found near the corner window, the alleged assassin's nest.

THE FINGERPRINT ON THE RIFLE

Originally, the Dallas Police stated that they located no fingerprints on the rifle that belonged to Oswald on the rifle. If Oswald didn't have any fingerprints on the rifle, he either didn't fire the rifle that day or fired the rifle and wiped off the prints or he fired the rifle and someone else wiped off the prints. Due to the fact that Oswald was found in the second floor lunchroom ninety seconds after the first shot was fired, he wouldn't have had time to wipe off the fingerprints. This leaves us with two possibilities:

a) Oswald didn't fire the rifle.
b) Oswald fired the rifle and then handed it to another person who
wiped off the fingerprints and hid the weapon on the opposite
corner of the sixth floor.

The Dallas police later said they found a fingerprint on the rifle after the rifle was disassembled. On the bottom of the rifle barrel, a palm print was found that belonged to Oswald. However, this palm print is highly suspicious as you will find when you investigate the details of how and when the palm print was found.

The rifle was in the custod: ' the Dallas Police Department from the time it was found at the Texas School Book Depository until is was flown to Washington on November 23rd for testing and examination in the FBI lab. Although extensive examination was made of the rifle at the FBI lab, no announcement that fingerprints were found on it was made. In a written statement made by Hoover, the FBI made an extensive examination of the weapon but found no significant fingerprints. What is curious is that the rifle was flown back to Dallas on the afternoon of November 24th after Oswald had been shot.

Dallas Police Lieutenant John Day says he discovered the palm print on the underside of the barrel on the night of November 22nd before he turned the rifle over to the FBI. However, no statement, record or photograph was ever made which is not customary and Day evidently didn't report his findings to anyone inside or outside the Dallas Police Department.

After Oswald's death he was taken to Miller Funeral Home in Fort Worth. On the night of the 24th, funeral home director Paul Groody said that agents from the FBI came into the funeral home and spent several hours with Oswald's body. Groody told assassination researcher Jim Marrs which Mr. Marrs quotes in his book, _Crossfire_, "I had a heck of a time getting black fingerprint ink off Oswald's hands."

Why was the FBI taking Oswald's fingerprints from his body when he had been fingerprinted at least three times while in the custody of the Dallas Police and his fingerprints had been found on various personal belongings? No one knows and no one knows why the rifle was flown back to Dallas either.

On November 26th, the rifle was again flown to the FBI in Washington but it was not until November 29th that the Dallas police turned over the fingerprint that was lifted of the bottom of the gun barrel. Thus we have the following strange facts concerning the fingerprint found on the rifle:

1) The rifle was examined by the Dallas police on November 22nd
and no announcement was made that fingerprints belonging to
Oswald was found.

2) During the early morning hours of November 23rd, the rifle was
flown to the FBI Lab in Washington.

3) The rifle was extensively examined by the FBI and Hoover issued
a written statement that no fingerprints were found.

4) On November 24th, after Oswald was murdered by Ruby, the rifle
was flown back to Dallas.

5) The night of November 24th, the FBI took fingerprints from Oswald's dead body even though Oswald had been fingerprinted alive several times.

6) The Dallas police turned over the rifle to the FBI a second time on November 26th, 1963 but no announcement was made that fingerprints were found.

7) November 29th, after the rifle was in the custody of the FBI for three days, the Dallas police released information that it had obtained Oswald's fingerprint on the underside of the rifle barrel.

THE THIRD MAN WITH A BULLET WOUND

James Thomas Tague was apparently hit by debris from a stray bullet during the assassination in the Southeastern corner of the plaza. His story did not surface until the summer of 1964. At the time his story did surface, the Warren Commission was widely under way with it's investigation and it was being reported that three shots where fired that caused the following damage:

A) The first bullet hit Kennedy's back
B) The second bullet hit Connally
C) The third bullet hit the President's head

The surfacing of Tague's story was very troubling for the Warren Commission as they now had to explain how one bullet had missed.

Apparently right after the assassination, Tague was not aware of the cut on his face. Deputy Sheriff Eddy Walthers encountered Tague moments after the assassination and told him he was bleeding from a small cut on his face. Walther's police report he filed is quoted in assassination researcher Jim Marrs work *Crossfire* on page 61 as follows:

"I immediately went to the Triple Underpass on Elm Street in an effort to locate possible marks left by stray bullets. While I was looking for possible marks, some unknown person stated to me that something had hit his face while he was parked on Main Street....Upon examining the curb and pavement in this vicinity, I found where a bullet had splattered on the top edge of the curb on Main Street....due to the fact that projectile struck so near the underpass, it was, in my opinion, probably the last shot that was fired and had apparently went high and above the President's car."

Late in the afternoon on the day of the assassination, Tague contacted the local FBI by telephone and reported the incident but the FBI never asked for his testimony or obtained any statements.

The Warren Commission asked the FBI to look into this incident on July 4th, 1964. The FBI checked the curb and reported back to the commission in a document that was dated July 17th which read in part:

"The area of the curb where the bullet or fragment hit was carefully checked and it was ascertained there was no nick in the curb in the checked area, nor was any mark observed."

But Tom Dillard, a news photographer for the _Dallas Morning News_ had taken a photograph of the mark on the curb that ended up in the custody of the Warren Commission. On July 23rd, 1964 Tague gave his testimony before the Warren Commission. After his testimony, the commission again asked the FBI to look into this matter and the FBI then physically removed the section of the curb and had an analysis made in the Washington Lab. The findings are as follows:

> _"Small foreign metal smears were found adhering to the curbing section within the area of the mark."_

THE BLOOD ON THE SIDEWALK STEPS

Jerry Coley and Charles Mulky worked for the _Dallas Morning News_ in the newspaper's advertising department. Coley sold ad space and on the day of the assassination he stopped making his rounds early in order to view the Presidential Motorcade in downtown Dallas. Coley and Mulky walked from the newspaper office to the front of the Dallas County jail where they watched the motorcade. As the motorcade turned left into the plaza area both heard shots and saw people running toward the top of the grassy knoll. Both men walked in that direction but were stopped by a policeman who asked them not to enter the area. They then walked around the School Book Depository Building and came out onto the grassy knoll from the other side. Coley and Mulky then walked down the grassy knoll in the plaza and noticed a dark red substance on the steps. Mulky's first thoughts was that someone had spilled a soft drink and said that the volume of the substance was more than a pint. Mulky bent over and stuck his finger in the red substance and tasted it. He then told Jerry Coley, "My God, Jerry...that's blood." The two raced back to the newspaper office to find newspaper photographer Jim Hood. Upon locating Hood, the three went back to the grassy knoll and located the pool of blood. By this time, the blood had begun to coagulate. Photographer Hood was able to take several photos of the blood.

In the following days, Coley states that he started receiving strange and threatening phone calls at his home. He was so scared, he sent his wife and family out of town for a few weeks and he himself decided to leave town for a week or so until things settled down. Upon returning to town and to work, a Times news reporter requested an interview with him and he refused.

A few days after the Times reporter requested an interview, two FBI agents came to Coley's place of employment and asked to interview Coley and Hood. The four men went into a conference room. The FBI agents immediately asked about the blood and the photographs without either one of them saying anything about it.

The FBI agents wanted all the photographs, all the negatives and wanted to look at the camera. Jim Hood got up from his chair and went to get the items requested. He was back in a few moments and handed the photographs and the negatives to one of the FBI agents. The FBI agents put the photos and negatives in an envelope and stated that, " _that was the end of the photographs, the end of the story and the end of the blood._ " The agent also said to both Hood and Coley, _"For your own benefit, it never happened. You didn't see it."_

Fearing for their lives and scared from the threatening telephone calls and the FBI agents, Hood, Mulky and Coley remained silent for 20 years. By the year 1988, all parties to the incident were dead except Coley. Coley had known Jack Ruby as Ruby spent a great deal of time at the newspaper office.

In 1988 a film crew asked to interview Jerry Coley about Jack Ruby. By this time, Coley's children had grown and he decided to tell about the pool of blood. The film crew spent three days with Coley and returned to Hollywood. However, the producer killed the story as the other witnesses to corroborate the story had died. This story had never been published until 1991 when writer Wallace O. Chariton included a chapter about it in his book called _Unsolved Texas Mysteries_ published by Worldware Publishing in Plano, Texas.

THE BODY OF THE PRESIDENT

The medical evidence of the Kennedy assassination is full of controversy and contradiction that started when the first doctor in Dallas attempted to save Kennedy's life. The first two doctors to treat the President at Parkland Hospital were Dr. Malcolm Perry and Dr. Kemp Clark. Dr. Perry was the first doctor to see the President. He noted a small round wound in the President's throat just to the right of his Adam's Apple. The hole was reported to be 3 X 5 mm. The doctors performed what is called a tracheotomy over the wound in the throat. This is an operation that involves placing a breathing tube down the throat. Perry made an incision in the throat wound and inserted the tube that altered the size and nature of the hole.

Both Perry and Clark held a press conference later that day stating several times that it was their opinion that the throat wound was an entrance wound. Their quotes were quickly spread throughout the world by the news media. However, the President was facing forward and if the throat wound was an entrance wound, then, someone had to have fired the shot from the front, not the rear. Both Dr. Perry and Dr. Clark seemed quite sure of their opinion on this and it was not until they testified before the Warren Commission that they changed their story to say that the throat wound could have been either an entrance or exit wound.

Perry and Clark were not the only two doctors who saw the President at Parkland Hospital before the tracheotomy was performed. A total of ten doctors and one nurse examined the President before the operation was performed. Only one described the throat wound as an exit wound. Here is their brief summary:

> *DOCTOR CARRICO: ENTRANCE WOUND*
> *DOCTOR PERRY: ENTRANCE WOUND*
> *DOCTOR CLARK: NO OPINION*
> *DOCTOR McCLELLAND: ENTRANCE WOUND*
> *DOCTOR BAXTER: ENTRANCE WOUND*
> *DOCTOR JENKINS: EXIT WOUND*
> *DOCTOR JONES: ENTRANCE WOUND*
> *DOCTOR AKIN: ENTRANCE WOUND*
> *DOCTOR PETERS: ENTRANCE WOUND*
> *NURSE HENCHLIFFE: ENTRANCE WOUND*

Other than the tracheotomy, no other surgical procedure was performed at Parkland on Kennedy. He was pronounced dead around 1:30 P.M. The emergency room doctors also described a wound in the right back section of the head of about 35 square cm. A casket was brought to Parkland hospital by a local funeral company and funeral director Aubrey Rike helped place Kennedy's body into an expensive ceremonial casket with bronze side bars. Rike stated that he had placed a mattress liner in the bottom of the coffin to protect the inside of the coffin from blood stains.

The casket was driven to Air Force One and flown back to Washington with Mrs. Kennedy, Lyndon Johnson and the rest of the Presidential party. The arrival was televised on nationwide television and those of us who watched can remember Mrs. Kennedy with her blood stained dress getting off the plane with the ceremonial casket and getting into a light colored ambulance. The body was taken to Bethesda Medical Hospital. However, several of the medical technicians remember details that just don't add up. Officially, Mrs. Kennedy rode with the expensive ceremonial casket to the front doors of Bethesda Medical Center but witnesses have a different story. Assassination researcher, David S. Lifton, interviewed several of the technicians that worked at Bethesda as part of his fifteen year research into the medical evidence of the Kennedy assassination for his best selling book, _Best Evidence_. Most of the witnesses he interviewed said that they had been ordered not to talk about what they knew and had to sign a statement to that effect which indicated that, if they did talk, they were subject to court marshall. These witnesses describe a plain grey shipping casket being delivered from the rear of the building in a black unmarked ambulance. Both Paul O'Connor, Bethesda medical technician, and Dennis David, Chief Of The Day, recall Kennedy arriving in this manner. David said that when he opened the plain grey casket, he found the President in a zipped up body bag. However, the Dallas funeral director, Aubrey Rike, insists that he didn't put Kennedy in any body bag and he didn't put him in a gray shipping casket. Both O'Connor and David recall Mrs. Kennedy arriving at the front entrance in the light colored ambulance with the ceremonial casket and both state that upon her arrival, Kennedy's body was already in the autopsy room.

Jerrol Custer was an X-ray technician that night and took the X-ray photos of Kennedy. Lifton interviewed Custer for his book, _Best Evidence_. He stated that he had already had X-ray photos of Kennedy in his hands when he saw Mrs. Kennedy arrive with the ceremonial casket. Custer also recalls that the brain was not in it's cavity and that he was able to place both of his hands inside the skull. This was at a time before the autopsy was completed.

The autopsy was witnessed by two FBI agents. In their report, they stated that upon examination of the President's body before the autopsy, a tracheotomy and surgery to the head had been performed. The tracheotomy had been performed at Dallas but certainly no surgery to the head. FBI reports also show that the back wound of the president was probed and no point of exit could be found. If no point of exit could be probed then the bullet that entered Kennedy's back did not come out his throat and, if this is the case, more than one gunman fired at Kennedy as the wound in the back and the wound in the throat had to have been caused by two separate bullets.

David Lifton's fifteen year research points that much had changed from the time Kennedy's body left Parkland Hospital and arrived at Bethesda Naval Center At the 1991 Assassination Symposium in Dallas, Texas in November, Lifton went over his evidence on this and summarized it as follows:

> A) When the body of the president left Parkland, the back head wound was described as a wound that was about 35 square cm. When it arrived at Parkland, the same wound was described as being about 170 square cm.
>
> B) When the body left Parkland, most of the brain was in the skull. When the body arrived at Bethesda, the skull contained no brain.
>
> C) When the body was placed in the casket in Dallas, only his head was covered in a white sheet. When the body arrived at Bethesda, it was in a zipped up body bag.
>
> D) When the body left Dallas, it was in an expensive ceremonial casket with bronze handles. When it arrived at Bethesda, it was in a

gray military shipping casket with no handles.

E) Officially, the President's body was taken from Andrews Air Force Base to Bethesda in a light colored Navy ambulance and entered Bethesda through the front door. Yet, witnesses at Bethesda state that the President's body arrived in a black civilian ambulance at the rear of the hospital before Mrs. Kennedy arrived in the front with the light colored ambulance.

In David Lifton's Book, *Best Evidence*, he points out the fact that somewhere between Parkland and Bethesda the body was altered in order to conform to the lone assassin theory proposed by the Warren Commission. The first edition of the Lifton book was published in 1980. A new edition was published in 1988 which includes autopsy photographs Lifton says he obtained from an FBI agent. The autopsy photographs given to Lifton and published in the latest edition of *Best Evidence* create more questions than they answer. A view of the President's head from the top show a massive wound or opening in the center of the President's skull. A rear right view of the head shows a flap of skull and skin toward the right frontal position of the head but reveals no back wound. An enlargement of the top view shows what Lifton describes as a pin or clip inside the cavity of the skull.

The Warren Commission used drawings of the President's wounds and stated that they did this in respect to the President and his family. The Select Committee went a little better and looked at the autopsy photographs but had scale drawings rendered for publication. The problem between the two official investigations is that the back wound of the President has moved. The Warren Commission drawing shows the wound higher up on the neck than the Select Committee drawings. This appears to be very strange. The Warren Commission also shows that the President's head is bent way down which causes the wound on the neck to come up quite a lot so the trajectory will line up properly with the exit wound in the throat. However, it is highly doubtful that the President would bend his head in such a manner. The Zapruder film shows the President behind a highway sign out of view when the first bullet struck. Yet, before he went out of view and after he came back into view, he didn't have his head tilted down. The only time his head tilts downward is when he is hit in the head.

The Zapruder film also shows that when the head explosion occurs, it occurs in the right frontal portion of the head, not the rear. It certainly appears to be a strike from the front. As the President is hit in the head, his head and body thrust backward and to the right which is certainly a sign that he was hit from the front. The explosion also caused debris to fly to the back and to the left of the President which is another indication that the shots did not come from behind.

In Lifton's latest editions of *Best Evidence*, he has published black and white photographs of the President's autopsy and claims many of them to be fakes. During the 1991 November Assassination Symposium in Dallas, Texas, computer image expert Tom Wilson presented evidence of his study of the photographs in which he removed gray scale color from the photograph and found that the autopsy photographs have been completely redone and touched up. Wilson has also done an electronic autopsy of photographic and x-ray evidence given to him by the famous lawyer and doctor Cyril Wecht. His conclusions are that the headshot is from the front. During the same symposium, David Lifton presented his evidence. No explanation from governmental authorities has come forward to explain the touched up autoposy photographs or any of the inconsistencies that are glaring from the evidence that has surfaced concerning the work of researchers and experts David LIfton, Dr. Cyril Wecht, and Tom Wilson.

THE BACKYARD PHOTOGRAPHS

The day after the assassination, the Dallas police released photographs of Lee Oswald holding the murder weapon in one hand and a copy of a communist paper in the other hand. These photographs, according to Dallas police, were taken in his backyard. One of the photographs appeared on the cover of *Life Magazine* in February of 1964.

Captain Fritz had shown Oswald this photograph during interrogation and Oswald said that he knew something about photography and although the photograph was his face, it had been pasted on the body and he had never seen the photographs before.

The photographs were found at 2515 West Fifth Street in Irving, Texas, the home of the Paines. On two searches on the day of the assassination of this address, the Dallas police did not locate the photographs. However, another search was made the following day and it was this third search in which the Dallas police say they found the photos. But the two photos were never listed on inventory sheets of Oswald's possessions. Neither was the black shirt and the black pants that Oswald had on in the photographs ever located. Officially, two photographs but only one negative were found. Yet, Dallas police Gus Rose says that there were also two negatives. Until 1967, these photos were the only ones known to be of the backyard pose.

The actual camera the alleged photographs were taken with was not found for several weeks but finally turned over by Robert Oswald, Oswald's brother. Oswald's brother said that he found the camera at the Paine home even though the Dallas police had searched the home several times for the camera. Robert said that the camera belonged to his brother Lee Oswald. This reflex camera was a very poor quality camera and Oswald was highly interested in photography. He owned several very expensive cameras and no one ever explained why he would use such a cheap camera for these photographs.

The Warren Commission said that the photos were taken by Marina Oswald, Oswald's wife, on March 31st, 1963 at the 214 W Neely address. The photos show a bright sunny day. But, a check on weather reports in the area that day reveal that it was cloudy and rainy all day.

The Warren Commission determined that the photos where real and had FBI agent Lindal Shangfield testify before it. The agent brought with him a photograph that had duplicated lighting taken with the reflex camera that might have determined the problems of the shadows on the face. However, this photograph was a photograph of an FBI man with his head cut off. The FBI did state that the actual photographs were compared to the simulated photograph to determine if they came from the same reflex camera which they stated that they did. However, Jack White pointed out that this could have easily have been done by taking composite photographs of the scene using the reflex camera.

In 1976 the Senate Intelligence Committee located a third photograph of Oswald with the backyard pose that was slightly different. The photo was found among the belongings of the widow of Dallas police officer Roscoe White. In the early 1990's Rosco White's son claimed that Rosco White was one of three gunmen that fired at the President which I will go into in another section.

In 1967 after he returned from Haiti, George DeMorenschild found a fourth photo of the backyard photograph that was still a slightly different pose among his personal belongings that he had in storage. On the back of this photograph is written:

The inscription was first written in pencil and then gone over in ink. Handwriting experts have revealed that the writing was not the handwriting of Oswald, his wife, DeMorenschild or his wife.

In 1970, Dallas news reporter Jim Marrs was looking into the backyard photographs when he interviewed Robert and Patricia Hester. The Hesters worked at the National Photo Lab in Dallas. They said they were very busy processing photographic material for both the FBI and the Secret Service the night of the assassination. In 1970, the Hesters told Marrs that the FBI had color transparencies of the backyard photographs the night of the assassination and had one color transparency that had nobody in the picture. Not only is this highly suspicious, this was the night before the photographs where supposed to have been found in the first place.

Photographic expert Jack White has studied these photographs for two decades and testified before the House Select Committee. His conclusion is that the photographs are fakes. His pointed findings include:

1) STANDING OFF CENTER: White concludes that Oswald is standing off center and outside the weight bearing alignment of his feet. A person could not stand in such a position.

2) PROPORTIONS: When the body proportions are brought into alignment from the knees to the head by adjusting the size of the photographs, one head is much larger than the other.

3) OVERALL BODY SHADOWS: Although the photos were supposed to have been taken just seconds apart, the overall body shadows in the photographs are all different. In 133-A the photograph has a 10 o'clock shadow, 133-B a 12 o'clock shadow and 133-C a 10 o'clock shadow again.

4) ARM AND ELBOWS: White said that the elbow is too high in one photograph and the elbow doesn't show up on the one photograph of the arm were Oswald is holding the rifle. This pose had been attempted to be duplicated but could not.

5) HANDS AND FINGERS: On the photographs the left hand and finger looks normal. Yet the right hand is missing fingernails and the hand looks stubby.

6) WATCH: The photographs reveal that Oswald is wearing a watch but all witnesses have stated that Oswald did not wear and didn't own a watch. No watch was found among the possessions of Oswald and he was not wearing one when he was arrested.

7) RIFLE: When the photographs are blown up to the actual height of Oswald that was 5'9", the rifle in the photograph is too long. When the rifle is adjusted in the photograph to it's proper length, Oswald's height is six inches too short.

8) SCOPE: White noted that in the photograph the rear end of the rifle scope is missing and pants wrinkles appear where the end of the

scope is supposed to be.

9) FACE: The face shows Oswald with a flat chin but Oswald had a clift chin. There is a line that breaks up the grain of the photograph that runs across the chin that many say is where the cut took place to paste Oswald's face onto the photograph.

10) PHOTOGRAPHIC OVERLAY: When Mr. White took 133-A and 133-B and adjusted and overlayed them, nothing matched up which isn't suppose to happen with two slightly different poses. However, the faces on the two photographs did.

11) FACE SHADOWS: Both photos show the same V shaped shadow below the nose. However, on one of the photos Oswald's head is tilted but the shadow does not adjust for this tilt.

12) NECK SHADOWS: On one of the photos there is light on the right side of the neck but the same photo shows the rifle casting a shadow to this angle.

13) COLLAR SIZE: The collar size can be determined from the photograph using a mathematical formula which came out to size 16. Oswald wore a six 14 1/2 collar and all his clothes found among his personal belongings were in the 14.5 to 15 inch range.

14) BACKGROUNDS: White determined that one photograph had the top cropped off and the other photograph had the bottom cropped off which made the photos appear like they had been taken at slightly different locations. However, except for small fractions, everything lines up on both photographs when the two were compared. That is, the camera did not change position and the only way to do this would be with a tripod which was not used.

15) SMALL DIFFERENCES: For many months White was puzzled by the small differences he noted in the backgrounds but they were not off much. After looking at the photographs some more he determined that on the background of one, the camera appears to be slightly tilted. He then took another copy of the photo by tilting it on a board and everything came perfectly into alignment.

During the 1991 JFK Assassination Symposium held in Dallas, Texas of November of that year, computer image processing expert Tom Wilson corroborated all of the White analysis and added that he inspected the feet on the man in the backyard photograph as to light refraction and compared this to official records of the day concerning the position of the sun. Wilson stated that the photograph was taken at 9:12 A.M. if it was taken on the day it was alleged to have been taken. But Marina Oswald's testimony stated that the photographs were taken in the early afternoon which is completely inconsistant with the Wilson study.

EVIDENCE OF OTHER SHOTS FIRED

A shot that hit cement close to a manhole cover on the middle part of the grassy knoll was located by several witnesses and bystanders. The manhole cover would be just east of where shots hit Kennedy and Connally in the motorcade. Deputy Sheriff Buddy Walthers recalls the bullet mark. A forty-five caliber slug was located near the bullet mark. This was picked up by a man identifying himself as an FBI agent. The bullet mark near the manhole traces back to a building across the street from the School Book Depository Building known as the Records Building or County Records Building.

Recently a person by the name of Dean Morgan came forward and stated that in 1975 her father had gone up on the roof of the Records Building to fix a large air conditioner. The roof of the building has a kind of lip that runs all the way around the building. On the side facing toward Dealey Plaza, a 30.06 bullet shell was found that was lodged under the lip of the roof. The shell appears to have been there for a long time as the side of it that was exposed to air and sunlight and was pitted.

In the Groden and Livingston book, _High Treason_, a photograph appears of the FBI agent picking up the slug. No one has ever been able to identify the FBI agent or bring forward any more information concerning this slug.

Several witnesses have also stated that the highway sign on the north end of the grassy knoll was hit by a bullet. The sign is the same sign seen in the Zapruder film. Either the afternoon or evening of the day of the assassination or in the early morning hours of the following day, the sign was removed. No one has ever been able to account for who removed this sign or why it was removed. It has also been determined that there is a splice in the Zapruder film during the time that the highway sign is in view. The Zapruder film does reveal the back of the highway sign and it appears that there is a slice in the film right at the point of the sign being hit by what looks like a bullet. In the frames directly after the slice, a slow motion study reveals bits and pieces flying away from the sign.

Another bullet mark was found just in front of where Zapruder was standing on the sidewalk. The mark tracks back to the previously mentioned manhole on the other side of the street and to the south.

The Warren Commission published photographs of the windshield of the Presidential limo. The vehicle had a bullet hole on the windshield and a dent from a missile on the metal frame that ran around the windshield. No further examination of the vehicle could be made by other investigators because President Johnson had the vehicle flown to Detroit and taken apart and rebuilt.

In 1974 Richard Lester was on the south side of the Triple Overpass with a metal detector and located a bullet fragment. Two years after his find, he turned the fragment over to the FBI and it was analyzed for the Select Committee. It was determined that this fragment was from a 6.5 millimeter weapon. Since this did not come from the rifle that was to supposed to have belonged to Oswald, it had to have been shot by someone else.

THE GENERAL WALKER HOUSE PHOTOGRAPH

The Dallas police department found a photograph of General Walker's home among Oswald's possessions. Chief Curry published a photograph containing some of the personal possessions the Dallas police obtained and the Walker photograph is clearly visible in this photograph. In the driveway of the Walker house is a 1957 Chevrolet. In the Curry photograph, the license plate is visible but you cannot read the numbers. When the Warren Commission published the photograph, there was a black spot where the license plate is supposed to be. Marina Oswald stated that when she saw the photograph, the license plate didn't have this black spot.

OSWALD'S ACTIVITIES AFTER THE ASSASSINATION

OSWALDS'S ESCAPE

The Warren Commission Report stated that Oswald left the School Book Depository Building through the front door at 12:33 P.M. despite the fact that they found no witness that saw him leave even though there were dozens of people and police officers around the area of the front of the building at the time.

The Warren Commission Report stated that Oswald walked about seven blocks passing about seven bus stops and then boarded a public bus at 12:40 P.M. that was traveling back towards the School Book Depository Building. The bus got snared in traffic because of the assassination and, according to the Warren Commission, Oswald got off the bus at 12:44 P.M. The bus evidence was determined based on the fact that Oswald had a bus transfer ticket in his top pocket at the time of his arrest and witness testimony given by Cecil McWatters, the bus driver. However, Cecil McWatters was not able to identify Oswald in a police lineup.

Other witnesses observed a different accounting of the man from the sixth floor window.

RICHARD CARR: Richard Carr was working on a building under construction near the School Book Depository Building. He stated that he saw a dark skinned person in one of the upper windows of the School Book Depository Building that looked either Spanish or Cuban. After the assassination, Carr went back down to the ground floor of the building and walked outside. He stated that he saw this person he had earlier seen on the sixth floor shortly before the shots rang out. Carr followed this man and saw him get into a Nash Rambler. Carr has been threatened, shot at and has had dynamite placed in his car's ignition and Carr's story, like many others who have been threatened, has changed from time to time but the above account is his original account.

DEPUTY SHERIFF ROGER CRAIG: Deputy Sheriff Roger Craig told the Warren Commission that shortly after the assassination he was standing near the Book Depository and saw a man run from the building down towards the grassy area were a light colored Rambler station wagon with a luggage rack had pulled up to the curb. The driver was a dark skinned male with short dark hair wearing a white jacket. Craig stated that he later identified this man as Lee Oswald and went to Captain Fritz's office to tell him. However, Fritz stated that no Deputy Sheriff was ever in his office during this time although someone had called about it. However, pictures speak better than words and in Chief Curry's book concerning the assassination called the *JFK Assassination File*, published a photograph on page 72 showing Craig standing next to Fritz in his office the early evening of the assassination. Craig stated that his witness testimony before the Warren Commission was changed in fourteen places and that he had been threatened, shot at and driven from the police force. He was the victim of an accident in which he injured his back and on May 15th, 1975, he died of a gunshot wound that was ruled a suicide.

Craig's account was verified by another witness by the name of Marvin C. Robinson.

> *MARVIN C. ROBINSON:* Robinson stated in an FBI report that he was driving west on Elm Street just after the assassination. As he crossed the intersection of Elm and Houston, he saw a light colored Nash station wagon stop in front of the School Book Depository Building and a white male came down from the building and got into the station wagon.

At 12:48 the Warren Commission report says that Oswald approached a cab at the Greyhound Bus Station which was a few blocks from the School Book Depository Building. He started to enter the cab but noticed a lady standing on the curb also appearing to be waiting for a cab. He offered this lady his cab but she declined stating that she could catch the next one. It is very hard to understand a man escaping from the murder of a President of the United States offering his cab to someone else. According to the Warren Commission, the cab drove Oswald to within one block of his rooming house in the Oak Cliff section of Dallas when he departed the cab a minute or so before 1:00.

> *WILLIAM WHALY:* The cab driver, William Whaly stated that he was able to identify Oswald in a police lineup before the Warren Commission. However, he said that during the police lineup Oswald was the only adult in the line and the rest of the suspect line consisted of teenagers. He gave this description:
>
> " *You could have picked him out without identifying him by just listening to him because he was bawling out the policeman, telling them it wasn't right to put him in a line with these teenagers and all of that and they asked me which one and I told them. It was him alright, the same man.*"
>
> It is also a well known fact that by the time Whaly was brought into the police station for the lineup, Oswald's picture had been plastered all over the news media and Whaly likely saw Oswald's photo beforehand.

Oswald entered his rooming house right around 1:00 P.M. Mrs. Earlene Roberts was in the living room watching television as Oswald came in. Oswald said nothing and appeared to be in a hurry.

SUMMARY

> *1) It's hard to belief that Oswald would walk past at least six bus stops to catch a bus. The bus driver could not identify Oswald.*
>
> *2) Two witnesses stated that they saw Oswald get into a Nash Rambler.*
>
> *3) It's hard to understand how a killer fleeing an assassination of the President of the United States would offer his cab ride to another person.*
>
> *4) Although the cab driver picked Oswald out of a lineup, he testified that the other people in the lineup were teenagers and Oswald was*

complaining about it.

OSWALD AT HIS ROOMING HOUSE

We have covered the time span between when Oswald left the School Book Depository Building up to the time he was driven by cab to his rooming house. As I moved on collecting more facts concerning Oswald's activities after the assassination, more and more facts surfaced that just did not fit into the official findings. During the time that Oswald was in his rooming house, some strange facts occurred that had been witnessed by an employee of the rooming house, Earlene Roberts. The following is ROBERTS facts she related to the Warren Commission:

> *EARLENE ROBERTS:* Roberts stated that while Oswald was in his bedroom, a patrol car pulled up to the curb in front of the house and lightly tapPed on the horn twice. Roberts looked out of a front room window to see if she knew the police officer but stated that she did not recognize anyone. She stated that she saw two uniformed police officers in the patrol car. Later study determined that Tippit's patrol car was the only police car in the Oak Cliff area at this time and he was alone. It was also the practice of the Dallas police department to only keep one officer in each patrol car in this area during day time patrols.

> Roberts also stated that she thought the patrol car had three numbers on it and indicated that one number was a one and one number was a zero. During this day, officer Tippit was driving patrol car number ten. During this time, it is also important to point out that Tippit had failed to respond to a radio call from the police dispatch.

After ROBERTS gave her statement before the Warren Commission, she disappeared. Several assassination researchers attempted to locate her for further interviews but she could not be found. ROBERTS died January 6th, 1966. Her death was ruled a heart attack.

Oswald was only in his room a few minutes when he walked through the living room again zipping up a light colored jacket. Oswald left through the front door. Roberts says that the last time she saw him, she had glanced out the front window and noticed him standing by a bus stop. The time was between 1:03 and 1:04 P.M.

SUMMARY

> *1) Roberts testified that a patrol car pulled up to her curb while Oswald was in his room and beeped on the horn.*

> *2) Tippit was the only patrol car in the area and the description of the number on the patrol car closely matches that of Tippit's patrol car.*

DESCRIPTION OF OSWALD BY DALLAS POLICE

A description of Oswald was broadcast over police radios about 12:45. How the police came to suspect Oswald at this point is not exactly known. Captain Gannaway explained that Oswald's description was broadcast as a result of a roll call of Book Depository employees that revealed he was the only employee missing. In Mark Lane's book, *Rush To Judgment*, Lane points out that not only was Oswald not the only employee missing from the building after the assassination, there

73

never was a "comprehensive roll call." Lane reveals that 48 employees were outside after the assassination and could not have gotten back inside the building for the roll call as the building had been sealed off by the Dallas police. Police Chief Curry stated on newscoverage found on local television station WFAA through interviews he did in the hallways of the police station that the description went out after the rifle was found on the sixth floor. This doesn't add up either as the rifle was not found until 1:22 and the broadcast went out at 12:45. The Warren Commission stated that the description went out from the eye witness testimony of Howard Brennan who saw a glance of the upper part of a man in the sixth floor window. However, his description could have fit just about any of the white males who worked in the building and he was unable to I.D. Oswald in a police lineup that night. No suitable explanation has ever been given as to why a description of Oswald was broadcast on the police radio at 12:45.

THE MURDER OF OFFICER TIPPIT

At 1:16 P.M. the police dispatcher received a call from the Oak Cliff area on a patrol car radio that said that an officer had been shot. The dispatcher asked the citizen for the location. The citizen replied to the effect that the location was East 10th Street just east of Patton. The citizen who called on the police radio was Domingo Benavides.

This location was almost a mile away from the rooming house. It has been established that there was no bus that traveled from the rooming house to the Tippit location. The only bus was traveling back towards downtown near the School Book Depository Building. No one has ever determined how Oswald traveled almost one mile between the time he was last seen by Roberts at about 1:04 standing at the bus stop until the Tippit shooting which had to have occurred no earlier than 1:12. It would have been physically impossible for Oswald to have walked almost one mile in 8 minutes.

HELEN MARKHAM: The only witness called by the Warren Commission was Helen Markham. Markham failed to identify Oswald in a police lineup just three hours after Tippit's shooting. Her Warren Commission testimony went like this:

> *MR: BALL: Now when you went into the room you looked these*
> *people over, these four men?*
> *MRS. MARKHAM: Yes, sir.*
> *MR. BALL: Did you recognize anyone in the lineup?*
> *MRS. MARKHAM: No, sir.*
> *MR. BALL: You did not? Did you see anybody, I have asked you*
> *this question before, did you recognize anybody from their face?*
> *MRS. MARKHAM: From their face, no.*
> *MR. BALL: Did you identify anybody in these four people?*
> *MRS. MARKHAM: I didn't know nobody.*
> *MR BALL: I know you didn't know anybody, but did anybody in*
> *that lineup look like anybody you had seen before?*
> *MRS. MARKHAM: No. I had never seen none of them, none of*
> *these men.*
> *Mr. Ball: No none of the four?*
> *MRS. MARKHAM: No one of them.*
> *MR. BALL: No one of all four?*
> *MRS. MARKHAM: No, sir.*

Mrs. Markham went on to state that she "picked" the second man in the police lineup as the man most closely meeting the description of the man she saw at the Tippit murder scene and she stated that when she saw his face, "I had cold chills just run all over me." Markham's testimony is very flimsy at best and the transcript itself reveals that commission members had talked with her

BEFORE her testimony. Although other witnesses saw the Tippit shooting, this is the only witness that testified before the Warren Commission.

> *WARREN REYNOLDS:* Statements of Warren Reynolds are even more suspicious. Reynolds was at work at his used car lot inside his sales office building which was about one block from the scene of the Tippit shooting. He heard shots and walked out onto the car lot and looked down the street in the direction he heard the shots from. Reynolds saw a man running from the shooting and attempted to follow him but lost the man as he went around the corner of a building. The FBI interviewed him on January 21 and handed Reynolds a photograph of Oswald. Reynolds could not identify Oswald as the man he saw. Just two days after talking with the FBI agents, Reynolds went down into the basement of his car lot to check a light switch and was shot in the head. Reynolds survived the shot and by the time he testified before the commission, he miraculously had a change of mind and stated that he could positively I.D. Oswald as the fleeing person.

Assassination critic Mark Lane who was hired by Oswald's mother as a lawyer and who later worked for Jim Garrison during his New Orleans investigation located another witness to the Tippit shooting and interviewed her. The witness's name was Acquilla Clemons.

> *ACQILLA CLEMONS:* Clemons stated that she saw two white males standing near Tippit's police car. One had a pistol which she described as short and heavy. She described the other man as, "tall and thin." Clemons also told Lane that in the weeks following the shooting, a man came to her house and told her not to tell anyone about what she had seen for her own protection. Clemons stated that she thought this person was some sort of police officer and stated that he wore a sidearm.

The Clemons statements would indicate that two people were involved in the killing of officer Tippit. I attempted to locate another witness who could confirm the Clemons story. I didn't have to look very far.

> *FRANK WRIGHT:* Frank Wright was another witness who's statements seem to go along with Clemons.WRIGHT was a resident of the neighborhood who lived about half a block from the shooting. Upon hearing shots he walked out his front door just as Tippit was hitting the ground from the shots. WRIGHT saw a man standing near the fallen officer who walked around the police car and entered a vehicle described as an older gray colored car. The vehicle drove off at a high rate of speed.

In Jim Garrison's book, *On The Trail Of The Assassins*, he points out on page 197 that FBI Director. J. Edgar Hoover ordered the Dallas office not to interview either Clemons or Wright.

Radio transcripts recorded by the Dallas police minutes after the Tippit killing reveal that officer H.W. Sumers called in a witness description of the killer that was described as a white male with wavy black hair with dark colored pants and a light colored jacket and was armed with a dark colored automatic pistol. Just a few minutes after that, the police transcripts have a Dallas police officer reporting that the shells recovered at the scene came from a 38 automatic. Oswald was carrying a pistol on him at the time of his arrest but it was not an automatic weapon.

When the autopsy was completed on Tippit the coroner located two different types of bullets found in Tippit's body. Four bullets were found. Three of them were Winchester bullets and the fourth was a Remington-Peters.

Only one bullet taken from Tippit's body was at first turned over to the FBI for analysis at the FBI lab in Washington D.C. The FBI lab analyzed this bullet and found that it did not match the revolver found on Oswald at the time of his arrest. It wasn't until the Warren Commission was under way that the commission asked the FBI to locate the other bullets and have them analyzed. Four months after the shooting, the FBI took possession of the other three bullets found in Tippit's body from the Dallas Police. From these four bullets, the FBI lab expert testified before the Warren Commission that the FBI was unable to state if these bullets came from the revolver found on Oswald at the time of his arrest.

The ejected shells found at the scene of the Tippit murder are even more puzzling than the bullets. Evidently the police located four shells and, at first, called the murder weapon an automatic because of the ejector markings found on the bullets. First of all, the shells do not show up on evidence inventory sheets the day of the murder. The shells were not turned over to the FBI for lab studies until almost a week after the murder. The FBI did conclude that the shells turned over matched the revolver found on Oswald at the time of his arrest. However, no one has ever been able to explain the automatic ejector markings as they were not present on the shells sent to the FBI lab. Officer Poe had marked shells found at the scene with his initials on the inside of the shell which is common practice in police work. During his Warren Commission testimony, Poe was shown the four shells but he was unable to identify any of his markings on these shells.

What has developed here is that it appears that two people where present when Tippit was shot. One walked or ran away from the shooting and another drove away. It also appears that an effort was made to suppress the eyewitness testimony of both Clemons and Wright. Hoover ordered the FBI office not to interview Clemons or Wright and Clemons stated that she was threatened about revealing what she saw. Reynolds, who couldn't at first state positively that Oswald was the man he saw running from the scene was shot in the head and later changed his mind that he could identify Oswald.

The weight of the physical evidence also reveals that there could have been two people who shot Tippit. Two different types of bullets from different manufactures were fired. The first bullet taken from Tippit's body did not come from Oswald's revolver. The other three bullets could not be identified as being from Oswald's revolver. Police officers appear to have at first identified spent shells as coming from an automatic weapon which Oswald did not have. The shells the Warren Commission ended up with could not be identified with chain of position markings from police officer Poe.

SUMMARY

1) *Oswald could not have physically traveled on foot from his rooming house to the Tippit murder location in the time allowed.*

2) *Two witnesses saw someone other than Oswald seconds after the shooting fleeing the scene.*

76

3) One bullet recovered from Tippit's body didn't come from Oswald's gun.

4) The other three bullets taken from the Tippit body could not be matched to Oswald's gun.

5) The bullets taken from Tippit's body were two different brands.

6) The first description of the shells found at the Tippit murder by police state that they came from an automatic weapon which Oswald did not possess.

THE ARREST AT THE MOVIE THEATER

Oswald was arrested inside a movie theater a short distance from the scene of the murder of the patrol officer. Like everything else about the Kennedy Assassination, the details concerning Oswald's arrest are very suspicious.

> *JOHNNY BREWER:* About 1:30 Johnny Brewer was working in a retail shoe store and listening to the accounts of the Kennedy assassination being broadcast over a local radio station. He had just listened to an account of the Tippit murder and heard sirens. He happened to look up and he saw a man duck into a doorway as police cars drove by. Brewer then watched this man as he continued his way up the sidewalk and lost sight of him just at a movie theater. Believing this person looked rather suspicious, Brewer walked down the sidewalk to the Texas Theater and asked the ticket agent in the window if she had just sold a ticket. She stated that she had not. Brewer then stepped into the lobby of the theater and asked a Mr. W. Burroughs who was standing behind the counter the same question. Burroughs replied that he had not sold a ticket but he thought he heard the door open as he was turned around. At about 1:45 another call came into the Dallas police dispatch that said that a man meeting the description of Oswald had snuck into the Texas Theater without paying for a ticket.

Police cars began to arrive at the Texas Theater within a few minutes. Sergeant Gerald Hill had the lights turned on inside the theater. Brewer went to the stage with two other officers and pointed Oswald out.

> *POLICE OFFICER M. MCDONALD:* Officer M. McDonald noted that there were about fifteen people in the theater. He stated that one man seated in the front row told him the man he wanted was in the third row from the rear. McDonald approached Oswald with his gun drawn. Oswald stood up and said:

> *"It's all over now."*

> Oswald then hit McDonald in the face and drew his revolver. A struggle took place between Oswald and McDonald. McDonald was trying to bend Oswald's hand and arm to get the gun barrel away

from him. He heard the hammer click. The gun misfired. Jim Marrs, in his book _Crossfire_, points out that the gun misfired because it had a bent primer. If the primer was bent and caused the gun to misfire at the theater, how was it that the gun discharged a few minutes before at the Tippit shooting.

GEORGE APPLIN: A witness who was sitting in the movie theater was questioned by the Warren Commission by the name of George Applin. Applin witnessed the arrest of Oswald. Applin told the Commission:

> ...but there was one guy siting in the back row right where I was standing at, and I said to him, I said, Buddy you'd better move....there is a gun. And he says.....just sat there.

In 1979 Applin told the _Dallas Morning News_ that this person was Jack Ruby.

Researcher Jim Marrs points out in his book, _Crossfire_ on pages 353 and 354 that two witnesses told him that Oswald was in the theater at 1:00, a time frame at least ten minutes before the Tippit murder. Marrs, in his excellent investigation, interviewed both. Here is a witness summary:

> _BURROUGHS:_ Mr. Burroughs who's now an assistant manager at the theater stated that he remembers Oswald purchasing popcorn and then went back into the theater and sat next to a pregnant woman. After a few minutes, the woman got up and walked upstairs which contained the public restrooms. Burroughs stated that this was about 15 minutes before Brewer came into the theater asking about someone sneaking in.

> _JACK DAVIS:_ Marrs also pointed out in his book that he interviewed a man by the name of Jack Davis who was only eighteen years old at the time of the assassination. Davis told Marrs that he remembers he was watching the opening credits for the movie which was aired just a minute or so past 1:00. It was at this time that Oswald came into the theater and sat down right next to Davis.

If Oswald did enter the movie theater at any time prior to about 1:20, he could not have been at the Tippit murder scene. Another witness, Bernard Haire provides even more suspicious facts concerning the arrest of Oswald.

> _BERNARD HAIRE:_ Bernard Haire, who worked in a retail store two doors down from the movie house, recalls watching police officers bring a suspect out the rear of the theater and putting this person in a patrol car. For years, Haire thought that he had witnessed the arrest of Lee Oswald. However, it's a well documented fact that Oswald was brought out of the theater by police through the front door of the theater. The Dallas police report on the murder of officer Tippit states that the suspect was arrested in the balcony of the movie theater. No one has ever come forward with official explanations on the police report or to explain Haire's statements.

SUMMARY

1) Two witnesses state that Oswald was in the movie theater just a few minutes before 1:00 which was before the Tippit murder.

2) One witness states that Jack Ruby, Oswald's murderer, was present in the theater.

3) One witness saw another man arrested being taken out the back door of the theater.

4) A police report indicates that Tippit's murderer was arrested from the balcony of the theater when Oswald was arrested on the main floor of the theater.

THE MURDER OF OSWALD

On Sunday, November 24th at 12:21 P.M. Oswald was being transferred from the Dallas Police Department to the county jail. He was being escorted through the Dallas Police Department basement to a waiting vehicle. The basement was crowed with newsmen and television cameras. A man by the name of Jack Ruby jumped forward with a pistol in his hand and fired into Oswald's stomach. Oswald was rushed to Parkland hospital and underwent surgery. He died at 2:07 P.M.

A police communications officer, Billy Grahamer was on duty taking incoming telephone calls for the Dallas Police Department on Saturday night. About 9:00 P.M. Grahamer received a call from a man who would not identify himself. Grahamer stated that he had thought that he knew who the party was but could not place him and that the caller used Grahamer's name. The unidentified caller told Grahamer that they needed to change the planes on moving Oswald the following day and if they did not change the planes, "we are going to kill him." Grahamer reported the call, and went off duty. He went home and went to sleep. When he got up the next day, he turned the television on and learned that Jack Ruby had killed Oswald. Grahamer states that it was at this point that he identified Ruby as the caller the evening before. Grahmer stated that he had known Jack Ruby for a number of years.

After shooting Oswald, Ruby was taken upstairs and placed in a jail cell. He was interviewed by police officer Don Archer. Archer has stated that Ruby was, at first, very hyper , sweating and had a very rapid heart beat. Archer stated that Ruby asked him for one of his cigarettes which Archer gave him and which he smoked. After word came to Archer that Oswald had expired, he advised Ruby explaining to Ruby that this would mean the electric chair. Archer has stated over and over with certainty that it was not until after Ruby was advised that Oswald had expired did he calm down and stop sweating even though Ruby had just learned that he was facing murder charges. Archer also stated that he offered Ruby another cigarette after he told him of Oswald's death but Ruby told him he didn't smoke. Due to the difference in behavior in Ruby prior to knowing if Oswald had expired and after he learned Oswald had expired, Archer has stated that he concludes Ruby acted as if his life depended upon the successful murder.

FOOTPRINTS OF INTELLIGENCE: EVIDENCE OF OSWALD'S INTELLIGENCE LINKS

PART ONE: INTELLIGENCE LINKS TO MILITARY CAREER

"A successful spy is never what he appears to be."

If one is to study the background of any real spy, one will find a smorgasbord of confliction. Spying simply works that way. It's filled with attempts at infiltration and double dipping (double agent). Infiltration takes place by appearing to be something you are not, appearing to be friendly to parties you are not, and appearing to have views that you do not. Double dipping appears to happen when the price is right. When you trace the background of the overwhelming majority of intelligence professionals, you'll find that their start in intelligence occurred when they were in the military. You'll also discover a life of confliction. By that, I mean the spy is never what he or she appears to be on the surface and is likely to be just the opposite of the projected appearance.

Another relevant point worth pointing out is that intelligence work tends to involve elaborate plans which can sometimes take years to come to a conclusion. Military people are trained in intelligence work every year. This might involve taking foreign language courses and other vital training for future purposes which have not even been developed. All countries, including the United States, intelligence agencies have what are commonly called agents in place or sleepers. A cover is developed for the agent's activities and he might not be used for years, if at all. These are often refered to as moles. Naturally, this type of work involves all aspects of an agent's life to maintain the cover story and most people who practice this tradecarft develop a life long infatuation with it which usually starts at an early age.

Robert Oswald, Lee's brother, described Lee's teenage years as a person who was introverted and a bookworm. Robert has stated that Lee's favorite television program was *I Led Three Lives*, a story of a spy and FBI undercover man who was involved in infiltrating communism. A close look at Oswald reveals beyond a reasonable doubt that he had been involved in intelligence work for several years starting with his military service record. This researcher did not have to look too deep to find Oswald's footprints of intelligence.

At the age of fourteen, Oswald developed an interest in anything Russian. After finishing the ninth grade, Oswald quit school. His only goal was to join the Marines which he could not do until he reached age seventeen. The next few years he spent most of his time reading and studying Marxism. His brother, Robert, remarked upon hearing this that he was surprised as Lee had never mentioned anything about his interests in communism to him. Evidently, Oswald was marked with the double life at a very early age.

In 1955, Oswald joined the local Civil Air Patrol. His trainer was one David Ferrie, a part time private investigator and private pilot with strong ties to the intelligence community. Later in

Oswald's life, Ferrie plays a significant role in Oswald's footsteps of intelligence in New Orleans.

A few days after his seventeenth birthday, Oswald enlisted into the Marines. On October 26th, 1956 he arrived at the Marine Recruit Station in San Diego to complete his basic training. Oswald was very outspoken about his Russian studies and many people in basic training with him nicknamed him, "Oswaldokovich" which Oswald himself seemed to like and encourage.

Oswald's footprints of intelligence seemed to already be in place. On one hand, Oswald proclaimed Marxism has his preferred political preference. On the other hand, his patriotism propelled him first into a Civil Air Patrol unit under the leadership of a person with strong ties to the intelligence community and second into the Marine Corps. Already a life of conflicting activity appear in Oswald's activities.

Although evidence suggests that Oswald's learnings towards things Russian was very much out in the open throughout his military career, this did not seem to effect his military occupation. Although his superiors would have known of Oswald's leanings towards things Russian, it didn't seem to concern them. When the whole record is studied, it's almost as if he was being encouraged. The only explanation could be that Oswald was being developed for intelligence use and his superiors knew this.

During Oswald's military training, it has been fairly well established that Oswald was not very good with a rifle.

Key Witnesses
Sherman Cooley: Cooley was a fellow Marine who went through basic training with Oswald. Cooley stated that, in basic training, Oswald also picked up the nickname "Shitbird" because of his poor marksmanship.

Nelson Delgado: Delgado was another fellow Marine recruit who went through basic training with Oswald. He too has reported that Oswald's marksmanship ability was very poor. He has also stated that he was bugged by the FBI after the assassination because of the remarks he had made concerning Oswald's poor marksmanship.

In December of 1959, Oswald finally qualified as a sharpshooter by just two points. Sharpshooter is a second grade of three in marksmanship. Shortly before leaving the Marines, he couldn't requalify for the designation.

In January, Oswald completed basic training and was sent to Camp Pendleton, California to complete basic combat training. Upon graduation, he was authorized for and graduated from radar school. His communist views did not seem to prevent him from obtaining security clearance for highly classified material.

In March, Oswald was sent to the Naval Air Technical Training Center in Jacksonville, Florida for radar air controller training. He was given a security clearance of Confidential and promoted to the rank of private first class.

Key Witness

Daniel Powers: Powers was a fellow Marine stationed at Jacksonville with Oswald. Powers has stated that Oswald spent the great majority of his weekend passes going to New Orleans. Oswald always stated that he was going on weekend visits to his family. However, his family had moved to Texas during this time. New Orleans was known as a mecca of the intelligence community at the time.

In May, Oswald was sent to Kessler Air Force Base in Mississippi. Here he attended an air traffic control course. Upon graduation, Oswald was given a MOS (Military Occupational Speciality) of Aviation Electronics Operator.

His first assignment was on a naval air station in Atsugi, Japan. This naval air station was the hub for the secret U-2 spy planes and housed some of the largest field operations centers for the CIA in the Far East. Being in radar communications, Oswald watched the secret U-2 planes take-off and land at the base while on duty. With his open remarks about his pro-Marxist views, he surely would have been recognized as a high security risk to the military unless intelligence operations had been involved and plans under way for Oswald. It appears that his intelligence assignments came very quickly.

Oswald's social life off base is of extreme suspect. He frequently went to a place called the Queen Bee which was a club that offered girls of the evening. At the time, Naval intelligence had a great deal of intelligence reports that the Queen Bee was filled with female spies who's job was to pump naval officers for information. Oswald started dating one of the girls who worked at the club. The Queen Bee was a rather expensive club that was usually financially off limits to enlisted men and tended to draw higher ranking military officers. Dates with girls from the club ran around $100 per night. Oswald's pay at this time was less than $100.00 per month.

In Jim Marr's book, *Crossfire,* he exposes medical records dated September 16, 1958 for which Oswald was treated for gonorrhea. Military regulations call for courtmarshall for such a thing. However, Oswald's record clearly reveals that no punishment was given and the record clearly states that the Gonorria was contracted in the line of duty. Oswald's off-base activities during this time became very closed mouthed and the fellow Marines that he was stationed with have stated that he simply would not discuss any of this activity even with his most trusted buddies.

Key Witnesses

Mark Bucknell: Bucknell was a fellow Marine buddy of Oswald's after his tour of duty in Japan was over. He was interviewed by assassination researcher Mark Lane. Bucknell told Lane that Oswald told him that while in Japan he went to the Queen Bee and was approached by a female who attempted to question him about his work on the base. Oswald reported this to his superior officers who referred Oswald to an intelligence officer. The Intelligence officer explained to Oswald that the female he spoke of was a Russian spy and that he could be used to give her false information which he did.

James Wilcott: Wilcott was a former CIA payroll officer who testified before the Select Committee on Assassinations in the 1970's. He told the committee that third parties within the CIA had told him that Oswald was an agent for the CIA while in Japan.

Oswald studied the Russian language during this time and began to speak fluent Russian. It's hard to believe that he did this in his spare time. More likely, he took a language course while stationed in Japan. It's highly likely that such courses we being taught in conjunction with some of the CIA activities going on at the base. The Russian language is very difficult to learn and you generally cannot pick the language up in a few months of spare time self-learning.

Key Witnesses

J. Lee Rankin: Rankin was the general counsel for the Warren Commission. Rankin made a slip of the lip one day concerning Oswald's language courses. He implied that the committee was attempting to find out which government school for accelerated language studies Oswald attended. The Defense Language Institute is the military's accelerated language teaching programs.

Owen Dejanovich: Dejanvich was another of Oswald's fellow Marines. He has stated that Oswald dated a girl while in Japan that was a, "round eyed Russian."

Oswald continued to voice stronger and stronger pro Marxist feelings with his fellow Marines. He went as far as to start referring to others as, "you Americans". It's hard to imagine why this did not present a security risk at such a base where top secret spy planes were based and where so much top secret CIA activity was going on if Oswald was not acting out the part of some sort of intelligence or counter-intelligence operation.

Within weeks of Castro's victory in taking over Cuba, Oswald was transferred to a base located in Santa Ana, California. With fellow employees, Oswald continued voicing his pro-Marxist leanings and talked of joining up with Castro's revolution. Again, there is no evidence that his superiors did anything from a security standpoint.

Key Witnesses

Nelson Delgado: A Puerto Rican Marine friend of Oswald's has stated that Oswald was in communication with the Cuban consulate in the Los Angeles area by letter and in person. Delgado has reported seeing letters around Oswald's personal area from the Cuban Consulate. Again, no one seemed to voice much concern about this Oswald with a secret clearance who was in communication with Cuban officials and proclaimed Marxism as his politics of choice. It's hard to understand why Oswald was not called down by his superiors for such conduct which would have certainly looked like a security problem.

Kerry Thonnley: Thonnley was another of Oswald's fellow Marine friends. He has stated that a lieutenant had found out about Oswald's Marxist thinking and that he subscribed to a Russian newspaper. The lieutenant attempted to make an issue of of it but nothing ever became of it. Surely the lieutenant reported this matter to his superior officers but nothing was ever done.

Mark Bucknell: Bucknell told assassination researcher Mark Lane that in 1959, Oswald and other Marines had been ordered to report to the CID (Criminal Investigation Division). Bucknell further stated that the CID office let a civilian come in and give a recruitment speech for the group on an intelligence operation concerning communists in Cuba.

FOOTPRINTS OF INTELLIGENCE
EVIDENCE OF OSWALD'S INTELLIGENCE LINKS

PART TWO: INTELLIGENCE LINKS IN THE SOVIET UNION

"A successful spy is never what he appears to be."

In the late 1950's, the office of Naval Intelligence developed a program in which military people would be used to infiltrate the Soviet Union and provide intelligence information. As the rest of the facts develop, you'll see Oswald in this program.

In 1959, Oswald requested an early discharge from the Military which was promptly granted. He stated that he was needed in New Orleans to support his mother. Contrary to taking some time for such a request to be granted or denied, Oswald's request was granted in record time. In September, Oswald applied for a passport for Russia and China. The passport was approved and issued in record time (six days). Oswald promptly left California and went to New Orleans. In New Orleans, Oswald withdrew the only funds he had in a savings account which amounted to $203.00. He booked passage on a freight ship in New Orleans bound for France. His passage ticket cost $220.75. Oswald's ship docked in France on October 8th. Although his family knew that he was discharged from the service, they had no idea he was going to France. They thought he had planned to return to New Orleans and obtain employment with an export business.

Bucknell remarked in the Lane interview that Oswald told him he was being discharged from the Marines to be sent to Russia for an intelligence mission and would return to the U.S. in 1961 as a spy hero.

Although Oswald arrived in France October 8th, one week later, he was in Moscow. He crossed eight country borders, applied for a visa into Russia in Helsinki which was granted in record time of only two days and had to have been using financial funds for all of this from an unknown source. It's hard to understand how Oswald got across all those borders and was issued a Russian visa in record time without intelligence connections and it's never quite been explained as to how he obtained the finances to do so if they had not been supplied to him.

On October 31st, Oswald showed up at the U.S. Embassy, renounced his U.S. citizenship and stated that he planned to reveal military secrets he knew about to the Soviets. He spoke with a consulate case officer, Richard F. Snyder on this date and handed Snyder a handwritten note that stated he wanted to revoke his American citizenship and defect to the USSR.

This was a Saturday and Snyder explained to Oswald that he would have to return on a weekday to complete all the paperwork to renounce his citizenship. Oswald never returned. From a legal standpoint then, he never really did officially discard his American citizenship.

Although a diary of his time in Russia exists, the diary has been proven to be fabricated and written at two or three settings, most likely during the time that he was traveling back to the US from

Russia aboard a ship. What Oswald really did while he was in Russia is not really known. However, when one approaches the study of the Oswald diary looking for hidden meaning, certain things become very revealing.

He states that he was sent to work in a radio and television factory as a factory worker and was paid more than the management who ran it. He talks about being subsidized by the Red Cross. Checking reveals that the Red Cross certainly would not become involved in subsidizing such a person. Oswald's use of the words "Red Cross" must have been some Russian agency. He was given an apartment that was, by soviet standards, upper class. Oswald lived and worked a very short distance from the KGB.

On May 1st, 1960 a U-2 spy plane with pilot Gary Powers was shot down by the Soviets. The Soviets had knowledge that spy planes were being flown over their air space, but the soviets did not have the radar equipment or technology to track them. When the plane was shot down, Gary Powers ejected his seat and landed safely by parachute. He was captured alive by Russian Intelligence. At first, the Eisenhower administration issued statements to the effect that a weather plane was missing. Eisenhower was advised by the CIA that the likelihood of Powers being captured alive was very remote. The Soviets issued their statement and caught the President in a down right lie. Powers was eventually traded back to the US for a captured Russian spy. After his return, he stated that he was interrogated by KGB people on dozens of occasions and noted that he was always placed in a room with one wall of mirrors that looked as if they could have been two way mirrors. Although Powers did not have much knowledge about the U-2 Base in Atsugi, Japan, the Russians seemed very knowledgeable on the subject and repeatedly questioned him on it. The only documented reference that Oswald ever made about Powers surfaced in a letter he wrote to his brother two years after the incident. The letter said:

"Powers seemed to be a nice bright American-type fellow when I saw him in Moscow."

It is very suspect that, of only two U-2 flights over Russia after Oswald entered the country, the Soviets suddenly developed the radar knowledge to track the spy plane and shoot it down. It is also highly suspect that Oswald, if he was a factory worker, would have seen Gary Powers unless he was deeply involved in some sort of intelligence activity.

Francis Gary Powers himself has stated publicly that he felt he was shot down because the Soviet Union obtained technical information about U-2 flights that were supplied by Oswald. Powers was evidentially exchanged for a Soviet spy, Rudolf Abel, while Oswald was still in the Soviet Union.

In looking through the Oswald diary which has been shown to be contrived, the first negative remarks about Russia occur the same day that the U-2 is shot down. After that, the diary continues to voice Oswald's concerns about living in the USSR. In February of 1961, Oswald writes a letter to the U.S. Embassy declaring that he wishes to return to the United States. In March of 1961, Oswald starts courting a Russian girl by the name of Marina Prusakova who comes from a high ranking family. Marina was residing with her uncle at the time who was a Lieutenant Colonel and believed to be involved in Russian intelligence. After dating for a few months, Oswald married

Marina in April of 1961.

Upon marriage, Marina applied to her government to leave the Soviet Union to go to the United States to live with her husband. Emigration is hardly ever granted in such cases by Soviet officials unless some intelligence activity is involved. From the U.S. side, American intelligence didn't look favorably upon Russian citizens marrying U.S. citizens and entering the country. Moreover, the U.S. was being asked to take back a man who renounced his American citizenship and stated that he would supply the Soviets with classified military secrets. Oswald and Maria had a child before final approval for their Soviet exit and entrance into the U.S. was granted. The American side, likely the intelligence community, was attempting to block the approval of Marina's entrance visa but the U.S. Department Of State finally approved it. Oswald, his Russian wife and Russian born daughter left Moscow on June 1st, 1962 in route for the United States.

The CIA has openly stated that they never debriefed Oswald or his Russian wife but, as a matter of practice, debriefed common tourists that took vacations to Russia. It's highly unlikely that the CIA did NOT debrief both Oswald and Marina and statements made to the contrary is a clear indication of the CIA attempting to distance itself from Oswald.

Under a Freedom Of Information Act request to the CIA in 1977, material surfaced that stated that OSWALD had what is called a CIA 201 file. Although the CIA gave the House Select Committee On Assassinations information to the effect that the 201 file opened on Oswald had to do with his potential intelligence use, several former CIA employees have stated that a 201 file would indicate that an intelligence relationship was already in place and that at 201 file is not the kind of file opened for merely exploring intelligence use. Assassination researcher Jim Mars quoted three former CIA officers who explained this in his book _Crossfire_.

In November of 1991 _Nightline_ aired the findings of journalist Forrest Sawyers who had spent some time at the offices of the KGB in the Soviet Union after the recent shakeup of the agency. Sawyers was permitted to look at some of the documents in the KGB file on Oswald and interview some of the citizens that knew Oswald while he was in the USSR. According to KGB officials, Oswald was under consistent surveillance during his stay in Russia as he was suspected of being a spy. The KGB concluded that Oswald was not a spy which is just the type of disinformation that would have been wanted by the United States. Soviet officials within the KGB told Sawyer that they did not believe that oswald could have committed the assassination of John Kennedy by himself. Although Sawyers was first told he would be able to see the complete file on Oswald, he was only given limited access and was not permitted to obtain a copy of it.

FOOTPRINTS OF INTELLIGENCE
EVIDENCE OF OSWALD'S INTELLIGENCE LINKS

PART THREE: INTELLIGENCE LINKS
BACK IN THE USA

"It was incomprehensible to me why he was so secretive all the time," Marina Oswald before the Warren Commission.

Upon his return to the United States, Oswald continued to engage in mysterious activity that points to some sort of intelligence related connection. A letter from FBI director J. Edgar Hoover surfaced long after the Warren Commission in which Hoover voiced concern that someone may be posing as Oswald at a time when Oswald was living in the Soviet Union

In 1962 Oswald returned to the United States. In October of that year Oswald obtained employment with a Fort Worth photographic and typesetting company called Jaggars, Chiles, Stonvall. This firm was involved in classified photographic and typesetting work for the Army Map Service. It's known that this work consisted of typesetting place titles on photographic maps that were being taken by the secret U-2 missions. It is interesting to note that Oswald's employment w h this firm started two days before U-2 flights photographed evidence of nuclear missile ranges being built in Cuba. It is also curious as to how Oswald obtained employment and a security clearance with the firm that worked with top secret military intelligence information.

After Oswald's arrest by the Dallas police, they located Oswald's address and telephone book. In it was a notation that said:

Jaggars-Chiles-Stovall
Typography
533 Browder
R111550
Micro dots

The Browder Street address was the address of Oswald's former employer, Jaggars, Chiles, Stonevall. Microdots is a photographic process that reduces a photograph to a small spec that can be placed in a period of a letter or behind a postage stamp which is a common practice for intelligence people to transmit photographs and other information.

During Oswald's employment with this company, he became friendly with another employee by the name of Dennis Ofstein. In Philip Melanson's book, *Spy Saga, Lee Harvery Oswald And U.S. Intelligence*, several pages detail various conversations Oswald had with his co-worker, Dennis Ofstein. Ofstein remembers Oswald asking him if he knew anything about microdots. He also recalls that Oswald knew a great deal about the Russian Military and the location of their planes and armored equipment. In his government testimony Ofstein said:

He also mentioned about the disbursement of military units, saying that they didn't intermingle their armored divisions and their infantry divisions and various units the way we do in the United States, that they would have all of their aircraft in one geographical location and their tanks in another geographical location, and their infantry in another, and he mentioned that in Minsk he never saw a vapor trail, indicating the lack of aircraft in the area.

Ofstein also recalled a visit to Oswald's apartment in which Oswald showed him a photograph of a Russian building and said that it was a top secret government building that was guarded day and night and that anyone even approaching it without proper credentials was shot on the spot.

During this same period of time, Oswald become friendly with a man by the name of George DeMohrenschildt. DeMohrenschildt was a Russian born nobleman who listed his official employment as an oil geologist. DeMohrenschildt was a very high society type person that traveled the world and appeared to be independently wealthy. Why such a high society international person would be personally interested in the lowly Oswald who couldn't even manage to come up with funds to pay rent on shabby apartments half the time is unknown. However, DeMohrenschildt visited Oswald's low rent apartment just days before he obtained employment at JCS. DeMohrenschildt certainly had associations with the intelligence community on an international scale and most researchers conclude that DeMohrenschildt had some sort of covert dealings with the CIA.

In March, according to official findings, Oswald was spying and photographing the home of retired General Edwin Walker who was an active member of the John Birch Society and an ultra-right-wing-extremist. On April 10th, someone attempted to shoot General Walker with a rifle but the Dallas police never solved the case. Seven months later, Oswald was dead and the US government was not only charging him with the murder of President Kennedy and patrolman Tippit, they where also blaming him for the attempted killing of General Walker.

Right after the attempted shooting of Walker, DeMohrenschildt left the Dallas area. The Select Committee determined that in May of 1963, DeMohrenschildt had a meeting with CIA people though they could not determine the exact nature or reason for the meeting. A few days after the DeMohrenschildt meeting with the CIA, he and his wife left the country for Haiti. In 1977 assassination researcher Edward Epstein interviewed DeMohrenschidt for his upcoming book *Legend*. Epstein had a number of meetings set up with DeMohrenschidt and it was during this time that DeMohrenschidt committed suicide. In 1983 Epstein was quoted in a newspaper article that was published in the *Wall Street Journal* that DeMohrenschildt had indicated to him that he was keeping an eye on Oswald for the CIA. Assassination researcher Henry Hurt, in his published work, *Reasonable Doubt*, devotes several pages to the established relationship between Oswald and DeMohrenschildt and DeMohrenschildt's established relationship to the intelligence community.

The Warren Commission said that DeMohrenschildt was Oswald's last known close friend. DeMohrenschildt was also a personal friend of Jackie Kennedy's parents.

In 1977 DeMohrenschildt told the *Dallas Morning News* that it was CIA officer J. Walton Moore who told him to develop a relationship with Oswald. In March of 1977, the House Select Committee wanted to interview DeMohrenschidt but was having a hard time locating him. This was at the same time that several Epstein interviews were taking place. The House Select Committee had finally located DeMohrenschidt in Florida and contacted him about an interview. Within hours after the phone call, DeMohrenschildt was found dead. The death was ruled a suicide and was determined to be caused by a gunshot in the mouth.

In April of 1963, Oswald moved to New Orleans and obtained employment with a company called the Reily Coffee Company. The owner of Reily Coffee Company, William Reily, was involved in and supported fundraising activities of the Cuban Revolutionary Council which was a CIA backed organization who's purpose was to overthrow the Castro government.

Right next door to the Reily Coffee company was the Cresent City Garage. The garage was an inside parking lot that maintained pool vehicles for various federal government agencies including the FBI and CIA. The garage was owned by Adrin Alba. Alba stated that Oswald spent a great deal of time in the waiting room of the business reading magazines. After the assassination, the FBI came into the business and took all of the gun magazines in the waiting room. According to the Warren Commission, it was one of these magazines that Oswald ordered the assassination weapon from.

Alba was interviewed by assassination researcher Henry Hurt for his book, *Reasonable Doubt* and told Hurt about an instance when he observed that raises a lot of questions. Alba had just had an FBI agent check out a governmental pool vehicle from the garage. He was sure it was an FBI agent because he recalls the agent showing him an FBI identification which was the standard custom. A few minutes later Alba says he saw this vehicle with the FBI agent in it pull up to the curb and stop. Oswald was walking by on the sidewalk and walked up to the vehicle. The FBI agent handed Oswald an envelope which Oswald took and then continued walking toward the Reily Coffee Company. The same thing happened the following day or a few days later.

During the first week of August 1963, Oswald was on Canal Street passing out flyers that were Pro Castro in nature. A few days before, he had gone to see a Cuban activist who was involved in attempted overthrows of Castro by the name of Carlos Bringuier. Oswald told Bringuier that he wanted to help. Somehow, Bringuier found out Oswald was passing out Pro Castro material on Canal Street a few days later and went to Canal Street, confronted Oswald and a fight broke out. Both men were arrested. Oswald conducted two radio interviews after this incident and was interviewed, at his request, by the local FBI office in which he provided them with copies of the material he had been passing out. Part of this material was a 40 page booklet titled *The Crime Against Cuba*. Inside this booklet was a rubber stamped address that said:

FPCC
544 Camp Street
New Orleans, La.

More such pamphlets with the FPCC address on them were found among Oswald's belongings by the Dallas Police after his arrest.

After his arrest in New Orleans, Oswald asked to see an FBI agent while in the custody of the New Orleans police. FBI agent John Quigly came to see him while he was in jail. Afterword, Quigly wrote a five page report detailing information on the Fair Play For Cuba Committee. During the same day, Willam Walker, who was a security clerk for the FBI, stated that Quigly called him and asked him to check local FBI files on Oswald. Walker said he found both a Security file and an informant file on Oswald. Quigly has stated that on orders from higher up, he destroyed notes pertaining to his interview with Oswald.

544 Camp Street was an address of a run down building that no one paid much attention to at first. However, the building had two entrances to it. One was an address known as 531 Lafayette Street and the other 544 Camp Street. The Lafayette address was the address of what appeared to be a detective agency called Guy Banister And Associates. The relationship between Oswald and Banister that develops is quite interesting, however, in order to understand the significance of this relationship, a short background on Guy Banister is needed.

Guy Banister was a FBI agent out of the Chicago office. He was good at his job and was in on the capture of public enemy number one, John Dillinger. Banister became head of the Chicago office of the FBI. Banister retired from the FBI in 1954. During World War Two he worked in Naval Intelligence. Upon retirement from the FBI, Banister moved to New Orleans to become the assistant police chief. However, in 1957 he was forced to retire at age 58 after he had pistol whipped a waiter in a local restaurant. Banister then opened a business called Guy Banister & Associates which, up front, appeared to be a private investigative agency. What it actually was had something to do with covert activities between Cuban Activities attempting to overthrow the Castro Government and other highly covert activities of the American intelligence arm. In 1983 a CIA document became public that was written in 1962 that indicated that Banister was the New Orleans FBI contact man for the CIA. Banister died of a heart attack seven months after the assassination.

The geographical location of the Banister office is highly suspicious. Within blocks was the local office of the CIA and the FBI. The Crescent City garage was also within a few blocks which was a parking garage that leased space to American intelligence departments such as the CIA, FBI and Secret Service. Also within a few blocks was a New Orleans post office which was known as a "drop" for intelligence agents and a major office of Naval Intelligence. Less than one block away was the address of the William B. Reily Coffee Company in which Oswald had obtained employment in the Spring of 1963.

Banister's office was located on the ground floor of 531 Lafayette Street. His office was very friendly with Cubans attempting to overthrow the Castro government and, according to the landlord of the building, Samuel Newman, Banister helped arrange an office lease for a group known as the Cuban Revolutionary Council. The CRC was a CIA sponsored group that was involved in the Bay Of Pigs invasion.

This makes the address Oswald stamped on his FPCC pamphlets highly suspicious but, at first, no direct linkage between Oswald and Banister could be found. However, when Banister died in the late 1960's his wife found a stack of Oswald's FPCC brochures among Banister's office positions. Assassination researcher Anthony Summers obtained more linkage from Banister's personal secretary, Delphine Roberts, who was called as a witness before the House Committee. Roberts told Summers which is detailed in the Summers book, *Conspiracy,* that she had noted Oswald in Banister's office a great deal during the summer of 1963 and that she had assumed Oswald was doing work for Banister. Roberts also said that she had noted Oswald passing out leaflets on the street one day and when she got back to the office she asked Banister about this. His response:

> *"Don't worry about him. He's with us...*
> *he's associated with this office."*

Roberts testified before the House Select Committee and stated the following when asked if Oswald was ever seen in Banister's office:

> *" I saw Oswald alot in Banister's office*
> *the summer of 1963 and thought Oswald*
> *was working for him."*

Two other witnesses were dug out by Summers that verify that Oswald had some sort of relationship with Banister's office and was present on many occasions during the summer of 1963. They were two brothers who also worked for Banister part time that went by the names of Allen Campbell and Daniel Campbell.

There are several other documented incidents of Oswald passing out these Pro-Castro pamphlets on the streets of New Orleans with the Camp Street address. On the one hand, he is directly linked with organizations Anti-Castro in nature. On the other hand, here he is publicly passing out Pro-Castro information and appearing on radio shows. It's certainly mirror or opposite activities of each other and certainly points to some sort of intelligence connection.

Oswald had started his own FPCC (Fair Play For Cuba) chapter in New Orleans and was, apparently, it's only member with a secretary for the group listed as A. Hindell, a fictitious name Oswald has used more than once. This was all occurring at a time when American intelligence organizations were heavily involved in attempts to infiltrate communist and Pro-Castro organizations and it certainly appears that Oswald was under the supervision of Banister.

Upon Banister's death, it appears several police and intelligence agencies where highly interested in his sensitive files. Some where removed by federal agents and have never seen the day of light. One half-filled filing cabinet ended up in the hands of the Louisiana State Police Intelligence Division. Much of these files were nothing more than indexes for other files but the subjects of the indexes themselves are quite interesting. They read in part:

CENTRAL INTELLIGENCE AGENCY
AMMUNITION AND ARMS

ANTI-SOVIET UNDERGROUND
CIVIL RIGHTS PROGRAM OF J.F.K.
B-70 MANNED BOMBER FORCE
DISMANTLING OF U.S. DEFENSES
U.S. BASES-ITALY
FAIR PLAY FOR CUBA COMMITTEE
INTERNATIONAL TRADE MART
LATIN AMERICA

These are hardly files that you would find in the offices of a private investigative agency. These are the types of files one would find in a federal intelligence agency. It certainly indicates that Banister was involved in some sort of intelligence work. The fact that Banister had a file on the Fair Play For Cuba Committee, along with the other linkage certainly proves that Oswald was involved with Banister in an attempt to infiltrate the organization and it certainly appears that Oswald was involved in infiltration activities.

The two witnesses who verified Robert's linkage of Banister to Oswald also threw some light on to Banister's activitie. The Campbell brothers were ex-Marines and worked for Banister part time. Summers interviewed these two brothers for his book, *Conspiracy*, and stated they they were very guarded with their comments. However, they did point out that one of the things that the Banister office did was infiltrate colleges in the area and hunt for pro-communist individuals and pro-communist groups.

In late August or early September of 1963, Oswald was observed in Clinton Louisiana under very strange circumstances. Clinton, Louisiana was a very rural town with a population of under 2,000 people. Just like many small communities in the south, the Congress of Racial Equality (CORE) was in the process of conducting a massive drive for voter registration for blacks. The day of the voter registration drive, there was a long line of blacks at the county registers office registering to vote. Fearing violence, the law enforcement community including the local police and federal marshal were on hand. Several witnesses including the mayor, the town marshal and the the clerk of the county register of voters have stated publicly that a black Cadillac arrived in the morning. There were three men in the vehicle. One man got out of the vehicle and went over to the long line of blacks who were registering to vote. This white male has been identified as Lee Oswald. Since he was the only white person in the line, he stood out like a sore thumb. Several witnesses later positively identified him. According to the clerk, Henry Palmer, when Oswald got to the front of the line, he attempted to registered to vote. Palmer asked Oswald for identification and specifically remembers him pulling out a Navy Identification card with the name Lee H. Oswald on it. Oswald told Palmer that he was attempting to obtain employment at a local state hospital and thought he would have a better change if he was a registered voter in the area. Palmer told Oswald that, since he was not a resident of the county, he could not register to vote. This was the end of the conversation. Oswald thanked Palmer and walked back out of the building.

Several CORE workers where highly suspicious of the black Cadillac parked in the street with the three white males. They contacted the marshal's office to have the vehicle checked out. Marshal John Manchester did so. Manchester went up to the vehicle and spoke with the man behind the wheel and determined that the vehicle was no threat to the peace. The black Cadillac remained parked in the area all day. Several witnesses described the other two occupants of the black Cadillac as follows:

MAN BEHIND THE WHEEL:
Large white male, grey hair, ruddy complexion.

THIRD PERSON IN THE CADILLAC:
White male with strange hair and eyebrows that didn't look real.

The description of the man behind the wheel certainly fits that of Guy Banister. The description of the third person certainly meets the description of David Ferrie.

It is important to point out that the U.S. intelligence community was deeply involved in domestic spying activities during the civil rights movement and voter registration drives of blacks were being monitored by the FBI's covert program called COINTELPRO.

The last week of September of 1963, Oswald obtained a VISA and traveled to Mexico, City Mexico aboard a commercial bus. Officially, his reason for going to Mexico City was to visit the Soviet and Cuban Consulates' offices in an attempt to get back to Russia through Cuba. The passport office application shows that Oswald's final destination was the USSR.

The person who applied for a VISA right before Oswald was a man by the name of William Gaudet. Officially Gaudet was editor of a newspaper called Latin American Traveler. However, he has admitted that he has done undercover CIA work for over twenty years. In a 1977 interview with Anthony Summers, author of _Conspiracy_, Gaudet said that he worked out of the basement of the Camp Street address and knew both Banister, Oswald and knew of the two men's relationship. He also told Summers that Oswald was a "patsy" in the Kennedy assassination. In 1978 Gaudet did another curious thing when he contacted authorities and provided details concerning Jack Ruby's 1963 trip to New Orleans. In 1978 the House Committee On Assassinations asked the CIA for information on Gaudet and the CIA responded only that Gaudet was used to obtain foreign intelligence information in the 1950's.

A man that sat right next to Oswald on the bus provides even more suspicion than Gaudet. A manifest of bus passengers listed him as a John Brown. The FBI had a very hard time tracking him down and when they finally did, they found out he used three different names, John Brown, John Howard Bowen and Albert Osborne. This man officially listed his work as a Missionary. He had international travel but no visible means of support. Federal authorities attempted to verify his missionary work but could never do so. Since early 1970, rumors have flown that this man had connections to the CIA but it has never been confirmed.

During Oswald's stay in Mexico City, he was most likely being impersonated. Although documentation has surfaced that Oswald visited both the Russian and Cuban Consulates' offices, witness descriptions from these offices by clerks did not match and the CIA produced a photograph of a man that was clearly not Oswald. The CIA routinely took photographs of people entering and exiting these offices but the one they produced of Oswald was clearly not him.

Two very interesting pieces of information have recently developed concerning OSWALD'S trip to Mexico City. First, FBI Agent Hosty, in his interview with _Investigative Reports_ mentioned earlier stated that the CIA was attempting to cover up or "cloak", as he put it, facts about OSWALD'S trip to Mexico City. In Mark Lane's new book, _Plausible Denial_, Lane devotes several pages that would indicate that the CIA invented the Oswald trip to Mexico. That is, OSWALD never really went to Mexico at all but a trail was created that would indicate that he did. The photo the CIA produced was certainly not of OSWALD. Lane points to several pieces of information that would lead to this conclusion including a female OSWALD was supposed to have talked with who first stated that the man was not OSWALD and the CIA had her covertly thrown into a Mexico jail until she did, "remember." At first, the HOSTY statements and the LANE evidence seem to be in conflict. But when you really think about it, it would make a great deal of sense for a covert operation. Invent a paper trail and then make surface appearances that would lead one to think the activity you had invented was being covered up. Anyone uncovering the activity and noting that attempts were made to cover it up certainly wouldn't think that it was false information planted by the party attempting to cover it up. It would make one think the exact opposite and the legend would become successful.

After Oswald's return from Mexico, he again returned to Dallas and took a room at the YMCA, October 3rd, 1963. During this time, his wife was living in Irving Texas with Ruth and Michael Pain. Michael Pain was a physicist and inventor working at the time for Bell Helicopter on new helicopter designs. Ruth Pain's father worked for an organization known as the Agency For International Development which had strong ties to the CIA. Michael Pain's brother also worked for the Agency For International Development and it has recently been learned that, at one time, DeMohrenschildt also worked for the agency.

Oswald spent time at the Pain home on the weekends. A few weeks before the assassination, Ruth Pain found a letter Oswald had authored after asking her if he could use the typewriter. The letter said:

> _Dear Sirs:_
>
> _This is to inform you of events since my interview with Comrade Kostine in the Embassy of the Soviet Union, Mexico City, Mexico. I was unable to remain in Mexico City indefinitely because of my Mexican visa restrictions which was 15 days only. I could not take a chance on applying for an extension unless I used my real name so I returned to the US._
>
> _I and Marina Nicholeyeva are now living in Dallas, Texas._
>
> _The FBI is not now interested in my activities in the progressive organization FPCC of which I was secretary in New Orleans Louisiana since I no longer live in that state._
>
> _The FBI has visited us here in Texas. On Nov. 1st agent of the FBI_

James P. Hosty warned me that if I attempt to engage in FPCC activities in Texas the FBI will again take an "interest" in me. This agent also "suggested" that my wife could "remain in the U.S. under FBI protection," that is, she could defect from the Soviet Union.

Of course I and my wife strongly protested these tactics by the notorious FBI.

I had not planned to contact the Mexican City Embassy at all so of course they were unprepared for me. Had I been able to reach Havana as planned the Soviet Embassy there would have had time to assist me but of course the stupid Cuban Consulate was at fault here I am glad he has since been replaced by another.

Upon reading this letter, Ruth Paid said that she immediately thought that Oswald might be some sort of spy.

While in Dallas, Oswald attended a meeting of the American Civil Liberties Union with Michael Pain. After the meeting, Oswald told Pain that he didn't think he could join such an organization. A few weeks later, he applied for membership though the national headquarters. The ACLU is an organization that would have been on the domestic intelligence gathering list of federal intelligence agencies. On November 1st, Oswald rented a new post office box at the Terminal Annex and listed both the American Civil Liberties Union and the Fair Play For Cuba Committee on a postal form to obtain mail at this box number.

Oswald also attended a meeting of the John Birch Society on October 23rd and listened to a speech given by General Walker with 1300 other people. It is now a known fact that all of the organizations Oswald was involved with, The John Birch Society, The American Civil Liberties Union and the Fair Play For Cuba Committee, were being closely monitored by domestic intelligence units within the intelligence organizations of the United States. It also appears that Oswald was attempting to create a paper trail that would link him to these organizations. This is exactly and precisely the way intelligence agents infiltrate such organizations and the way other intelligence agents in the field were approaching their assignments at this time in history.

About two and one half weeks before the assassination, Oswald went to the local Dallas office of the FBI and asked to speak with Special Agent James Hosty. He was informed that Hosty was not in and left a note for Hosty with the secretary. The note said something to the effect that Oswald wanted Hosty to stop bothering his wife. Hosty was ordered by his superior to destroy the note after Oswald was shot by Ruby so he tore it into pieces and flushed it down a toilet.

In Jim Garrison's book, *On The Trail Of The Assassins*, Garrison states that he interviewed an FBI agent by the name of Carver Gazen who worked with James Hosty in the years after the assassination in Seattle Washington. Gazen told Garrision in this interview that Hosty admitted to him that Oswald was a paid informant of the FBI.

On January 22, 1964, Texas Attorney General Waggoner Carr contacted the general Counsel of the Warren Commission, J. Lee Rankin, by telephone and told him he had information that Oswald was an informant for the FBI. He stated that his information came from Dallas District Attorney Henry Wade and that Oswald became an FBI informant on September of 1962. His information also revealed that Oswald was being paid $200.00 per month and that his informant number was S-179.

Carr flew to Washington and appeared at an executive session of the Warren Commission to explain this information. During this session which was sealed until 1975, Rankin stated that he had obtained other information from the Secret Service that Oswald was an FBI informant. Rankin stated that the Secret Service traced the source of this information to a Dallas Deputy Sheriff by the name of Allan Sweatt. During this session, Allan Dunes stated that he thought that the transcript of this meeting should be destroyed. The official finding of the Warren Commission was that Oswald was not an informant of the FBI.

In 1976 the CIA released documents that show in a report that three days after the assassination the CIA indicated that they had interest in Oswald. The document said in part:

> "we showed intelligence interest...
> discussed the laying on of interviews"

In 1977 CIA documents were released that revealed that Oswald had a 201 file within the CIA. The CIA has admitted that a 201 file existed but stated that a 201 file merely shows a possible future interest in a person. 201 files are personnel files and Jim Marrs, in his book, _Crossfire_, researched this further and found the following witnesses who shed light on 201 files:

> VICTOR MARCHLTTI: Marchltti was an assistant to the CIA Deputy Director. He said that, "if Oswald had a 201 file he was an agent."

> BRADLEY AGERS: Agers was a CIA officer involved with the Cuban exiles. He stated that a 201 file would indicate, "either an agent or had some sort of CIA assignment."

> PATRICK MCGARVEY: McGarvey, another former employee of the CIA, stated that a 201 file, "means he's a professional staff employee."

This is very interesting news since back in the 1960s, the CIA was stating that they had never interviewed Oswald and had no interest in doing do. It is even more interesting that the CIA was regularly being briefed by almost all tourists who traveled to the Soviet Union but had no interest in Oswald who had defected and lived there for a number of years.

In the Garrision book, _On The Trail Of The Assassins_, Garrison points out that a witness by the name of C.A. Hamblen has stated that during the months of the assassination he worked as the night manager for the Dallas office of Western Union. Ten days before the assassination, Oswald came into the office and sent a telegram to the Secretary Of The Navy in Washington D.C. Hamblen also stated that Oswald used to come in in the evening hours quite often and pick up funds that were being sent to him. Hamblen says that Oswald used a library card and a Navy card for identification.

During one of the searches of the Pain home, Dallas police detectives, Gus Rose and R.S. Tovall found a sea bag that belonged to Oswald. Inside was a Minox camera which was a typical spy camera used by agents in the 1960s. The camera was a miniature type camera about three inches long. The camera shows up on a November 26th, 1963 inventory sheets. However, by the time the inventory was detailed by the FBI, they were calling it a Minox light meter.

Detectives Rose has stated that he's sure it was a Minox camera but that federal authorities asked him to change his position and state that the item was a light meter.

Dallas news reporter, Earl Golz researched this incident further by contacting the Minox Corporation. Golz interviewed Kurt Lohn who was the distribution manager for Minox. Lohn stated that the serial number on the camera was not " commercially available" and that Minox didn't make light meters at the time. If the company didn't make light meters at the time, the camera could not have been a light meter. If the company didn't have this serial numbered camera available commercially, Oswald must have obtained it from U.S. government sources.

In 1979 the FBI released twenty five photographs with documentation that stated that Lee H. Oswald had taken these photographs with a Minox camera. Of the twenty five photographs, most were of buildings from overseas. Five were of military facilities in Asia.

Other inventory of Oswald's possessions include:

15x Wollensak Telescope
Nippon Kogaku Binoculars
Several Camera Filters
Slide Viewer
Ansco Flash Assembly
35 mm Camera
Another Pair Of Binoculars
7 X 18 Telescope
Compass
Pedometer
Variety Of Film
Several Other Cameras

RUBY'S MISSING LINKS:
THE STRANGE FOOTPRINTS OF JACK RUBY
Mysterious Bedfellows And Amazing Coincidences

Ruby was born in 1911 and grew up in a poor family with seven other children in the Chicago ghetto. His father was a drunk and his mother had mental problems. At the age of ten, his parents separated. Ruby spent the rest of his childhood and teenage years in foster homes.

His first jobs included operation of a push cart on the streets of Chicago, errand boy for Al Capone, scalping sporting event tickets and selling music sheets which violated copyright laws.

In the early 1930's, he moved to California were he sold tip sheets at horse race tracks. In 1937, he moved back to the Chicago area and started a business in which he sold watches at suspiciously low prices.

In 1937, Ruby went to work for the Scrap Iron And Junk Handler's Union. It was about this time that organized crime infiltrated and took over the union. Ruby first had duties that involved organizing and collection of dues but he quickly moved up to a leadership position.

On December 8th, 1939, the union's top man, Leon Cooke, was shot and died over some missing funds. An arrest was made of Ruby for the murder but he was released. It was during this time period that Guy Banister was head of the local FBI office. Banister's name comes up again in a later chapter concerning the Garrision investigations in New Orleans. A man by the name of Paul Dorfman became the leader of the union and the union changed it's name to the Waste Material Handler's Union. Robert Kennedy, in his book *The Enemy Within* described Dorfman as a person with connections to organized crime. Dorfman brought the union under the control and direction of the Teamsters. During this time, the state of Illinois seized the books of the union and stated that they believed it was a front for organized crime but nothing became of the investigation.

Ruby left his job with the union and started selling punch boards out of the trunk of his car and living in expensive hotels. In mid 1943, he went into the Air Force were he served until 1946.

Upon discharge from the service, according to official accounts, Ruby went into a sales business with his brothers that didn't pan out. The sales business sold novelties and punch boards. Yet, David Schem's research documented in his book *Contract On America: The Mafia Murder Of President John F. Kennedy*, points out several witnesses interviewed by the FBI point to other activity:

> *PAUL ROLANF JONES:* Jones stated that Ruby sold a set of salt
> and pepper shakers and that these items were sold by the case. But,
> inside was a case of whiskey.
>
> *JOHN CAIRNS:* Cairns told the FBI that Ruby hung around mob
> controlled night clubs. He also stated that he had heard rumors from
> many people that Ruby was the connection for narcotics traffic.
>
> *EDWIN MORRIS JR.:* Morris explained to the FBI that Ruby
> managed a mob controlled striptease bar called the Torch Club in the

1950's.

> ROBERT SHORMAN: Shorman told the FBI that Ruby was
> involved in a floating craps game operation in the Chicago area in
> the late 1940's and early 1950's.

From the time Ruby got out of the Air Force until 1956, the Social Security Administration has stated that Ruby reported no income. Yet, during this time Ruby was living in the most expensive hotels in the Chicago area.

In 1947, Ruby was about to be called as a witness before a congressional committee investigating crime in Chicago. Then U.S. Congressman Richard Nixon wrote a letter to the committee on behalf of Ruby so he would not be called to testify. The letter said:

> *It is my sworn statement that one Jack Rubenstein of Chicago,
> noted as a potential witness for hearings of the House Committee
> on Un-American Activities, is performing information functions for
> the staff of Congressman Richard Nixon, Republican of California.
> It is requested Rubenstein not be called for open testimony in the
> aforementioned hearing.*

One of the most interesting things about Ruby's coincidental links to various people it that Nixon was in Dallas the night before the assassination to address a convention of Soda Bottlers. Several witnesses have stated that they witnessed Jack Ruby at the same hotel in which Nixon was staying. Nixon left the following morning before the assassination occurred and made statements in later days that he could not recall being in Dallas during this time period.

It was just after the Nixon letter that got Ruby of the hook to testify at a congressional committee that Ruby moved to Dallas and had his real name, Jacob Rubenstein changed to Jack Ruby. Officially Ruby moved to Dallas to help his sister open a nightclub. Yet, it's apparent that it was about this time that the Chicago mob was attempting to move into and control the rackets in the Dallas area and Ruby's background reveals that he was part of the rackets. Sheriff Guthrie stated that Jack Ruby was one of several gangsters that was involved in attempting to bribe his office during this time.

It is common knowledge that Ruby was involved in the Dallas underworld in which he conducted business operations for prostitution, drugs, gun smuggling and gambling.

WILLIAM ABADIE: The FBI interviewed Abadie for the Warren Commission. During his interview he stated that he was employed by Jack Ruby as a slot machine and juke box mechanic and he also would take tickets for bookmaking.

JACK HARDEE: Hardee told the FBI that, at one point, he attempted to set up a numbers game in the Dallas area. However, he was told he had to have clearance from Jack Ruby to conduct such an operation.

HARRY HALL: Hall told the FBI that, at one time, he had operated a gambling operation in Dallas. He gave Ruby 40% of his take as Ruby could keep the police away from him.

CARL MAYNARD: Maynard was a restaurant owner in the Dallas area who happened to employ a waitress who was a former employee of Jack Ruby. Maynard stated that the waitress told him that all Ruby's girls at the night club would work dates for $100.00 per night and that Ruby got 50% of that income.

His first night club was in partnership with his sister and called the Singapore Club. In 1953 he opened a striptease club called the Vagus Club. His business partner in the Vagus Club was Joe Bonds AKA Joe Locorto. Locorto went to prison for eight years in the 1950's for sodomy with a fifteen year old girl.

In Seth Kantor's book, *Who Was Jack Ruby,* he states that a 1956 FBI report names Jack Ruby as the narcotics man in the Dallas area. Anyone wishing to deal drugs within the county was required to obtain the permission of Ruby.

In David Schem's book, *Contract On America*, he points out the following links to Jack Ruby concerning his friendship and business associations with individuals known to be members of organized crime:

> *BOBBY CHAPMAN:* Chapman was a known Dallas Texas bookie. Chapman was arrested on gambling charges by the FBI. On December 13th, 1963 Chapman told the FBI that he had known Jack Ruby for ten or twelve years.
>
> *JAMES H DOLAN:* Dolan has a criminal record that includes convictions concerning race track fraud, impersonating a federal law enforcement officer and arson. He had a business relationship with Ruby that included the production of a musical.
>
> *JOSEPH BONDS:* Bonds was a one-time partner with Jack Ruby in one of his clubs in Dallas. His arrest record includes murder charges, assault, grand larceny, rape and sodomy. He served jail time for the sodomy conviction mentioned earlier. Bonds also used an alias of Joe Bonds.
>
> *ISADORE MILLER:* Miller was also a known bookie in the Dallas area. In 1965, he was convicted on gambling charges. Miller's name was found among Ruby's personal belongings and Miller admitted to authorities that he had known Jack Ruby since the late 1940's.
>
> *MEYER PANITZ:* Panitz worked for various mob owned hotels and gambling casinos in the 1950s. Panitz told the FBI in an interview that he was a good friend of Jack Ruby's when he lived in the Dallas area from 1947 to 1958.
>
> *JOHN PATRONO:* Patrono was another bookie in the Dallas area who also owned a liquor store and a nightclub. In 1963 Patrono stated that he knew Jack Ruby for about eight years before the assassination and Ruby had given him a loan at one point.

There is a solid link between Ruby and mafia crime boss Santos Trafficante. Trafficante owned several hotels and casinos in the Havana area. When Castro came into power, he closed down these casinos and placed Traffincante in jail at a place called Trescornia Camp which was near Havana.

> ROBERT MCKEOWN: McKeown had owned a business in Cuba and was forced out of business by Castro. He returned to the United States in 1957. In 1958 he was convicted on charges that involved the transportation of illegal arms to Cuba. McKeown has stated that Ruby called him just a few days after Traffincante was arrested in Cuba and informed him that his interests in Las Vegas had funds to help release three prisoners being held in Cuba. McKeown stated that a few weeks later, he had a meeting with Ruby in Houston. At the meeting Ruby said that he would give McKeown $25,000 for a letter of introduction to Castro.

During this time period, Ruby made several trips to Havana. The House Select Committee said in it's report that Ruby made as many as six trips to Cuba. The committee also stated that, on at least one occasion, Ruby was running gambling money out of Cuba to Miami. It appears that Ruby visited Trafficante in jail during at least one of these trips.

> LEWIS MCWILLIE: McWillie was a casino manager for some of the Trafficante owned hotels around Havana. He said that Ruby visited Trafficante in jail in Cuba in 1959.

> JOHN WILSON: Wilson was a journalist from England who had been jailed by the Castro government for a short time. Wilson has stated that he remembers Santos Trafficante meeting with a man by the name of Ruby during the summer of 1959.

There is significant evidence that points to the fact the Ruby and Lewis McWillie were good friends. McWillie, as stated above, was employed as a casino manager for Santos Trafficante and in later years worked in casinos in Las Vegas. McWillie had also lived in the Dallas area and was involved in illegal gambling operations. Ruby stated in his Warren Commission testimony that he called McWillie frequently and saw a great deal of him.

It is also apparent when you conduct a study of Jack Ruby that he was very friendly with Dallas police officers and knew at least half the police force.

> *NANCY HAMILTON:* Mark Lane interviewed a former employee of Jack Ruby's by the name of Nancy Hamilton in the state of Maine in his video production *Rush To Judgment.* Hamilton told Lane that she was employed as the manager of Ruby's club in 1963 and that she obtained the job from a referral through the Dallas Police department. Hamilton stated that Ruby was well known by the Dallas police and that he personally knew from one-half to two-thirds of the police force. Lane told Hamilton in the interview that, at

the time of the assassination, there were about 1200 employees of the Dallas police force and asked if Ruby could have known 600 of them. Hamilton replied that he knew at least 600. Hamilton also stated that Ruby furnished free drinks to Dallas police officers and that the police officers and other public officials had their own private stock at Ruby's club. She also stated that she personally knew that district attorney Henry Wade was one of the officials that would come into the club. Hamilton also said that Ruby provided "booze, gambling and girls" for the police department. She also stated that Ruby was given certain favors such as being able to serve drinks after hours and although it was common knowledge that Ruby's business was gambling, women and booze, the police department left him alone.

I have conducted Reverse Speech analysis which I will go into later on the Hamilton interviews and determined that she was telling the truth. I also determined through this investigative technique that Ruby's club had a private entrance for police officers and other officials.

> JOSEPH W. JOHNSON: Lane also interviewed Johnson who was a piano player and had worked for Jack Ruby for about six years in the mid 1950's. Johnson stated in the interview that Ruby knew about half the Dallas police force that consisted of about 600 officers. He also said that police officers would come into the club both on duty and off duty.

I have also conducted Reverse Speech tests on the truthfulness of the Johnson statements and conclude that he is telling the truth.

> ROBERT SHERMAN: Sherman was another musician that worked for Ruby in his club. He has said in FBI statements that he had witnessed from 150 to 200 Dallas police officers coming into Ruby's club including Captain Will Fritz. They were given both free food and drinks.

> JAMES RHODES: Rhodes was a bartender for Ruby. He has stated that Ruby always gave Dallas police officers free food and special drinks that were on the house and that police officers came into his club all the time.

> JAMES BARRIGAN: Barrigan was another night club operator in the Dallas area. He has stated that Ruby could serve drinks after hours because of his relationship with the Dallas police.

> PAUL ROLAND: Ronald was a friend and financial backer of Ruby's. Roland has stated that Ruby could put on strip shows that were actually against the law but he could do it because of his relationship with the Dallas police and he was likely paying them off.

JANET CONFORTO: Conforto was a dancer who worked for Ruby that was his feature attraction for awhile. Ruby had located her in New Orleans. Her stage name was Jada. Conforto has stated that Ruby was in a position to allow strip shows that no one else in town could perform because of his friendship with the Dallas police.

Being involved in investigative work most of my adult life and having done a number of investigations concerning people who owned seedy topless night clubs such as RUBY owned, I can state that the majority of those involved in the topless bar business that I have had under investigation had suspicious ties to criminal elements. I believe that there is enough evidence here to state with a fair amount of certainty that RUBY had too many ties to organized crime to not have been involved in it.

Assassination researcher Mary Ferrall present evidence at the assassination symposium in November of 1991 that Jack Ruby became an FBI informant in March of 1959, a few days within the time frame that Oswald started his travels to Russia and ended his informant status by official documents (that Ferrall has) on October 10th, 1959. October was a time period when Oswald was already in the USSR. It's interesting to note that a memo written by J. Edar Hoover indicated that Hoover through someone was posing as Oswald in the United States.

TRACING RUBY'S FOOTPRINTS FOR SEVERAL CRITICAL DAYS

Starting a few days before the assassination, Ruby's activity seems to involve too many coincidences that would point to some part of conspiracy activity. Dr. Jerry Rose, publisher of the Kennedy Assassination newsletter, *The Third Decade*, described this time period as, "Ruby's hyperactive weekend." I thought it would be important and relevant to compile background information that would trace those footsteps and see if there are any links to either Oswald or involvement in the assassination.

On Saturday, November 17th, 1963, one week before the assassination, Harvey Norman and Jean Bostick visited Ruby's club, the Carousel at 1312 1/2 Commerce Street in downtown Dallas. On the following Sunday morning, Ruby sent the couple a telegram asking them to come back to the Carousel as his guest. Many assassination researchers indicate that this could have been done for the establishment of an alibi.

On Thursday, November 21st, 1963, one day before the assassination Ruby talked with a girl by the name of Connie Tramall who was looking for a job in the Dallas area. Ruby attempted to employee Tramall as a stripper in his club but Tramall was not interested in that type of work. Tramall told Ruby that she had a tip that Lamar Hunt, the son of H.L. Hunt was opening a bowling alley and she wanted to apply for a job. Ruby offered to drive Tramall to the Hunt office so she could apply for the job. According to Tramall, Ruby drove her to the Hunt office to apply for the job. The House Assassinations Committee investigated a letter that surfaced from one Lee Harvey Oswald to a Mr. Hunt dated November 8th, 1963. The letter is on file in the National Archives. The letter is handwritten which states:

November 8, 1963

Dear Mr. Hunt,

I would like information concerning my position.
I am asking only for information. I am suggesting that we discuss
the matter fully before any steps are taken by me or anyone else.

Thank You,
Lee Harvey Oswald

Later that day, Ruby appeared at the Assistant District Attorney's office of William Alexander located within the county sheriff's office. His visit allegedly concerned a bad check he had obtained and was attempted to inquire as to what to do to collect on it. In front of six people in the outer waiting rom, Ruby made the remark:

" I'm Jack Ruby. You don't know me but you will."

That evening, Ruby had dinner and drinks with Lawrence Meyers and Jean West who were in town from Chicago at the Cabana Hotel. We will document later that David Ferrie had made at least one telephone call to the home telephone number of Jean West. Jim Braden was checked into this hotel and was later picked up for questioning concerning the assassination but was released.

On the day of the assassination, several witnesses have stated that they observed Ruby in front of the Dallas Police Department during the early morning hours. At the time of the assassination, Ruby stated before the Warren Commission that he was at the Dallas Morning News checking and preparing ad copy for his newspaper ads on his two nightclubs. The Dallas Morning News is only a few blocks from Dealey Plaza, the assassination site and all of Ruby's time between noon and one o'clock has not been accounted for despite the fact that the Warren Commission concluded that Ruby was at the Dallas Morning News.

I never really noticed how close the Dallas Morning News was to Dealey Plaza until I made an effort to find the newspaper on one of my many trips to Dallas. If Dealey Plaza and the newspaper building were houses, they would be right next door to each other. The Dallas Morning News is located just beyond the South grassy knoll in the plaza. The last person to see Ruby at the newspaper office was Don Campbell. Campbell last saw Ruby at 12:20. This would have given Ruby a full ten minutes to make it to the front of the School Book Depository Building and my time study reveals that this was more than enough time.

You will recall that Mercer stated that she observed Ruby an hour or so before the assassination parked on the side of the road in a green panel truck. You will also recall Hill stated that she observed a man in the area she thought was Ruby standing in front of the School Book Depository Building and walking towards the area behind the picket fence. You will also recall that Hoffman describes a man that fits the description of Ruby in the area behind the picket fence handing what looked like a rifle to a railroad worker who bent down behind a railroad switch box. You will also recall that Tilson, an off duty police officer, observed a man coming down the inbankment on the other side of the railroad bridge carrying something in his hands that meets the description of

Ruby. Vickie Adams, an employee of the School Book Depository Building also states that she saw Ruby standing on the corner of the School Book Depository Building right before the assassination waving his hands and making jesters. You will also recall that Phil Willis stated that he had taken a photograph of the School Book Depository Building in the background of a man who looked like Jack Ruby. The Warren Commission published this photograph but had the photograph cropped so the man Willis thought was Ruby would not be in the picture.

So we have six witnesses; Julia Mercer, Vickie Adams, Jean Hill, Phil Willis, John Tilson, and Ed Hoffman, all describing a man meeting the description of Jack Ruby right before, during and right after the assassination. Four witnesses, Mercer, Hill, Adams and Willis have stated that they are certain it was Ruby. Tilson and Hoffman describe a man meeting the description of Ruby. Tilson has made statements that the man looked like Ruby. Hoffman isn't sure. Based on the testimony of these witnesses and the Willis photograph, I conclude that Ruby was in front of the School Book Depository Building moments before the assassination. Based on the testimony of Hill, Hoffman and Tilson, I would tend to believe that Ruby started his brisk walk from the School Book Depository Building at the time the shots rang out towards the area behind the fence. Based on the testimony of both Hill and Hoffman, information from the Rosco White diary which we will get into a little later and photographic evidence from the badgeman photograph I would tend to believe that Ruby took the rifle from the man behind the fence and continued his brisk walk over to a railroad worker over by the railroad tracks and handed him the rifle. Based on the Hoffman account, Ruby then turned and walked back towards the picket fence and likely had something to say to the assassin who we will later identify. He then walked towards the other side of the bridge were Tilson observed him coming down a grassy incline and getting into a vehicle. Tislon took down the tag number of this vehicle and called it into Captain Fritz's office. No record has ever been found of the tag number.

Although Ruby stated before the Warren Commission that he was never at Parkland Hospital on the day of the assassination, there are three witnesses and one photograph that would indicate that he was. Newsman Seth Kantor, and Roy Stamps both stated with certainty that they witnessed Jack Ruby at Parkland. Wilma Tice also stated that she saw Ruby at Parkland. In the Penn Jones work, _Forgive My Grief III_, he published a photograph taken at Parkland Hospital that shows that back of Jack Ruby. In the absence of any other motivation for Ruby to have lied to the Warren Commission about his presents at Parkland, I conclude that Ruby most likely planted the magic bullet.

There is considerable evidence that would tend to indicate that someone was attempting to cover up both the sightings of Ruby at the assassination site, and the sightings of Ruby at Parkland. The Warren Commission called Seth Kantor as a witness and stated that he was simply mistaken as to his revelation of seeing Ruby at Parkland. A photograph that might have revealed Ruby in front of the School Book Depository was cropped so the man in the photograph would not appear in the Warren Commission Report. Hill stated that she was told while being interviewed right after the assassination by officials that, "it would pay to keep your mouth shut." Tice stated that she received a telephone call after she was notified that she was to testify before the Warren Commission about her sighting of Ruby at Parkland. The unidentified caller told Tice, "It would pay you to keep your mouth shut." One photograph was altered and two witnesses were told not to talk about it.

Later in the afternoon, Ruby went to a synagog were he has stated that he ran into Leona Miller.

Leona Miller's telephone number was found in Ruby's personal belongings. However, this telephone number was actually listed to a Virginia Davis who was an Oak Cliff resident who had witnessed the Tippet murder.

During the evening of November 22nd, Ruby went to the Dallas Police Station with sandwiches he had prepared for police officials. He was informed by Detective Simmons that they didn't need the sandwiches so Ruby stayed around to witness a press conference given by District Attorney Henry Wade. The Wade press conference was video taped by newsman and was put on the air on the national networks. Wade made a remark that Oswald had been a member of a Free Cuba Committee. Wade didn't quote the name of the organization right and Ruby, who was standing in the back of the room remarked:

" It's the Fair Play For Cuba Committee"

If Ruby didn't know anything about Oswald as he claimed, how is it that he had inside knowledge about the Fair Play For Cuba Committee Oswald had started in New Orleans. An employee of Ruby's by the name of Wally Weston talked privately with Ruby on visits with him during the time that he was held by the state of Texas. Weston states that Ruby told him during one of these visits:

They are going to find out about New Orleans.

During the early morning hours of November 23rd, Ruby took two friends, George Senator and Larry Crawford to a location in Dallas that contained a sign about the Chief Justice Earl Warren. The sign had banner letters that said:

IMPEACH EARL WARREN

Ruby took photographs of this sign and noted a post office box number on the sign. Ruby and his two friends drove to the post office to see if the box number quoted on the sign had any mail in it. You will recall that Earl Warren became the head of the Warren Commission.

Warren Reynolds, you will recall, was a witness concerning the Tippet murder in which he saw a man running down the street from the murder sight. Reynolds, you will recall, first stated that he could not make a positive identification of Oswald but after being shot in the head in the basement of his used car lot, changed his mind and positively identified Oswald. Darrell Wayne Garner was arrested for the shooting by the Dallas police but a witness came forward and stated that Ganner was with her during the time that Reynolds was shot in the head. The girl's name is Betty McDonald. Based on McDonald's testimony, Ganner was let out of jail and no inditement was made. Betty McDonald was employed as a stripper by Jack Ruby. McDonald apparently used two names. She went by the name of Betty McDonald but was also known by the name of Nancy Jane Mooney. About one week after McDonald provided the alibi for Garner, she was arrested and jailed for a fight she had had with her roommate. Two hours after she was placed in jail, she apparently committed suicide in her jail cell.

On Sunday morning, Jack Ruby had spoken with another employee by the name of Karen Carlin. Carlin was a stripper at the Carousel Club and had contacted Ruby to obtain an advance on her pay. Carlin lived in Forth Worth. Ruby agreed to provide the advance and made arrangements to have funds wired through Wester Union from Dallas to Fort Worth. Ruby went downtown to wire the funds right before he entered the Dallas Police parking garage and murdered Oswald. In 1966, Carlin herself became a homicide statistic when she died of wounds from a gunshot.

Apparently, three more strange homicides eventually resulted from activity that day involving three witnesses who had gained entrance into Ruby's apartment. Bill Hunter and Jim Koethe were both news reporters who were able to obtain entrance into Ruby's apartment on the day Ruby murdered Oswald. Tom Howard was Ruby's first attorney and Howard had been in Ruby's apartment that same afternoon. Bill Hunter died on 11/24/63 when he was "accidently" shot by a police officer. Jim Koethe died of a blow to the neck in September of 1964. Koethe was working on a book on the assassination at the time of his murder and some of his documented research material was taken. In 1965, Tom Howard died of a heart attack.

At about 9:00 P.M of November 23rd, 1963, the evening before Ruby murdered Oswald, Billy Grahamer was on duty in the Dallas police communications room taking calls as the came in. he stated that he received a call from a an individual he, at first, could not identify. Grahamer said that he thought he recognized the voice but he could not put a face or name with the it. The caller stated that the police department needed to change the plan to move Oswald from the Dallas Police jail to the Sheriff's jail. The caller said that if the plan to move Oswald was not changed, "we are going to kill him." Grahamer reported the call to authorities which must have went all the way up the communication lines to Washington as J. Edgar Hoover was awoken from sleep with a call from headquarters that there was a plan to shot Oswald. Apparently, this warning made no difference as the plans to change Oswald's transfer from the Dallas police jail to the custody of the Sheriff's jail was not changed.

After the call, Grahamer went home and went to bed. The following day, he woke up and turned on the television set. As soon as Grahamer had turned on his television, he heard that Jack Ruby had murdered Oswald. At this very moment, Grahamer said that he was able to place the voice on the telephone to Ruby. Grahamer says that he knew Ruby and that Ruby knew him. Grahamer was recently interviewed for the television program _Investigative Reports_ which aired in October of 1991. I made a tape recording of this interview and performed Reverse Speech analysis on the Grahamer interview and concluded that Grahamer was telling the truth.

How Ruby got into the basement of the Dallas Police parking garage is not known. The official version given by the Dallas Police Department and published in the Warren Commission is that Ruby had slipped passed a police officer who was guarding the vehicle entrance to the basement when the police officer's attention was distracted. However, Ruby seemed to know so many police officers and was so friendly with the police department,the weight of the evidence seems to suggest that he could get in and out of just about any restricted area.

After Ruby murdered Oswald, he was taken into custody and taken upstairs. He was interrogated by police detective Don Archer. Archer stated that Ruby was, at first very hyper, perspiring and had a very rapid heartbeat. Ruby was stripped down for security reasons and asked Archer for one of his cigarettes. Archer gave Ruby a cigarette and placed him in a jail cell. Archer says that Ruby continued to be very nervous for several hours until Archer was informed by the Secret Service that Oswald had expired at Parkland. Upon hearing the news, Archer relayed the message that Oswald had died to Ruby. According to Archer, it was during the time that he told Ruby that Oswald had died and that he would likely get the electric chair, that Ruby started to calm down. In a recent interview with _Investigative Reports_ concerning Archer's interview with Ruby in which he advised Ruby that Oswald had died, Archer said:

> " I said, Jack it looks like it's going to be the electric chair for you.
> Instead of being shocked he became calm, he quite sweeting, his
> heart slowed down. I asked him if he wanted a cigarette and he
> advised me that he didn't smoke. And I was just astonished that this
> was a complete difference in behavior than what I expected. I would
> say that his life had depended on him getting Oswald "

Ruby first stated that he shot Oswald in order to spare Mrs. Kennedy the need to testify at the Oswald trial. However, it has since surfaced that he told his second attorney that his first attorney told him to say that. Archer's account and conclusion based on Ruby's behavior after he was taken into custody for murdering Oswald is consistent with remarks made by Ruby himself at a later date he which he said:

> "RUBY: Everything pertaining to what's happening has never come
> to the surface. The world will never know the true facts of what
> occurred, my motives, ah in other words, I'm the only person in the
> background that knows the truth pertaining to everything relating to
> my sentence.
> REPORTER: Do you think it will ever come out?
> RUBY: No because, unfortunately, thank God, they they have so
> much to gain and have such an ulterior motive to put me in the
> position I'm in, we'll never know the true facts.
> REPORTER: Are they people in high places.
> RUBY: Yes"

In a later chapter we will go over this Ruby statement using a new investigative technique.

SUMMARY

1) Ruby had enough links and activity to organized crime that would tend to prove that he was involved in organized criminal activity. Much of this evidence was known to the FBI which was apparently not given to the Warren Commission.

2) Ruby lied to the Warren Commission about a number of trips to Cuba. The House Select Committee determined that Ruby made a number of trips to Cuba that involved connections with members of organized crime members.

3) The weight of the evidence would suggest that Ruby went to see Santos Trafficante during one of his trips to Cuba and would suggest that Ruby was involved, in some way, in activity to get Trafficante out of a Cuban jail.

3) Ruby lied to the Warren Commission about his reasons for shooting Oswald. In the absence of any other motivation for his deception, he likely shot Oswald to silence him.

4) Ruby lied to the Warren Commission about being at Dealey Plaza during the assassination. In the absence of any other motivation for his deception, he likely had some involvement in the assassination.

5) Ruby lied to the Warren Commission about being at Parkland Hospital. Based on the absence of any other motivation for his deception, he likely planted the magic bullet.

7) Ruby's connection to the Dallas police and statements made by several witnesses would indicate that Ruby developed relationships with massive numbers of police officials and the weight of the evidence would indicate that the Dallas Police Department and the FBI was attempting to cover this fact up.

8) Ruby's mysterious telephone call to the Dallas Police taken by Billy Grahamer and his behavior after murdering Oswald observed by Detective Archer along with his statement after his trial as well as his apparent deception during his Warren Commission testimony would tend to prove that Ruby was forced into the murder of Oswald by unknown parties.

9) The murder of Oswald by Ruby and the mysterious deaths of people involved with Ruby and the assassination including Betty McDonald, Karen Carlin, Bill Hunter, Jim Koethe and Tom Howard combined with the threats made to Jean Hill and Wilma Tice would tend to indicate that a cover-up of the truth was taking place.

MISSING LINKS: OSWALD AND RUBY
COVERT AND OVERT COMMUNICATION BEFORE THE ASSASSINATION

The assassination of JFK was executed with more than one gunman. This means that it was the result of a conspiracy. The House Select Committee was unable to identify the gunman on the knoll. One must keep in mind that their investigation was conducted years after the event and traces of physical evidence had long vanished.

Oswald was forever silenced by his murderer. He was silenced by Jack Ruby. Why did Jack Ruby shoot Oswald? During his trial, Ruby stated that he shot Oswald to spare Mrs. Kennedy the thought of coming to Dallas and testifying at Oswald's trial. However, Ruby told his second attorney that that was not the reason and his first attorney told him to say that. Thus, he was not telling the truth. Evidence developed by the House Select Committee also establishes that Ruby was not likely telling the truth about his number of trips to Cuba and his reasons for going to Cuba. Ruby also stated that he was not present at Parkland Hospital the day of the assassination. However, we have developed corroborative evidence in another section of this investigation that he was present based on three eyewitnesses and one photograph. Ruby stated that he did not know Oswald. However, if he was not telling the truth about the reason he killed Oswald, if was not not telling the truth about being at Parkland and if he was not telling the truth about the number and nature of his trips to Cuba, could he have been also not telling the truth regarding his relationship to Oswald before the assassination.

If evidence could be established that Oswald and Ruby were in communication before the assassination, then not only did Ruby lie at his trial and to the Warren Commission as he had done on other issues, it would tend to implicate him in the conspiracy. Due to the fact that Ruby had stated flatly that he did not know Oswald, if evidence proves otherwise then surely Ruby was part of the conspiracy. What other purpose would he have for not telling the truth?

A criminal conspiracy to murder the President of the United States certainly was not an everyday undertaking. The mere fact Ruby himself shot Oswald is reason enough to take a very close look into any other ties he might have to Oswald. Our focus questions become:

> A) *Is there any evidence that points to indirect communications or links between RUBY and OSWALD?*
>
> B) *Is there any evidence that provides direct communications between RUBY and OSWALD?*

At first, I thought that the collection of evidence that points in this direction would be rather difficult. I soon found that I did not have to dig deep. However, before looking for actual evidence my thinking lent me towards a study of how covert communication between two people takes place. What quickly developed is a technique of washing communications much the same way someone washes dirty money.

A study of dozens of so called organized crime killings will reveal several techniques used by those who plan murder conspiracies. The most obvious is the laundering of communication. Almost never will the hit man know who ordered the job. Not only would he be oblivious to whom he was working for, he would not know exactly who paid him.

In dozens of so called Mafia murder conspiracies, a patsy is set up to take the rap if something goes wrong. The police are misdirected to the patsy which buys time for the real criminals to get away. Once the patsy is in the hands of the police, the police would be unable to make much sense out of the incident because the patsy himself was fed false information. But in order to get the patsy to conduct the job, some form of communication must take place with him.

The effective technique of laundered communication has long been a favored technique for not only organized criminal elements but any type of intelligence undercover or covert operation. There are two ways to pass information between two persons. The first is often referred to as a cutout. A cutout involves at last three people. A wants to get information to C so it is passed along to B who is in communication with both parties. In this chain of communication exchange, B is the cutout. Cutouts can be used without their knowledge if codes are used. For example, let's say A wants to get a message that means Yes to C. The code used for yes will be that the cutout had a fish sandwich for dinner last night and the code for no is the cutout had a pork sandwich last night. All that is required to pass the information is for A to take the cutout (B) out for a fish sandwich if his answer is yes and a pork sandwich if his answer is no. All B needs to find out the following day is what the cutout had for dinner last night. and C does not even have to bring up A's name. Using this technique, the cutout himself isn't even aware that he or she is being used to pass on information. Such advanced methods of passing information have been utilized by the intelligence community and in private undercover work for hundreds of years.

In highly secret and important cases, it is common for people using such a technique to use more than one cutout between the two parties. This technique is often called a multi-cutout technique. This makes it even more difficult to link the two parties in covert communication together and gives further distance between them. For example, let's say A wants to communicate with D. In order to do so he gives a message to B who passes the message along to C who then passes the message to D. B and C become the cutouts. It's a little more complicated than the fish or pork sandwich but covert information can be passed along a planned chain of people when they don't even know they are being used.

If there is any evidence that Ruby and Oswald were in communication with each other in the planning stages of a conspiracy, it's likely that much of that communication would involve the use of a cutout technique. In consideration of a theory that RUBY used OSWALD as a patsy, certainly RUBY would want to put as many cutouts between himself and OSWALD that he could. In consideration of a theory that RUBY was not using OSWALD as a patsy but was helping set up the assassination, again, he would want cutout communication as described above.

All that would be needed to study possibilities of cutouts, is to locate evidence of third and forth parties that could be linked together in the cutout chain. It should be pointed out that one such communications chain could be considered a coincidence. However, the odds of more than one such chain surfacing would be almost conclusive evidence that OSWALD and RUBY were using the CUTOUT technique for communication because it becomes a statistical improbability of a coincidence once you go beyond one possible cutout.

EVIDENCE POINTING TO CUTOUT COMMUNICATIONS

1) THE CARTER/KILLAM CUTOUT LINK

JOHN CARTER LINK TO OSWALD

John Carter was a boarder at the 1026 North Beckly Rooming House, the same address as OSWALD'S. At the same time he was residing at this address, he was dating a girl by the name of WANDA JOYCE KILLMAN.

WANDA KILLMAN LINK TO RUBY

WANDA KILLMAN was the girlfriend of one John Carter, a person that was employed by JACK RUBY and worked at RUBY'S club up until about two weeks prior to the assassination.

2) THE EARLENE ROBERTS/ BERTHA CHEEK LINK

EARLENE ROBERTS LINK TO OSWALD

EARLENE ROBERTS was the owner of the rooming house at the Beckley Street address making her LEE OSWALD'S landlord. She must have seen OSWALD daily. Roberts had a sister she was very close to named BERTHA CHEEK. The bedroom that OSWALD rented was not usually for rent. This room had no room number and connected directly to an adjoining bedroom used by ROBERTS. OSWALD was registered at this address under the name of O.H. LEE. Under direct communications evidence we find that someone in RUBY'S club told OSWALD not to use his real name and that he would be using the name O.H. LEE. As it turns out ROBERT'S close sister was good friends with RUBY.

BERTHA CHEEK LINK TO RUBY

BERTHA CHEEK was the sister of ROBERTS and from information developed they had been very close. CHEEK was a friend of JACK RUBY and there is evidence that CHEEK and RUBY had business dealings together. On November 18th, 1963, just four days before the assassination, CHEEK had a meeting with RUBY at RUBY'S club. The meeting was called by RUBY and concerned an idea for a new club in Dallas. RUBY presented his plan to CHEEK concerning the new club and asked CHEEK if she wanted a financial interest in the club. CHEEK refused. The next day, she talked with her sister who was OSWALD'S landlord.

3) DAVID FERRIE/JEAN WEST/LEWIS MEYERS CUTOUT

DAVID FERRIE
LINK TO OSWALD

FERRIE was a New Orleans resident who was a prime suspect of the Garrision Investigation. FERRIE worked for a private investigation agency owned by GAY BANISTER called the BANISTER AGENCY. Banister's business address was the same address used by OSWALD for his Fair Play For Cuba pamphlets and Banister's secretary has stated under oath that OSWALD was also employed by Banister for a short time. OSWALD was also a member of a Civil Air Patrol in New Orleans for some time. FERRIE was the Air Patrol squadron commander. The record shows that OSWALD joined FERRIE'S squadron in August or September of 1963. Witnesses Edward Voebel, Frank O'Sullivan (New Orleans police detective) Collin Hammer, Anthony Atzenhoffer and John Irion have stated that OSWALD and FERRIE knew each other and have testified to each other's presences together. FERRIE also worked part time for Guy Banister and Associates and in another section of this investigation we also find evidence that OSWALD was involved with this private investigative agency.

FERRIE TO JEAN WEST
TO L.V. LEWIS

Telephone records reveal that On September 24th, 1963 DAIVD FERRIE placed a telephone call to 944-4970. This is the same day that OSWALD left for Mexico City less than two months before the assassination. This telephone number belongs to JEAN WEST. Jean West is an associate and friend of one LAWRENCE V. MEYERS. MEYERS is a personal friend of JACK RUBY'S.

LEWIS V. MEYERS
LINK TO RUBY

MEYERS has testified under oath that he knew JACK RUBY. Two days before the assassination MEYERS had been visiting Dallas and had dinner with JACK RUBY. Telephone records show that LEWIS MEYERS made long distance telephone calls to the telephone number belonging to JEAN WEST about this time. MEYERS has also testified that JACK RUBY called him the night before he shot OSWALD and talked about twenty minutes. Telephone records confirm this statement.

4) THE RUBY/OSWALD/NEW ORLEANS ORGANIZED CRIME LINK

RUBY TELEPHONE CALLS
TO MEMBERS OF THE SYNDICATE

One month prior to the assassination, RUBY made long distance telephone calls to several men known to be associated with the Marcello Crime Syndicate. In fact, a study of telephone records show that during the last thirty days prior to the assassination, RUBY made many long distance telephone calls to various known members of organized crime. The New Orleans connection include Nofio J.

Pecora, a known Marcello associate. The one telephone call to Pecora was made by RUBY October 30, 1963.

OSWALD LINKED TO
UNDERWORLD & PECORA

OSWALD was raised by his uncle Charles Murret. Murret was more like OSWALD'S father. He was also a minor underworld figure who worked for the Marcello Crime Family. When OSWALD's was arrested in August 1963 in New Orleans for the street disturbance involving his Fair Play For Cuba activities, records show that NOFIO PECORA was the representative who arranged for OSWALD'S bail.

5)THE OSWALD/TIPPET/RUBY LINK

Since OSWALD had been charged with the murder of Office Tippet after his arrest, and since OSWALD'S landlord ROBERTS testified that a police car pulled up in front of her house and honked the horn during the time that OSWALD was in his room changing his clothes right after the assassination, it would be important to know if OSWALD knew TIPPET and if RUBY knew TIPPET.

RUBY KNEW OFFICER
TIPPET

RUBY was asked by the Warren Commission if he had known an officer Tippet. RUBY stated that he did know an officer TIPPET but that he did not think this was the same officer that OSWALD murdered. RUBY went on to say that there were three police officers on the Dallas Police Department with the last name TIPPET. However, if this was not the TIPPET that RUBY knew, how was it that he knew that there were three of them on the force. RUBY'S final answer concerning whether or not the TIPPET he knew was the TIPPET that OSWALD murdered," I was incarcerated too soon to find out." TIPPET'S last known position before he was shot was next to a house where an off duty policeman by the name of Harry Olsen was working as a security guard. It has been established with certainty, that officer Olsen was very good friends with RUBY.

OSWALD OBSERVED
WITH TIPPET

Two Dobbs House waitresses testified under oath that two days before the assassination, OSWALD was present as the Dobbs House Restaurant at the same time Tippet was there. In Priscilla Johnson McMillian's book *Marina And Lee*, which required extensive interviews with Marina Oswald, McMillian states that Marina was told by Oswald that he often ate dinner at the Dobbs House Restaurant.

The Tippet communications cutout technique is significant in that OSWALD was charged with murdering the police officer after the assassination. The EARLENE ROBERTS account of a police car pulling up to OSWALD'S rooming house and honking the horn is provides more weight as the TIPPET police car was the only patrol car in the area at the time. ROBERTS made this statement before the Warren Commission. After her statement she apparently went into hiding. Reporters attempted to locate her but they could not. Newspaper reporter Penn Jones made the remark that he thought this was very strange. ROBERTS finally surfaced as a homicide statisistic in January of 1966. The cause of death was listed as a heart attack.

6) THE OSWALD/FRALIER/CRAWFORD/RUBY LINK

JOHN CRAWFORD:
FRIEND OF RUBY
Crawford was a good friend of Jack Ruby's. The two knew and saw each other socially. CRAWFORD also knew a fellow by the name of WESLEY FRALIER. Crawford died in a plane crash in April of 1969.

WESLEY FRALIER
WORKER OF OSWALD's
Fralier was a co-wroker of OSWALD's and gave statements before the Warren Commission. Fralier worked with OSWALD at the School Book Depository Building and had driven OSWALD to work on the morning of the assassination. You will recall that this person testified about the long brown package OSWALD had with him on that morning which the Warren Commission concluded contained the murder weapon which we have determined could not be carried under the arm pit as described.

By developing my hypnosis, studying the way it's been done in other cases and then looking for evidence that that's what was happening, you can see that the conclusion is that there is a very high possibility that OSWALD and RUBY were engaging in covert communication using the cutout technique.

In developing the facts surrounding this situation, I also reasoned that there also might be other forms of covert communication. Again, I turned to a study of how covert communication operates and again another technique started to surface. Undercover operations in intelligence and covert communications of underworld figures also use another technique in which communications can be passed from one party to another in a more direct method. Since the assassination of a U.S. President would involve a higher degree of communication than simply passing yes and no answers back and forth, my gut feelings were that there had to be times in which more direct communications must take place. I began to hunt for evidence that would point to drop off points (commonly called dead drops in the intelligence community) by presenting evidence that would indicate that both OSWALD and RUBY were present or could have been present in the same public places. One of the most all time favored places to communicate in this manner among the intelligence community is the U.S. Post Office. It didn't take long to put several pieces of information together like I did with the cutout technique to present a true picture of what was going on.

POST OFFICE
BOXES IN DALLAS
On November 1st, 1963 OSWALD opened a P.O. Box under a fictitious name. OSWALD used this box as a mailing address and this is the address that the mail order for the rifle OSWALD later ordered was sent to. On November 7th, 1963, just seven days after OSWALD opened his P.O. Box, JACK RUBY opened a P.O. Box at the same post office. The box that RUBY obtained was only eight feet

from the box that OSWALD used. RUBY'S box was opened by the Warren Commission and they determined that it was never used as a layer of dust which was very thick was present.

ADDRESS LINK TO OSWALD AND RUBY

On October 7th, 1963 OSWALD obtained a room at 621 Marsalis Street. This address is on the direct path that RUBY would have to take going to and from his club and apartment which was located at 223 South Ewing. RUBY'S apartment address was only one and one half miles from OSWALD'S address. Dozens of sources have stated over and over that in the course of RUBY'S activities he would make many trips to and from his club and apartment daily. Since RUBY was a night club owner, most of his workday was in the evening. This being the case, RUBY would pass directly by OSWALD'S rooming house several times during the evening hours. The housekeeper's son at the Marsalis address has stated that OSWALD spent almost every evening out on the porch sitting in a chair and keeping his eyes on the road watching every car go by.

YMCA LINK

For a short time OSWALD took up residence at the YMCA and investigation reveals that he used this room to sleep in. Records also show that during this same time, RUBY became a member of the same YMCA although no one can recall him using the benefits of membership.

THE ATTORNEYS OF OSWALD AND RUBY

Under a Freedom Of Information request, Secret Service document CO-2-34030 was released in the 1970's. It revealed that the first attorney OSWALD requested after his arrest was a Mr. Ept. Ept was a partner of L. Belli, an attorney retained by JACK RUBY. A few months after the assassination Attorney James Martin was retained by the OSWALD family. When RUBY'S roommate first found out that RUBY had shot OSWALD, he went to the offices of Martin. Martin has admitted under oath knowing JACK RUBY.

In this communication study, I also reasoned that witnesses might exist that could place both RUBY and OSWALD in direct communication with one another. Just like the first hurdle in developing covert communications links, I assumed that this would be a long and difficult question to answer but the evidence had already been compiled in dozens of places as I began to look through indexes of witnesses that could place the two in two way communication with each other. I was astounded of what I learned.

117

SEPTEMBER 13th, 1963:
POSSIBLE MEETING

This is the same week that OSWALD ended his relationship with the U.S. Marines. After he departed the armed services, and before he made his famous trip to the USSR, he first went to New Orleans. On September 13th, 1963, RUBY was on his way back from Cuba to his home base, Dallas. Instead of flying directly from Miami to Dallas (studies show that flights such as this could have been booked) he flew instead from Miami to New Orleans and spent the night before flying on to Dallas.

The chances of OSWALD and RUBY ending up in the same city on the same day during this time are very remote. However, no witnesses could be found that could state that they communicated. However, as I moved forward with this study, I find more conclusive evidence of OSWALD and RUBY in contact.

RAYMOND KRYSTINK
PAIN FAMILY FRIEND

This witness testified before the Select House Committee.

KRYSTINK stated that he was friends with the Michael Pain family. The Pain family was the family that permitted OSWALD'S wife to reside with them for several months and permitted OSWALD to stay with them on the weekends. KRYSTINK and Michael Pain worked together for Bell Helicopter. KRYSTINK stated that Pain introduced him to LEE H. OSWALD in October of 1963 when they all went to an American Civil Liberties Union meeting together. After the meeting KRYSTINK stated that the party went to JACK RUBY'S nightclub, the Carousel. KRYSTINK could not remember a great deal of detail concerning this event but he stated that he remembers the party being introduced to JACK RUBY, the club owner.

Compelling evidence that OSWALD and RUBY were being at least seen in public together but hardly conclusive evidence that they were communicating with each other on a ongoing basis. I didn't have to look too much more to find what I was looking for. The next item I found was remarks made by Madeleiar Brown in an obscure publication concerning an unrelated article on her son's right to the LBJ estate.

MADELEIAR BROWN:
LBJ MISTRESS

BROWN is a Dallas resident who has later been identified as LBJ's mistress. She was a professional women in the 1960's who worked in the downtown Dallas area. Several evenings per week, she would spend time with her friends in Dallas nightclubs. One of the nightclubs she often went to was the Carousel Club owned by Jack Ruby. In the Spring of 1963, BROWN stated that she and a group of friends were at RUBY'S club discussing the recent attempted shooting of General Walker. She stated that RUBY told the group that a man by the name of LEE OSWALD was the person who shot at General Walker.

How did RUBY even know about OSWALD'S attempted killing of WALKER when nobody, not even official law enforcement, knew such a thing. I started looking for more witnesses who could place OSWALD at RUBY'S club. Again, it didn't take long.

RAYMOND CUMMINGS: Cummings was a Dallas
DALLAS CAB DRIVER   cab driver. He told the
                                           Garrison investigation
that he had drove both DAVID FERRIE and LEE OSWALD to RUBY'S club in the
early part of 1963.

WILLIAM CROWE: CROWE was an enter-
RUBY ENTERTAINER   tainer at RUBY'S club.
                                           he did a magic act at
the club in the weeks prior to the assassination. He has stated that OSWALD was at the
club and was a subject of his act about one week before the assassination. OSWALD
began to emerge as a regular in RUBY'S club but harder information would be needed
that showed OSWALD directly in communication with the club's owner, RUBY. I
began to collect the names of RUBY employees and employees who operated in that
type of business along with Dallas citizens who went to such places. Again, it didn't
take long to develop important evidence.

BEVERLY OLIVER: OLIVER was a Dallas
DALLAS SINGER   singer who was
                                           employed at various
clubs in the Dallas area. She has stated that about two weeks before the assassination,
she stopped in at the Carousel Club to see RUBY. When she entered the club RUBY
was sitting at a table with one of his dancers and another man. RUBY introduced
OLIVER to this man referring to him as, "my friend Lee from the CIA." OLIVER has
identified RUBY'S friend Lee as LEE OSWALD.

JANET CONFONTO: CONFORTO was one
RUBY DANCER   of RUBY'S dancers
                                           who   went by the
name of Jada. She has told several newsmen that she had seen OSWALD several times
at the Carousel Club owned by JACK RUBY. CONFONTO also backs up the Oliver
story about OSWALD being introduced by RUBY as, "my friend from the CIA."

KATHY KAY: KAY was another of
RUBY DANCER   RUBY'S dancers. She
                                           told   the Dallas
Times Herald in 1985 that she danced with OSWALD at RUBY'S club at the insistence
of RUBY. She stated that RUBY ask her to dance with OSWALD in order to make
OSWALD'S face turn red which was suppose to be a joke.

At last! Some words that revealed that RUBY actually knew OSWALD! I dug a little deeper. My
question became, could we place OSWALD in RUBY'S club within weeks of the assassination?
Another issue was corroborated by two witnesses, CONFRONTO and OLIVER who state that

119

RUBY introduced OSWALD to them as a CIA agent.

WALTER WESTON:
RUBY EMPLOYEE

WESTON was employed at RUBY'S club as master of ceremonies in the weeks before the assassination. In the mid 1960's he told news reporters for the *New York Daily* that he had observed OSWALD and RUBY together at the club a few weeks prior to the assassination.

Great! A few weeks before the assassination. But I still needed at least two witnesses who could say that RUBY and OSWALD were actually talking with each other about things that were of a more serious nature. Could anyone state that OSWALD and RUBY were involved in something covert? I started scanning indexes again of already compiled testimony and old newspaper files. Like always, it did not take long to come up with two witnesses.

ESTER ANN MASH:
RUBY WAITRESS &
GIRLFRIEND

MASH was a waitress at RUBY'S club and one of his girlfriends. She stated that in the spring of 1963, she was asked by RUBY to serve drinks for a private meeting RUBY was having in one of the private rooms at the club. She said that RUBY would not let anyone other than MASH enter the room. MASH stated that five "gangster types" attended the meeting along with OSWALD.

CARROLL JARNAGIN:
DALLAS ATTORNEY

Jarnagin was a Dallas attorney who had business with RUBY. He has stated that on October 4th, 1963 he went to RUBY'S club to discuss with him a legal case concerning one of Ruby's employees. He walked into the club and took a seat in one of the booths. He overheard RUBY talking with another man in another booth. This is what he recalls hearing, "Don't use my real name. I'm going by the name of O.H. LEE." This is the name that OSWALD used to rent a room in Oak Cliff around the same time.

So the communication run the whole spectrum of covert communication to actual communication taking place in RUBY'S club which reveals from what was overhead that something was up. Something was up indeed. RUBY was a co-conspirator in the Kennedy Assassination.

SUMMARY

1) Six cutout lines of communication have been established between OSWALD and RUBY. One or maybe even two might be considered a coincidence but five certainly provide a high probability that covert communications were taking place.

2) Seven possible dead drop links have been found in the investigation. Again, the location of just one or two such physical locations could be considered a coincidence. Seven presents a high probability that, without a reasonable doubt, one can assume that OSWALD and RUBY were using drop off communications techniques.

3) Seven witnesses place OSWALD at RUBY'S club and two state that OSWALD and RUBY were in direct communication.

4) Two witnesses state that OSWALD was introduced by RUBY as a CIA agent.

CONCLUSION

1) Based on the six means of cutout communications and the seven dead drop links, I conclude that Jack Ruby and Lee Oswald were engaged in covert communication.

2) Based on the witness accounts of Keystink, Brown, Cummings, Crowe, Oliver, Confronto, Kay, Weston, Mash and Jarnagin, I conclude that OSWALD had been present in RUBY'S club the weeks and months before the assassination and the RUBY nad OSWALD were in direct communication.

3) Based on the accounts of CONFONTO and OLIVER, I conclude that RUBY introduced OSWALD as, "his friend from the CIA."

We have come full circle. Oswald and Ruby were engaged in both covert and overt communication. Ruby was involved in organized crime and Oswald was involved in intelligence work. The exact nature of Oswald's intelligence work can not be determined but two witnesses state that he had been introduced by RUBY as being a CIA agent.

CONSPIRACY INDITEMENT IN NEW ORLEANS
THE GARRISON INVESTIGATIONS

Two days after the assassination, both the FBI and the Secret Service questioned a man by the name of David Ferrie in New Orleans. Ferrie was a rather strange person who had several off beat interests and occupations. He was a self-ordained bishop in his own church called the Orthodox Old Catholic Church Of North America. He was kicked out of two seminaries. He was an airline pilot and was dismissed from his employment with Eastern Airlines. It is worth noting that Guy Banister flew to Miami to testify at a hearing by Eastern Airlines in Ferrie's behalf. Ferrie was also a Soldier Of Fortune, and a homosexual. In his spare time, he was engaged in cancer research in his apartment were he kept dozens of white mice in cages. Ferrie suffered from a disease known as Alopecia which caused him to lose all of his body hair. He wore a red wig and glued what looked like pieces of carpet to his eyebrows. Ferrie was a sometimes private investigator and worked part time for Guy Banister.

On the day of the assassination, Ferrie was in court as he had been working as a private investigator for New Orleans mobster Marcello. After the court hearing, Ferrie drove for several hours in a rain storm to Houston Texas and entered an ice skating rink. He didn't do any ice skating but sat by a pay phone for several hours waiting for it to ring. The phone rang and Ferrie had a short conversation after which he left Houston and returned to New Orleans. The Secret Service wanted to know if Ferrie had ever lent his library card to Lee Oswald. Questions concerning why the Secret Service was asking Ferrie about his library card has never surfaced. Ferrie's library card was not on a list of inventory by the Dallas police at the time of Oswald's arrest.

Jim Garrison was district attorney in New Orleans. He took a personal interest in the Kennedy assassination and became a student of the Warren Commission when the Warren Commission report came out. Garrison first felt that something was not right with the Warren Commission findings after reading it. He started to study it in depth. As his study progressed, he felt that the report just didn't add up. He knew that Oswald had spent some time in New Orleans the summer before the assassination and he decided to dig into that. He quickly developed two things:

1) THE CAMP STREET ADDRESS

The Camp Street address looked familiar to Garrison but he could not quite place it. (Camp Street was the address Oswald stamped on his Fair Play For Cuba Committee brochures covered earlier) As soon as he visited this address himself, he remembered that this was the building that Guy Banister had his office in. As the local district attorney, Garrison knew that Banister's office was involved in covert intelligence work for the US government and had something to do with the Cuban exiles. It didn't take Garrison a great deal of time to determine that witnesses would place Oswald in Banister's company and that it appeared that Oswald was involved in some sort of covert activity through Banister's office.

2) THE INCIDENT IN CLINTON

The Clinton, La. incident was covered earlier. Oswald had come to the small town during a voter registration drive for blacks. He was with two other individuals who hung around in a black limo. Garrison determined that one of these men was none other than David Ferrie. Ferrie was a kind of weird person that was a sometimes pilot and sometimes private investigator deeply involved with the Cubans. His description is unmistakable. He wore a fake wig and fake eyebrows as he had a disease that would not permit him to grow his own hair. Garrison learned that the local law enforcement officials in Clinton had run the tag of the black limo. It was registered to the New Orleans International Trade Mart. The manager of the International Trade Mart was Clay Shaw and the description of the driver of the vehicle matched Shaw's description.

Garrison thought that he was developing something that might have to do with the Kennedy assassination and felt that it was his duty as district attorney to look into the matter.

Garrison learned that both Ferrie and Clay Shaw had some sort of ties to the intelligence establishment in the United States. Ferrie was involved with Guy Banister's office. There certainly seemed to be a link between Oswald, Ferrie, Shaw and Banister. Garrison started his own investigation that, at first, was kept secret. He quickly developed his own witnesses.

SHAW AND FERRIE CONNECTION

JULES RICCO KIMBLE: Stated that David Ferrie introduced him to Clay Shaw in a bar in New Orleans. He also stated that he had taken a plane ride with Ferrie to Montreal Canada and Clay Shaw came along and sat in the back seat of a Cessna 172. Upon landing, Shaw went his own way. On the return trip the following morning, Shaw returned around take-off time and had another man with him that was either Cuban or Mexican. It was learned latter that Kimble was a paid informant of the CIA.

DAVID LOGZAN: Logan stated that Ferrie introduced him to Shaw at a bar called the Dixie.

NICHOLAS RTADIN: Rtadin stated that he had joined Ferrie at the airport to take flying lessons from him. Upon his arrival, he saw Ferrie talking to a man he later identified as Clay Shaw at the front of an airport hanger.

RAYMOND BROSHEARS: Broshears stated that he had drank with David Ferrie and Clay Shaw at the Dixie Bar. He also remembers an occasion when he was having lunch with Ferrie at a sidewalk cafe when a man in a black car pulled up. Ferrie went over and talked to the driver of the car and Bronshears later identified the driver as Clay Shaw.

Broshears also stated that Ferrie was quite closed mouthed about the Kennedy assassination unless he had too much to drink. Since Broshears was a drinking buddy of Ferrie's, he had been with him on several occasions when Ferrie did mention the Kennedy assassination. Broshears has stated that he recalls Ferrie saying that he did not have that big of a part only to pick up a fellow by the name of Carlos at an ice skating rink in Houston who had been involved in the assassination.

EDWARD WHALEN: Whalen was a criminal on the run when he ran into Ferrie at a place called the Abington House in New Orleans. Whalen told Ferrie that he was on the run. Ferrie helped Whalen with the understanding that he could use Whalen for a job he was planning. Ferrie put Whalen up in a hotel and gave him a car to drive. The following day, Whalen said that he had a meeting with Ferrie and Clay Shaw and they informed him they were planning a murder. Whalen later learned that the killing was a hit on DA Jim Garrision as Ferrie had learned about the Garrison investigation in advance. Ferrie offered him $10, 000 up front to do the job and another $10,000 upon completion. At a meeting in Shaw's apartment, Whalen turned the job down. Ferrie called him outside and told him that he was making a big mistake, that Shaw could help him and that Shaw had helped Lee Oswald quite a bit.

DAVID FERRIE: When the newspapers started publishing that Garrison was involved in a secret investigation that involved the Kennedy assassination, Ferrie called the DA's office and told a Garrison assistant that he, "was a dead man." Ferrie called back the next day and asked a lot of questions concerning the investigation and wanted to know if they were still interviewing Cubans. A few days later, he called again and stated that the news media was hanging around his apartment and needed some help. The DA's office put Ferrie up in a hotel room for a number of days to keep him away from the news media.

A few days after that, Garrison was having a meeting with his staff that concerned whether or not they should obtain a grand jury inditement on Ferrie. During this meeting, an assistant walked in and told Garrison the problem on this had been solved as Ferrie was just found dead in his apartment. Garrison summoned his staff investigators and himself to Ferrie's apartment. By the time they got there, the body had already been taken to the morgue. Ferrie was found naked on his living room coach. Two typed and unsigned suicide notes were found. Garrison stated that he found several empty pill bottles with caps opened. One was for a drug called Porloid. He check out this drug and found that it was used to increase body metabolism. It was known that Ferrie had hypertension. Garrison contacted experts and learned that people who have hypertension should not take the drug as it could cause a blood vessel to explode. The autopsy concluded that Ferrie had died of natural causes. The cause of death was listed as a ruptured blood vessel in the head.

The same day Ferrie died, one of his friends whom he had worked with on anti-Castro activities also died. Elidia del Valle was found in a parking lot in Miami shot through the heart and his head split open with an ax. This crime was never solved.

CLAY SHAW: Garrison turned his investigation towards Clay Shaw. Based on the Garrison investigation, Shaw was arrested for murder conspiracy in the Kennedy Assassination on March 1st, 1967. Police officer Aloysius Habighorz was the booking officer for Shaw. He filled out his paper work and asked Shaw if he had any aliases. Shaw replied that he went by the name of Clay Bertrand.

The Garrison team took possession of Shaw's address book. It contained names and telephone numbers of people. There were two items that didn't list names and telephone numbers in the address book. They were:

LEE ODOM P O Box 19106
NOTATION: OCT AND NOV. -DALLAS.

The same notation of a PO Box 19106 was in Oswald's address book. No such box number existed at the time in Dallas. It was also learned that Clay Shaw had called a lawyer by the name of Dean Andrews about representing Oswald. At Shaw's hearing, Garrison called the following witnesses:

PERRY RUSSO: Russo stated that he knew Ferrie quite well and had attended a number of parties at Ferrie's residence. In September of 1963, he attended a party at Ferrie's house with his girlfriend, Sandra Moffett. The party had several Cubans, a gray haired older fellow by the name of Clem Bertrand Russo identified as Shaw and a young slim white male by the name of Leon Oswald. After the party started to break up Ferrie, Bertrand and Oswald started talking about assassinations. Ferrie stated that it would be impossible to assassinate Castro but it would be quite easy to assassinate Kennedy. Bertrand made the remark that they would have to be in a public place during the time that the assassination took place. When it actually happened, Shaw was giving a speech in California and Ferrie was in a court room for a trial he was working as a private investigator for. Rucco further stated that it was just after the Kennedy assassination that Ferrie purchased a service station business. He had gone to the service station to visit Ferrie and saw this man, Clem again talking to Ferrie.

VERNON BUNDY: Bundy was a heroin addict in jail for parole violation. Garrison found this witness during a time period when he was behind bars in New Orleans. Evidently, after the assassination Bundy told the jailer that he had information on Oswald. Garrison's staff interviewed him and believed that he was telling the truth so he testified at the hearing. He stated that in July of 1962, he had been at Lake Pontchartrain sitting on the sea wall. A young man drove up and got out of a car. This young man remarked that it was a hot day. Bundy identified this man as Lee Oswald. After a few minutes, another man came down toward the sea wall. This man Bundy identified as Clay Shaw. He said that the two talked for about fifteen minutes and that he saw Shaw hand Oswald what looked like a, "roll of money." After the incident, Bundy noted some yellow flyers Oswald had left behind that had something to do with Cuba.

Years after the trial, Victor Marchetti who was an executive assistant for the director of the CIA and coauthor of the book called The *CIA And The Cult Of Intelligence* stated that both Clay Shaw and David Ferrie were contract employees of the CIA. Marchetti also stated that the CIA was very interested in the trial of Clay Shaw and was covertly attempting to do everything in it's power to help him.

Although Shaw was found not guilty at his trial, Garrison claims that the federal government successfully ruined his case against Shaw and used some of the CIA controlled new media sources such as Life Magazine. They attempted to portray Garrison as a power hungry DA attempting to use the Kennedy assassination as a stepping stone to national public office. There is a great body of facts that indicate Garrison's claim is true. The federal government refused to honor several subpoenas Garrison had issued. Every state failed to honor summons Garrison had issued for people and witnesses involved who had moved out of state. Garrison's office and his investigation was infiltrated and Shaw's lawyers had managed to obtain copies of all of Garrision's files.

After the trial, Garrison attempted to file perjury charges against Shaw and, for the first time in the history of the United States, the federal government intervened and blocked the charges. Garrison was later arrested and tried for criminal charges and was acquitted. Today, Garrision is a Judge of the Louisiana Court of Appeal for the Fourth Circuit, New Orleans. He has written two books on the subject, _A Heritage Of Stone_ (now out of print) and more recently, _On The Trail Of The Assassins._ copyright 1988, published by Sheridan Square Press, New York.

INTRODUCTION TO REVERSE SPEECH
A New Investigative Frontier

In my ten year search for the truth of what happened on Dallas on November 22nd, 1963, I had always reasoned that a new investigative technique would one day be discovered that could help bring back some of the evidence that has since vanished. The problem with the Kennedy Assassination is that it happened almost thirty years ago. A new investigative technique never before used would help bring to light some of the mysteries the assassination has been cloaked in. After years of being on the lookout, I found the new investigative technique with Reverse Speech.

When you look at the history of major discoveries and breakthroughs, you'll find that many of them were discovered by accident and many weren't accepted by people when first revealed. Reverse Speech is no exception. It was discovered by mistake. It's very hard to accept and I thought it was another new phenomenon that didn't have much validity until I made a complete study of the subject when I first found out about it. I ask that you look at this with an open mind. In this article, I am going to explain what Reverse Speech is, describe my tests for the validation of it, explain how this new frontier can be used as an exciting and new investigative tool and give you some actual examples of Reverse Speech.

WHAT IS REVERSE SPEECH: Reverse Speech is a newly discovered form of human communication that exists outside of conscious awareness. This extra form of communication co-exists and occurs simultaneously with, our normal speech process. As the brain constructs the necessary speech sounds to form intelligible language, it constructs them in such a way that at least two messages are communicated. One forwards, which is constructed and heard consciously, and one in reverse which is constructed and heard unconsciously.

This unconscious form of communication or Reverse Speech, occurs constantly throughout the human speech process. Every minute of every day all of us are delivering and receiving speech reversals each time we engage in conversation. As we speak consciously in forward speech, we say what our conscious mind chooses to say. At the same time our unconscious mind is also expressing itself, backwards, in those very same sounds that we previously assumed came only from the conscious area of the mind.

What polygraph technology , PSE technology and body language attempted to achieve has now been given to us via an extrasensory means of perception that has always existed. However, Reverse Speech takes us much further into the subconscious mind. By analyzing speech in reverse, not only can we spot deception, we can also locate unconscious thoughts. Reverse speech is a voice of the unconscious mind. It has the potential to reveal true thoughts and true feelings sometimes in direct contradiction to what has been spoken forward.

This new discovery is very hard to accept when you first hear about it and, again, I ask you to keep an open mind about it until you get to the end of this article. My first thoughts about this was "hogwash" until I looked at it a little closer and did my own verifications. Please read on! In order to understand how this works, I am going to briefly describe how it was discovered by psychologist David J Oates.

David Oates is an Australian psychotherapist who worked with street kids in halfway houses. About ten years ago, some of Mr. Oate's young clients came to him and wanted to know his thoughts on what has now come to be called backwards masking. Backwards masking is a term used to describe popular bands deliberately placing hidden messages on records that were recorded backwards. Mr. Oates developed an interest in this fad as a direct result of some of these teenagers coming to him wanting his thoughts on backwards masking. He rigged up a recorder that would play in reverse so he could study backwards masking further. What he found out was that these hidden messages where occurring on all records and even occurred on some of the first records produced in the 1930s. David Oates also learned that these messages where present on all forms of music including Rock and Roll, Gospel, and County And Western and appeared to have a direct relationship to what was being said forward in the song. In 1984 David Oates, after conducting extensive testing, became personally convinced that unintentional backwards messages on records did exist. Over the next two year period, he found numerous reversed messages across a wide section of recordings ranging from songs to advertisements to political speeches to normal conversations.

In 1987 David was joined by associate Greg Albrecht who assisted him in his research for most of that year. During this time they devised the theory of "Reverse Speech And Speech Complimentary" and isolated many common patterns to this phenomena. Speech Complimentary has to do with the fact that the messages found in reverse have a direct bearing to messages stated at the conscious level. In November of 1987, this research team officially announced their findings to the Australian public. The media interest in Australia was intense and their work was featured on numerous current affairs television programs, magazines and radio broadcasts. Reverse Speech was used successfully by an Australian police force to solve a crime. Mr. Oates was offered a job in Brisbane to use Reverse Speech in a therapeutic situation. He then began to develop the technology further, refining procedures and theories and collecting extra information that supported the hypothesis of Reverse Speech.

In 1989, the first official research institute for Reverse Speech was formed in Brisbane, Australia, and David Began to lecture on the topic extensively, conducting training and instigating further research programs. In June 1989 he travelled to the United States to lecture on Reverse Speech. The reception he received was overwhelming and, as a result, he moved to Dallas, Texas in August 1989 to establish a research base in the United States.

In an Australian television interview with a man suspected of murder, Mr. Oates made an analysis of the soundtrack to prove his point that Reverse Speech can be used as an investigative tool. This is just one example David provides in his presentations and tapes. The two sentence soundtrack consists of a reporter asking the suspect if he ever threatened the victim with the suspect's response. The transcript goes like this:

DID YOU EVER THREATEN?
NO I NEVER THREATENED... I NEVER REMEMBER
THREATENING ALTHOUGH HE DID ON OCCASION TELL
THE POLICE I THREATENED HIM.

David Oates located a speech reversal that said:
REVENGE KILLING THE LAD.

About one month ago, I attended a lecture on Reverse Speech at the University Of Texas given by David Oates. The lecture lasted several hours and David gave example after example of the Reverse Speech phenomena. I was, at first, very skeptical. One of the first things I did was contact the police department in Australia to verify that they had used Reverse Speech in one of it's investigations which Mr. Oates revealed in his lecture. After making several telephone calls getting to the right person, I did verify that a murder weapon was located in the basement of a suspect using the Reverse Speech process. With that verified, I obtained one of David Oate's modified tape recorders to test some of his examples on my own as I thought that some of this stuff could have been some kind of technological trick. One of the more famous soundtracks Mr. Oates uses in his examples is a sound track of man's first spacewalk by Neal Armstrong. Where the soundtrack says, "That's one small step for man", David reversed the tape and it said, "Man will spacewalk."

> *EXAMPLE:*
> *NEAL ARMSTRONG: That's one small step for man, one giant*
> *leap for mankind.*
> *REVERSAL: Man will spacewalk.*

I went to a video store and obtained a documentary video tape of our space program and located the soundtrack on the video. I then tape recorded the soundtrack of, "that's one small step for man," and then played it backwards. Sure enough I found that when I played the tape recording backwards, the sentence, "Man will space walk," was found. I had proved to myself that David Oate's Reverse Speech examples were not some sort of technological trick that involved doctored soundtracks. I also did this with several other examples Mr. Oates presented in his lecture and all provided that David's soundtracks had not been doctored.

My next thoughts ran along the lines that this thing might just be some sort of coincidence. I talked with several language experts and statistical mathematicians at the local university proposing "what if" type questions and asking them if such coincidences could occur. Their basic answer was that speech spoken forward may produce a random audible word now and then when played in reverse but the idea that reverse speech could make complete sentences or phrases that related directly to what was being said forward was a statistical improbability. I tested the "one small step for man" further by recording these words into a tape recorder myself and having several other people do it thinking that I might come up with the same sentence in reverse, Man will space walk. Not only did I not hear " Man will space walk" when I played these tracks in reverse, I heard a completely different sentence with some individuals. On my own voice I recorded over and over again, I finally heard (after several hours of listening) , " Maybe this is valid." On another person who had somewhat of an idea of what I was doing, I heard, "Ralph's flipped out."

> *EXAMPLE:*
> *RALPH THOMAS: That's one small step for man, one giant leap*
> *for mankind.*
> *REVERSAL: Maybe this is valid.*

> *EXAMPLE:*
> *SUBJECT: That's one small step for man, one giant leap for*
> *mankind.*
> *REVERSAL: Ralph's flipped out.*

Mr. Oates's research clearly shows that reversals occur in normal speech about one time every 15 seconds. During highly emotional conversation they occur about once every two seconds. In prepared speeches and that sort of thing they only occur about once every five minutes. With the proper equipment and the proper training, Reverse Speech will become a new and exciting investigative technique.

After hours of testing, I started listening to other soundtracks of news interviews and have located several reversals. I have also signed up for David Oate's course on Reverse Speech. Through my own experimentation, I have learned that reverse speech is indeed valid but that one needs training to become a Reverse Speech Analyst as the actual reversals are very hard to pick up among the gibberish when you play a tape recording in reverse. Mr. Oate's course teaches professionals how to locate and identify reversals and how to utilize a screening process he has developed to make sure the reversals heard are valid. There are only a handful of people who are actually trained and certified as Reverse Speech Analysts. No one in the investigative sector is yet certified. Certainly one of the greatest opportunities in investigation exists with Reverse Speech.

I had become so excited about this new technology that I traveled to Dallas, Texas to spend some time with Mr. Oates. During our talks, Mr. Oates handed me some of his tape recordings and printed material. His research is well documented and contains a wealth of third party verifications attesting to it's validity from doctors, lawyers, professors and other professional and academic people.

I want to cite one more example of Mr. Oate's research that graphically illustrates the principle of speech complementarity where the reverse dialog reveals extra concerns that the speaker has concerning what the speaker has said forward. This example also proves how beneficial this technique can be for any type of investigation. It is an interview with John Lennon recorded immediately after the death of the Beatles manager, Brian Epstein. The reporter asks what advice the maharashi had given him.

> (REPORTER) I understand that this afternoon the maharashi conferred with you all. Could I ask you what advice he offered you?

> (LENNON) He told us that, ah, not to get overwhelmed by grief and ah whatever thoughts we have of Brian to keep them happy because any thoughts we have of him, have of him, will travel to him wherever he is.

> David Oates located a speech reversal in this soundtrack that says,
> Can't be Beatles now.

This example is significant for several reasons. First, many Rock And Roll historians claim that Epstein's death lead to the eventual disbandment of the Beatles. Lennon's reversal certainly reveals unconscious concerns. Secondly, this example uses an actual name in reverse, the Beatles which is a common occurrence in reverse speech. Thirdly, the reverse speech speaks in a distinct British accent.

After a very careful study of Reverse Speech, I have come to the conclusion that it is one of the major discoveries of all times as an investigative science and that Reverse Speech will revolutionize many aspects of the private investigative business. Since the lecture given by Mr. Oates in early 1991, I have taken the certification course in Reverse Speech and have been appointed to the board of directors of the Reverse Speech Institute and have been appointed to head up the investigative division of Reverse Speech. I also wrote a book on the subject for the investigative profession called Reverse Speech: A New Investigative Frontier.

Naturally, I started collection of audio recordings on people and witnesses involved in the Kennedy Assassination and started conducting testing and Reverse Speech analysis of these recordings. I am very excited about this new investigative process as it relates to the Kennedy Assassination. When doing the tape analysis, I couldn't help but think that this new application would bring about new evidence. I was right. The results are amazing and they are reported in the next chapter as well as on the audio cassette tape.

REVERSE SPEECH AND THE THE KENNEDY ASSASSINATION
"NEW EVIDENCE WITH A NEW TECHNOLOGY"

After becoming certified in the use of Reverse Speech as an investigative technique, I began to explore the assassination with my knew found knowledge. Naturally, I needed tape recordings made by the key players in the assassination. My first attention turned to Lee Oswald.

OSWALD: Very little comments made by Oswald have been captured on tape. Although he was interviewed by the Dallas Police Department after his arrest, the official story is that no tape recording was made during the twelve hours of interrogation by Dallas Homicide Detective Will Fritz. The reason given by Captain Fritz for not tape recording the interview is that he did not have access to a tape recorder and that he had requested the purchase of a tape recorder for quite some time. I find this hard to swallow. One of the largest and one of the best police departments in the country in the early 1960s certainly had to have a tape recorder and I am certain that it's use would have been considered with an interrogation with the suspect of the crime of the century. It is a well documented fact that Captain Will Fritz was ordered to stop his investigation by the federal government by President Johnson. Sources reveal that Johnson called Captain Fritz and stated that he had his man and in the interest of national security, "stop your investigation." Based on my research which would be too lengthy to go into in this article, I believe that Will Fritz likely had made tape recordings but they have either been suppressed or destroyed. I think that it is also important to point out that Will Fritz was known among police circles as one of the best police detectives in the country and whatever took place, Captain Fritz was following orders from his government.

There are some comments made by Oswald after his arrest and before his murder that have been captured on tape. He was permitted a very brief news conference and was recorded by newsmen as he made his way to and from the police interrogation room and his jail cell before he himself was shot down.

The following is the transcript with speech reversals of the news conference.

> (OSWALD) Ah I really don't know what this situation is about nobody has told me anything.
> (*No Reversal found, poor quality track. Too many news reporters talking in the background*)
> I've be accused of ah, of ah murdering a policeman.
> [I know nothing more than that.]
> *(R) I'm the lonely camelot. (VALIDITY 5)*
> I do request that someone [to come forward]
> *(R) I mustn't , I mustn't. (VALIDITY 6)*
> To give me [ah legal assistance.]
> *(R) We need more help. (VALIDITY 5)*
> (NEWS REPORTER) Did you kill the President?
> (OSWALD) [No I have not been charged with that in fact nobody] has said that to me yet.
> *(R) got one problem that 's nasty unknown. (VALIDITY 4)*
> The first thing I heard about it was when the newspaper reporters in the hall ah [asked me that] question.
> *(R) I didn't scratch (VALIDITY 4)*

That was the end of the news conference. It is apparent from the video of this news conference that the Dallas police cut it off. Oswald appeared frustrated at this point. It's my feeling based on additional research that the news conference was cut off by the Dallas police because they had not intended for a question and answer session to take place at all. The news conference was held in the police lineup room. Oswald was first displayed to the news media on the other side of the glass but reporters were complaining. The Dallas officers then escorted Oswald out onto the main floor of the lineup room and the reporters were able to ask the few questions. One reporter asked him as he was escorted away something about the cut above his eye and Oswald responded that a policeman hit him but the soundtrack was of very poor quality at that point with too many reporters talking in the background.

I was able to locate a few recordings from old news reels as Oswald was moved through the hallways of the police station. Here is one of those comments along with the reversals.

> (News Reporter) Did you fire that rifle?
> (OSWALD) I don't know the facts that you people have been given but I [emphatically deny these] charges.
> *(R) See now I'm the give-up. (VALIDITY 4)*

Still another comment was recorded in the hallway when reporters asked Oswald's involvement.

> (Oswald) These people have given me a hearing without legal representation or anything.
> *(R) That killer was gifted (VALIDITY 3)*
> (Reporter) Did you shoot the President?
> (Oswald) I didn't shoot anybody.
> *(R) Are they all going to dish it out? (VALIDITY 4)*

I have located eight speech reversals that Oswald made after his arrest and before he was shot down. In summary they are:

> *(R) I'm the lonely camelot.*
> *(R) I mustn't , I mustn't.*
> *(R) We need more help.*
> *(R) got one problem that nasty unknown.*
> *(R) I didn't scratch*
> *(R) Help! See now I'm the give-up.*
> *(R) That killer was gifted.*
> *(R) Are they all going to dish it out?*

Perhaps the most significant reversal is where Oswald says in reverse when a reporter asked him if he shot the President, " I didn't scratch." (NOTE: There is a faint word on the end of this reversal that could be "him" which would make the reversal, "I didn't scratch him. However, the final word was not audible enough for analysis.) Since speech reversal is the voice of the unconscious mind, they cannot be consciously controlled and they do not lie. What we have here is conclusive evidence using speech reversal as a kind of lie detector that Oswald did not kill the President.

The reversal that Oswald uses where he says forward, I request someone to come forward to provide legal assistance that says, *"We need more help,"* is also significant in that he is using the word we. This certainly indicates that Oswald was referring to some other party or parties other than himself. It certainly is evidence that points to more than one gunman.

The reversal that Oswald uses when he said forward, "These people have given me a hearing without legal representation or anything," (R: *That killer was gifted)*, certainly indicated that Oswald's subconscious mind thought whoever the killer was did a very good job and it certainly implies that it was not Oswald.

The speech reversal where Oswald says, *I mustn't, mustn't,* might have something to do with his subconscious wanting to tell something. Perhaps Oswald knew more than he would tell. The reversal that says, *You've got one problem, that nasty unknown,* is in direct relationship to Oswald not being the assassin.

The reversal that says, *Help! I'm the give-up,* certainly goes alone with Oswald telling the Dallas Police that he didn't kill the President and that he was just a patsy.

The reversal that says, *I'm the lonely Camelot,* is harder to reach an opinion on. The word Camelot comes up again and again in reverse speech as an Archetype which has meaning that has to do with very deep unconscious thought patterns and is believed to be one of the archetype words in the reverse speech vocabulary that is passed down from one generation to the other. It is important however to remember that Camelot is the name of a song that Kennedy listened to over and over again and that news reporters have since coined the Kennedy Presidency as Camelot. This makes it impossible to determine what type of reversal we have here.

CONCLUSION OF OSWALD TAPES: Based on the Reverse Speech tests, I conclude then that Oswald may have had some knowledge of the assassination but he didn't fire any shots.

CORROBORATION OF THE REVERSE SPEECH CONCLUSION ON OSWALD

1) PSE TESTING: PSE testing conducted by George O'Tool, Mike Kradz and Doctor Gordon Barland published in O'Toole's book, *The Assassination Tapes*, drew to the same conclusion I did. Their conclusion stated that Oswald likely did not fire the rifle but likely had some knowledge of the assassination. Although I had been researching for O'Toole's study several months, I was not able to locate it and review it until nine months after I completed the Reverse Speech analysis and I had no idea of what their conclusions were. As a former PSE examiner, I reviewed the tests conducted by O'Toole, Kradz and Doctor Gordon and reached the same conclusions that they did. I believe that it is important to point out that test results indicating deception are subject to the examiner opinion and it is much more difficult and complicated to make a conclusion of deception being present than it is to conclude no deception is present. Stress levels that would indicate deception can sometimes be tricky as the stress can sometimes be caused by external irrelevant factors. However, the exact opposite is the case when no stress is present and the subject is not engaged in deception. It is cut and dry. Oswald was telling the truth when he said he didn't shoot anybody.

2) WITNESS ACCOUNTS: You will recall that only one witness gave testimony that would tend to show that Oswald was the person pulling the trigger in the sixth floor window. This lone witness, Howard Brennan, could not identify Oswald in a police line up, kept changing his mind concerning a positive identification and failed PSE testing conducted by O'Toole and verified by myself. Aside from Brennan's own inconsistency, his account is inconsistent with at least four other witnesses. Arnold Rowland, Carolyn Walther, Ruby Henderson and John Powell all describe two men in the sixth floor window neither of which match the description of Oswald in any way.

3) PARAFFIN TEST: You will recall that the paraffin test revealed that Oswald could not have fired a rifle. If Oswald didn't fire a rifle on November 22nd, 1963, he didn't shoot Kennedy. A positive result was found on his hands but a negative result was found on his face. If Oswald would have fired a rifle, he would have tested positive on both hands and his face. The Dallas

Police and the District Attorney would only state that Oswald fired a gun (not a rifle) stating that the test results revealed positive results on both hands. But if Oswald had discharged a small firearm, this action is usually executed with one hand which would have resulted in a positive on one hand and a negative on the other hand. The positive test from both hands likely came from external chemicals in the form of lead based paint he had come into close contact with on November 22nd, 1963. It's been established that the floors of the School Book Depository Building were being painted on the day of the assassination and the close contact with the chemicals of such a paint would have likely caused a positive result. The paraffin test then tends to show that Oswald didn't fire either a rifle or a side arm on the day of the assassination and tends to corroborate my Reverse Speech analysis tests.

OTHER REVERSE SPEECH TESTS

Several additional news conferences and on the spot interviews were recorded with other officials involved in the investigation of the assassination. Henry Wade was the district attorney in charge of the Oswald case. Jessie Curry was the Dallas Police Chief at the time of the assassination. Most of these can be located on various videos in the form of short news clips. Here are transcriptions of the ones I have located and analyzed:

> DISTRICT ATTORNEY WADE:
> (REPORTER) Has he told anybody he killed the President?
> (WADE) He hasn't admitted killing the President to anyone.
> I don't know what he said,...he says he didn't do it.
> [We're still working on the evidence. This has] been a joint effort by the Secret Service, The Federal Bureau Of Investigation, The Dallas Police Department, The Sheriff's Office, my office, and Detective Will Fritz has been in charge of it.
> (R) This is the way....you won't believe this. (VALIDITY 4)

AUTHOR'S COMMENTS: I believe that it is important to point out that my research shows that Henry Wade had been asked by the federal government to cut off any comments concerning conspiracy theories. My research reveals that Wade had been contacted by high ranking federal government officials (most likely Lyndon Johnson or J. Edgar Hoover) and briefed about this. The reversal, "this is the way...you won't believe this," strongly implies that Wade was attempting to follow the guidelines and instructions he had been given by the federal government. "This is the way," certainly implies that he wanted the news reporters to believe that Oswald was the assassin. "You won't believe this," implies that there is more to the story. During the later part of my research, I developed the fact that the first official document inditing Oswald for the murder of Kennedy quoted Oswald as being part of an international conspiracy. The White House contacted Wade and had the references of a conspiracy removed from the inditement.

> (REPORTER) How would you describe his mood during the questioning?
> (WADE) [Very arrogant.]
> (R) Very ignorant. (VALIDITY 6)
> [Has been all along.]
> (R) More Water Sir? (VALIDITY 5)

AUTHOR'S COMMENTS: It is hard to tell what Wade was referring to in his reversal, "Very Ignorant." Was he saying that he felt Oswald was an ignorant person or was he saying Oswald was ignorant when it came to the assassination? My research reveals that Oswald was not an ignorant person and, in fact, he was a well read individual. Based on this research, my opinion is that Wade was referring to Oswald being ignorant of the assassination. It is also my opinion that the reversal, "more water sir," is unconscious thoughts coming out of someone asking Oswald if he wanted more water during the interrogation.

> (REPORTER) How do you sum him up Ah as a man based on your experience with criminal types?
> (WADE) I think he's a man that ah [planned this] murder [weeks or months ago and]
> *(R) No boy just had the skill   (VALIDITY 4)   (R) some help. (VALIDITY 4)*

AUTHOR'S COMMENTS: This reversal certainly indicates Wade's thoughts that one person could not have had the skill to pull off the assassination of the President Of The United States and his thoughts that Oswald had some help.

> as and laid his plans carefully and carried them and out [as planned at that time what he was going to tell] the police that are questioning him at present.
> *(R) Influence make Leo mad that's going to help you. (VALIDITY 3)*

> I would say that without any doubt he's the killer, the law says [beyond a reasonable doubt] until a moral certainty which I'm, there's no question that he was the killer of President Kennedy.
> *(R) There's a problem here. (VALIDITY 4)*

AUTHOR'S COMMENTS: The reversal, "there's a problem here," certainly implies that Wade thought that the evidence that was collected up until this time had at least one major problem proving Oswald's guilt.

> (REPORTER) Will you ask death in the electric chair for Lee Oswald?
> (WADE) [Yes Sir]
> *(R) I think so. (VALIDITY 2)*
> [we'll ask the death penalty.]
> *(R) I'd pay to sell him. (VALIDITY 5)*
> (REPORTER) How many cases of this type have you been involved in where the death penalty has been involved.
> (WADE) Since I've been district attorney, we asked, I've asked the death penalty in 24 cases.
> (REPORTER) How many times have you obtained it?
> (WADE) 23

ANOTHER SHORT NEWS CONFERENCE WITH WADE'S REMARKS:

> (WADE) Yes I haven't gone into that. The paraffin tests show that he had ah, recently fired a gun, it was on both hands.
> (REPORTER) Both?
> (WADE) Both hands.
> (Cannot hear question)
> (WADE) [A gun]
> *(R) A rifle. (VALIDITY 5)*

AUTHOR'S COMMENTS: A paraffin test measures chemical elements on a subject's hands and face that would be strong evidence concerning the firing of a weapon. Paint is one thing that will produce a positive result with a paraffin test and fresh paint was being used on plywood floors at the Texas School Book Depository Building the day of the assassination. Oswald's test results were positive for both his hands and negative on his face. A negative result on the face would indicate that a rifle was not fired by the suspect. If Oswald didn't fire a rifle, he could not have assassinated the President. Wade commented that the results revealed Oswald fired a gun in forward speech. He said, "a rifle" in reverse. There is a big difference.

DALLAS POLICE CHIEF CURRY

(REPORTER) What was his comments?
(CHIEF CURRY) He doesn't give any motive except he denies them both.
(REPORTER) We understand that no one actually saw this man pull the trigger of the the rifle that apparently killed the President. Is that correct?
(CHIEF CURRY) That is correct up till this time in our investigation.
(REPORTER) What about the ballistics tests chief?
(CHIEF CURRY) On the [ballistics test] we haven't had a final [report but] it is, I understand will be favorable.
(R) The throat (VALIDITY 4)   (R) take me too him. (VALIDITY 5)

AUTHOR'S COMMENTS: Curry's reversal about the throat is interesting. I assume that Curry is referring to Kennedy's throat wound and the reversal indicates he would like to see it. Kennedy's body had already been removed from Dallas to Washington D.C. which was actually an unlawful act of itself according to Texas law. The Parkland Hospital doctors who had treated Kennedy had stated in a news conference that the throat wound was an entrance wound. If the throat wound was an entrance wound, then the shot was fired from the front. If it was fired from the front, Oswald could not have fired it as his position at the time of the shooting was behind the President.

(REPORTER) Do you think the smudged fingerprints found on the rifle which killed the President will be able to establish the identity of the killer.
(CURRY) We hope so but I couldn't say positive at this time that they will be.
(REPORTER) Will it be enough to convict him?
(CURRY) I don't know if it will be enough to convict him or not. If we can put his prints on the rifle ah it would certainly connect him with the rifle. We want to say this that this investigation has been carried on jointly by the FBI the Secret Service, the rangers and the Dallas Police Department Captain Fritz has been in charge.

ANOTHER NEWS CONFERENCE WITH CURRY

(REPORTER) Was their any surveillance ah, was the police aware of his presence in Dallas?
(CHIEF CURRY) We and the police department here did not know he was in Dallas. [I understand the] FBI did know he was in Dallas.
(R) Pay ransom off. (VALIDITY 4)

AUTHOR'S COMMENTS: This is the first time the word ransom comes up from members of the Dallas Police. This word comes up again which is documented towards the end of this study. The specific meaning of this is not clear but it is apparent that the police chief's thought patterns were centered on the payment of a ransom.

(REPORTER) The FBI informed the police?
(CHIEF CURRY) [Yes]
(R) Save me! (VALIDITY 6)

136

We did not have knowledge.

AUTHOR'S COMMENTS: The reversal, "Save me," certainly implies that Curry was concerned about his comment. The FBI did, in fact, know of Oswald, knew that he was in Dallas and had interviewed him several times in the months before the assassination. It is also apparent that the FBI had an ongoing investigative file on Oswald in the Dallas field office.

> (REPORTER) You were uninformed.
> (CHIEF CURRY) We had not been informed of this man.
> (REPORTER) Chief do you have any concern for the safety of your prisoner in view of the high feeling among the people of Dallas over the assassination of the President?
> (CHIEF CURRY) No because his, [ah necessary] [causes will be] taken of course.
> (R) *His sentence. (R) That's because he's hostage.*
> *(VALIDITY 4)*

AUTHOR'S COMMENTS: The two reversals, "His sentence," and "That's because he's hostage," are interesting. It is my opinion that Curry was referring to Oswald's court sentence which would be death in the electric chair for the assassination. If he was referring to his sentence which was carried out by Jack Ruby, the same result of Oswald's death and silence becomes the issue. The reversal concerning Oswald being a hostage is also interesting. Hostage is defined in the Funk & Wagnalls International Dictionary as: A person held as a pledge for the performance of some stipulation.

> (REPORTER) Chief we understand you have the results of the paraffin tests which were made to determine whether or not Oswald fired a weapon.
> (CURRY) I understand it was, I understand it was positive.
> (REPORTER) But what does that mean?
> It only means that he fired a gun.

AUTHOR'S COMMENTS: Although I didn't find any reversals in Curry's response, his forward speech implies that Oswald didn't fire a rifle only a gun. Again, if Oswald didn't fire a rifle, he didn't kill the President. I also believe that it is significant to point out that neither Curry or Wade ever directly pointed out that the test was negative on the face which indicates Oswald did not fire a rifle. They just left that part of the test out.

COMMENTS MADE AFTER RUBY SHOT OSWALD
DALLAS POLICE CHIEF CURRY

> (CURRY)[The suspect's name is Jack]
> *(R) That's the man that does it. (VALIDITY 4)*
> Rubinstein I believe
> [He goes by the name of Jack] Ruby
> *(R) That's the man and a druggy. (VALIDITY 4)*

AUTHOR'S COMMENTS: My research indicates that Ruby was an underworld figure and a major contact for drug traffic. " That's the man that does it," implies that Ruby kills people and "That's the man and a druggy, indicates that the police chief knew Ruby was involved in drugs.

Dozens of witnesses who were employed by or knew Jack Ruby and dozens of Dallas police officers have stated that a large number of police officers in Dallas knew Jack Ruby but both the police department and the federal government attempted to cover this point up.

DISTRICT ATTORNEY WADE

(REPORTER) Did you know Ruby before this?
(WADE) [No Sir. Saw him in this very same] room Friday night
(R) Yes Sir! Send me Dallas night clubs. (VALIDITY 4)
when we had the defendant up here.
If some of you [will recall he asked a question] from out here
(R) Help me! Said he knew Oswald. (VALIDITY 2)
Na it was an answer to a question..he was standing right back here and I didn't
know who he was. I thought he was a member of the press and he told me as I
walked out of here that he was a night club operator.

AUTHOR'S COMMENTS: The first speech reversal indicates that Wade did know Ruby. My
research of Ruby's employees at his nightclub indicates that Wade had been a guest at Ruby's club
in the past and that Ruby did know him. The second reversal above, "Help me! Said he know
Oswald," indicates that Ruby had a relationship with Oswald. My research and documentation of
several witnesses clearly support the fact that Oswald and Ruby did know each other before the
assassination. Wade already knew this fact and it appears that he withheld it.

(REPORTER) What question did he ask you?
(WADE) What?
(R) No
(REPORTER) What question did he ask?
I don't remember but he [he, ah maybe it was an answer but] I.
(R) That's him him forget about it. (VALIDITY 3)

AUTHOR'S COMMENTS: In my opinion, this reversal indicates that Wade wanted to get off this
question.

DETECTIVE JAMES R. LEAVELLE INTERVIEW

Detective James R. Leavelle was the police officer who was handcuffed to Oswald when Oswald
was shot by Ruby.

(REPORTER) Can you tell us what happened, ah where handcuffed to him?
(LEAVELLE) I was handcuffed to him and also had ahold of waistband of his
trousers. I saw this man come from the crowd and at the time he emerged from this
crowd of these people he was not more than six [or seven feet from us] from me.
(R) Mafia restaurant. (VALIDITY 5)
(REPORTER) Did you see the gun in his hand as he came?
(LEAVELLE) I saw the gun in his hand as he emerged from the crowd but [being
such a short distance from me]
(R) He's a mobster this bullshit let's hit him. (VALIDITY 4)
ah I had time to say anything.
(REPORTER) Ah when Oswald fell to the ground was he unconscious at that
point?
(LEAVELLE) [I would say if he was not he was near ah nearly so.]
(R) What's he doing ah, Ransom, ransom he paid us off. (VALIDITY 5)

138

Ah just as soon the ah my partner on the other side Mr. Graves grabbed ah Jack's hand with the gun in such a manner that he wouldn't fire it anymore.
(REPORTER) Did you recognize him when he came through?
(LEAVELLE) Yes I have known Jack Ruby for a number of years and I recognized him just as soon as he emerged from the crowd.

AUTHOR'S COMMENTS:

The three reversals I found are:
   (R) Mafia restaurant.
   (R) He's a mobster this bullshit let's hit him.
   (R) What's he doing ah, Ransom, ransom he paid us off.

The first two reversals clearly indicate that Ruby was a member of organized crime and my research into Ruby's background certainly points in this direction. For the second time in my findings, I find the word ransom again by a member of the Dallas Police. When considering the forward dialog, it implies that Leavelle is referring to the fact that Ruby paid someone off.

RUBY AND THE DALLAS POLICE DEPARTMENT

The following is a televised statement issued by Police Chief Curry concerning the number of Dallas Police officers Jack Ruby had known. Within minutes after Ruby shot Oswald, rumors circulated that Ruby was well known to the Dallas Police. Dozens of employees such as Nancy Hamilton and a piano player by the name of Johnson have stated that Ruby not only knew at least half of the 1200 members Dallas police department, he gave them free drinks and free food at his clubs.

POLICE CHIEF CURRY STATEMENT:

We have 1200 men in our department and we ah, had each to man submit a report regarding his knowledge or acquainted with Jack Ruby. Less than 50 men even knew Jack Ruby. And less than a dozen had ever been in his place of business. Most of these that had been in his place of business had been in there because they were sent on investigations or answered a call for ah police service. Ah I believe there was four men in our department that we were able to determine had been there socially. That is of duty, in the presence, ah ah [and were present in his night] club.

(R) Johnson is there for me.

It is my opinion that the reversal, *Johnson is there for me*, is referring to President Johnson who had talked with Police Chief Curry by telephone after Ruby shot Oswald. This implies that this is a story that was developed to squash the flying rumors that over half the members of the Dallas Police Department knew Jack Ruby. My research reveals that Ruby did in fact know a large number of Dallas police officers, permitted them to come into his night clubs to drink and eat free of charge.

PRESIDENT JOHNSON'S FIRST PUBLIC STATEMENT
AFTER KENNEDY ASSASSINATION

After the assassination November 22nd, 1963, Lyndon Johnson took the oath of office aboard Air Force One in Dallas and then flew directly to Andrews Air Force Base outside of Washington D.C. Upon his arrival and departure from Air Force One, he gave his first public statement as President. The following is a transcript of his dialog along with reversal analysis:

> This is a [sad time for all people.]
> *People are mad.*
> [We have suffered a loss] [that cannot be weighed.]
> *Sorry depress by you.*
> *Yeah we saw an extra.*
> For me it is a deep [personal tragedy.] [I know that the world shares] [the sorrow] [that Mrs. Kennedy] and [her family bare.]
> *Get yourself gone sir.*
> *Fresh dope, we have to go now.*
> *Her loss*
> *He done it, she didn't do.*
> *That's a mouth full*
>
> [I will do my best.] That is all [I can do.] I ask [for your help] and God's.
> *That damn hood. Poor Ralph.*
> *You'd make out.*
> *I Hurry up.*

THE REVERSALS LOCATED ARE:

> *People are mad.*
> *Sorry depress by you.*
> *Yeah we saw an extra.*
> *Get yourself gone sir.*
> *Fresh dope, we have to go now.*
> *Her loss*
> *He done it, she didn't do.*
> *That's a mouth full*
> *That damn hood. Poor Ralph.*
> *You'd make out.*
> *I Hurry up.*

The first reversal, *People are mad*, is most likely Johnson's subconscious thoughts about the events that had taken place concerning the assassination of Kennedy. The second reversal, *Sorry depress by you*, is an interesting reversal but it's exact meaning remains a mystery to me. Did Johnson mean that he was depressed by Kennedy or was he referring to being depressed by the assassination?

Yeah we saw an extra, is a reversal that could mean that the authorities knew that there were more trigger men. It is important to point out that this news conference occurred Friday night after landing in Washington. Oswald was already under arrest.

I believe that the reversal, *get yourself gone sir*, is internal dialog. Johnson is telling himself to get going and get the news conference over. It goes along with the last reversal, *I hurry up*. The reversal, *fresh dope, we have to go now*, also implies that Johnson is in a hurry. I believe that the words, fresh dope, is referring to information. Certainly as the new president, Johnson had a great deal on his mind. Does fresh dope refer to new information on the assassination?

The reversal, *he done it she didn't do*, is another interesting reversal. Johnson is talking about Mrs. Kennedy in the forward dialog. Does he mean she didn't do it in reverse? I believe that is the case. Although the presidential family was often shown as a happy family, there is evidence that the Kennedys only stayed married for political and image reasons. Who is he? That is not exactly clear.

The reversal, *That damn Hood, Poor Ralph*, is the most significant reversal found. That dam hood implies a member of organized crime. The top crime boss of Dallas was Ralph. Did Johnson know that organized crime was involved in the assassination? What ever is the answer to that question, I conclude from Johnson's reversals that, although he might have known more about the assassination than he lead the public to believe, he had nothing to do with it. I do believe that it is relevant to repeat something that was covered earlier about Johnson. That is, after his retirement from the White House and before his death, he indicated that he did not believe that Oswald acted alone.

JACK RUBY'S LAST PRESS CONFERENCE

The following dialog is the last press conference of Jack Ruby. The press conference was very short and recorded on the spot by a local television station. The quality was not good. This interview took place directly following Ruby's sentence. I have placed in brackets in the forward dialog where the reversals I found occur. The reversals follow the forward dialog in italic.

[Everything pertaining to what's happening has never come to the surface.]
You dust him forever. Christ wasn't finished. You killed him.

[The world will never know the true facts] of what occurred, my motives, ah in other words, [I'm the only person] in the background [that knows the truth] pertaining to everything relating to my sentence.
Wish I wouldn't have.
Certainly not.
I pushed on my roll.
REPORTER: Do you think it will ever come out?

[No because, unfortunately,] thank God, they they [have so much to gain and have such an ulterior motive to put me in the position I'm in, we'll never know the true facts.]

He is the first, let's get one.
I'm pushed to the limit. They asked me to name'am.
REPORTER: Are they people in high places.
[Yes]
Hate them

The forward dialog certainly shows that the true facts concerning the assassination of Kennedy and the killing of Oswald is not now known and will never come to the surface. It is interesting to note that Ruby uses the word "everything" in his forward statement. He didn't use the words some facts but implies that the whole story given to the American people is not true. Ruby is saying forward that he never revealed his true motive for his murder of Oswald. He also indicates that he was forced to kill Oswald. Ruby also indicates forward that those who were involved would never permit the truth to come out.

I located seven reversals from the Ruby press conference. They are:

> *You dust him forever. Christ wasn't finished. You killed him.*
> *Wish I wouldn't have.*
> *Certainly not.*
> *I pushed on my roll.*
> *He is the first. Let's get one.*
> *I'm pushed to the limit. They asked me to name'am.*
> *Hate them*

The first reversal is a three sentence reversal *"You dust him forever. Christ wasn't finished. You killed him."* The forward dialog where this occurs is, " Everything pertaining to what's happening has never come to the surface." This is an expansive external reversal in which Ruby says that he murdered Oswald. The word "dust" is a kind of slang in the underworld. The second sentence, *"Christ wasn't finished,"* certainly implies a mission that Ruby carried out and goes along with what he says forward when he later implies that he was forced into the mission to kill Oswald. This whole thing certainly implies that Ruby killed Oswald in order to silence him. My research and investigation set out in my book Missing Links shows that the Dallas police and Captain Will Fritz thought they had Oswald at a point where he was about ready to break before he was taken down into the basement to be transferred to the county jail. It was at this time that Oswald was murdered by Ruby.

It is my opinion that Ruby's reversal, *"Wish I wouldn't have,"* shows remorse for his killing of Oswald. This is another expansive external reversal were Ruby says forward, "The world will never know the true facts." He is referring to his murder of Oswald which I conclude was a mission given him by unknown parties. This reversal is congruent with his forward statement that implies that he was forced into the mission which he never wanted to perform. His reversal, " *I'm pushed to the limit. They asked me to name'am,"* certainly goes along with this. In this reversal, I assume that Ruby is referring to law enforcement and government officials who interrogated him. They asked Ruby to name the other conspirators and Ruby implies in his reversal that he didn't name any names. From these reversals, my conclusion is that people within the government knew the assassination was a conspiracy but didn't know who the conspirators were.

The next reversal, *" certainly not,"* is a contradictory external reversal which contradicts Ruby's forward statement that he's the only one who knows the true facts. Ruby knew, therefore, that there were other people who knew the real story.

Ruby's reversal, *"I pushed on my roll,"* is a first level reversal that picks up slang again from the underworld. "Push my roll," is slang that has to do with paying someone off. Roll refers to a roll of money. My research shows that Ruby always had a large roll of cash in his pocket. Push refers to pushing someone by giving them cash in return for a favor. It's a payoff. This reversal is corroborated with the ransom reversals found in the reversal analysis of police officials previously published.

Jack Ruby's reversal, *" He is the first. Let's get one."* is another first level reversal which is very expansive as to his thoughts. It's my opinion that the first sentence, *"He is the first,"* is referring to Oswald. Ruby is saying Oswald was the first person known to be involved in the assassination. His second sentence, *"Let's get one."* implies that other persons were involved in the assassination and that Ruby would like to see at least one of them caught. Since he says let's get one, there had to be at least two more persons involved.

Ruby's final reversal in which he says,"Hate them," is another expansive reversal. The reporter asked Ruby if the people involved were in high places. Ruby replies forward that they are. In reverse he says that he hates them. It's relevant to note that Ruby was found guilty and given the death penalty. His attorneys had appealed the sentence. It is not clear who the reporter or Ruby were referring to when the reporter asked the question about high officials.

Ruby later got sick and was transferred to a hospital. He has stated while in jail that a medical person was giving him injections he thought would kill him. Ruby died of cancer while in the hospital.

THE JANET CONFORTO INTERVIEW

Janet Conforto was the feature act at Jack Ruby's club and went by the stage name of JADA at the time of the Kennedy assassination. Conforto had only worked at Ruby's club for a few months. Prior to her employment at Ruby's club, she worked in New Orleans as a stripper at a place called the Sho-Bar. The Sho-Bar was owned by New Orleans crime boss, Carlos Marcello. Using the stage name "Jada", Conforto was considered the hottest act in town. A few months before the assassination, Ruby had traveled to New Orleans to watch Conforto's strip act in the Sho-Bar and apparently developed a contract with her to become the feature attraction at his night club in Dallas. In the months following the Kennedy Assassination and the murder of Oswald by Jack Ruby, Conforto mysteriously disappeared. Although several independent investigators attempted to locate her, she could not be found. Finally, she became the victim of a homicide statistic in a motorcycle accident in the state of Louisiana. The day after Ruby murdered Oswald, Conforto was interviewed by newsmen. On Monday, November 24th, 1963 she appeared on WFAA television in Dallas. I obtained video coverage of this interview and performed reverse speech analysis on the interview. Here is the dialog:

REPORTER: How long did you know Jack Ruby?
CONFORTO: [I knew Jack Ruby] for approximately [four, five], six months.
You can't do that.
You asshole.

REPORTER: In what relationship?
CONFORTO: I was employed as the ah feature at the Carousel Club [and I had known Jack before] I went to work there and ah I had a [slight hassle with Jack] and I had left and ah that was the end of my association with Jack.
I wonder about that.
You'll find out.

REPORTER: What kind of a man was he?
CONFORTO: Jack Ruby was [ah a fanatic, he was very ah nervous] man, a very [violent man] he would ah cause hassles and harassments and ah always running around very energetic aahm.
You better not, he knew what drove me. You better shut up.
And Knew Oswald

REPORTER: Would you say he had a violent streak in him?
CONFORTO: Oh yea, very much so. [Yes he would get carried] away by something and lose all lines of rational thinking. He would just go off zoom [and just ah]...he has to ah prove something. He had to be somebody.
They greased him.
That ass done it.

143

REPORTER: I've heard some stories about him being a generous type. They tell a story that when a customer at one of his clubs would call for a taxi, Jack would put fifty cents aside in the event the customer left and then the cab driver would come up and have to go away empty handed he'd give him the fifty cents. Does this square with his character as you knew it?

CONFORTO: Oh yes, Jack ah was almost a dual nature. He would be ah very nice and very helpful to me. He ah would change completely then in the next few minutes he'd be your worst enemy an he'd be against you and he'd want everybody to support him against you and very irrational and very ah emotional.

(No reversals found)

REPORTER: Did he ever carry a gun?

CONFORTO: I don't know. I don't know him that well but I had seen him with a gun and ah [I presume he carried] it every night. It seemed to be a habit of his.
You going to get shot.

REPORTER: What about politics. Did he seem interested in politics particularly regarding the Kennedys.

CONFORTO: [I've heard Jack talk about] the Kennedys and I've been trying to think and it's so [confusing] today. But I believe he [disliked Bobby] Kennedy.
The horrible cost, I've heard that.
He did it.
If I tell you.

REPORTER: Got no recollection about what he said about the President?

CONFORTO: Ah [yea he followed that statement up about] Bobby with something about [Jack Kennedy but I can't] for the moment [form it in my mind.]
Horrible thought, he did it, you lousy thing.
Jack, yea he did it.
Now your minimal

REPORTER: Do you think that ah Jack Ruby was the type of man that was capable of killing the assassin of President Kennedy out of love for Kennedy, out of political motives.

CONFORTO: Ah [I don't think he loved Kennedy] that much. Ah [I don't know why] he would do it. I would say he would be perfectly capable of an act like that ah very much so.
He did it, love, he didn't care for them.
I don't know that.

SEVENTEEN REVERSALS FOUND IN ORDER OF OCCURRENCE

You can't do that.
You asshole.
I wonder about that.
You'll find out.
You better not, he knew what drove me. You better shut up.
And Knew Oswald.
They greased him.
That ass done it.

You going to get shot.
The horrible cost, I've heard that.
He did it.
If I tell you.
Horrible thought, he did it, you lousy thing.
Jack, yea he did it.
Now your minimal
He did it, love, he didn't care for them.
I don't know that.

Within the reversals, I believe that we have four that point to the fact that Conforto thought that Jack Ruby has something to do with the assassination. They are:

That ass done it.
He did it.
Horrible thought, he did it, you lousy thing.
He did it, love, he didn't care for them.

I do not believe that these reversals are referring to RUBY murdering OSWALD but refer to RUBY having something to do with the assassination of Kennedy. The last three reversals are specifically referring to the Kennedys and not to Oswald. Since there is and never was a question as to wether or not RUBY shot OSWALD in anyone's mind, I do not believe that the first two reversals are referring to Ruby shooting Oswald at all. They are all revealing that RUBY had something to do with the assassination. These reversals are corroborated by witnesses who place RUBY at the assassination site just before and right after the assassination and the witnesses and photographic evidence that place RUBY at Parkland Hospital were he most likely planted the magic bullet.

We have one reversal that points to the fact that Ruby had a relationship with Oswald prior to the assassination. That reversal is:

And Knew Oswald.

According to J. Gary Shaw of the JFK Assassination Information Center, Conforto stated privately that she had observed Oswald talking with Jack Ruby at the night club and that she was introduced to Oswald by Ruby as, "my friend from the CIA." This account is corroborated by Beverly Oliver (still alive) as Ruby had introduced Oswald as a CIA agent to both Conforto and Oliver. Conforto's private statement about Ruby introducing her to Lee Oswald as a CIA agent comes from Bud Shrake who was a local spotscaster in Dallas and was dating Conforto. Shrake is alive and well today and is an escort for Texas Govorner Ann Richards. So the reversal, And knew Oswald, can be confirmed through not only private statements Conforto had made, but through the account of Beverly Oliver who also recalls the incident.

I believe that we have several reversals that point to the fact that Conforto knew more than she was telling. The reversals that point to this are:

You can't do that.
You'll find out.
You better not, he knew what drove me. You better shut up.
You going to get shot.

I believe that the first and second reversal are directly related to her reversal about Ruby knowing Oswald. The first reversal, you can't do that, is internal dialog in which Conforto is telling herself not to expose that fact about the Oswald and Ruby relationship before the assassination. The next reversal, You'll find out, indicates that she believes that the media is going to find out anyway. The next reversal, you better not, he knew what drove me. You better shut up, also reveals that Conforto knew something she better not tell and that something was the fact that Oswald had been in Ruby's club and that Conforto knew that Ruby and Oswald had been communicating.

The reversal, you going to get shot, is internal dialog which gives the reason why Conforto would not tell everything she knew. Since she later mysteriously disappeared and then died under suspicious circumstances, I believe that the reversal, You going to be shot, is highly relevant and corroborative with the known events that took place after the interview. Since we have a reversal that came out that exposes the fact that Conforto knew that RUBY and OSWALD were in communication before the assassination and that OSWALD was introduced to CONFORTO by RUBY as a CIA agent, I conclude that this is what CONFORTO knew but did not want to expose in her forward speech.

One reversal indicates that someone was paying Ruby off. That reversal is:

They greased him.

This is, again, underworld slang that tends to indicate a payoff. The word "greased" refers to being paid off. It's my opinion that this reversal goes along with the "ransom" and "payoff" reversals we located and would tend to indicate that RUBY was given funds to make a payoff and a percentage of it was his to keep.

The conclusions drawn from the Conforto analysis is:

1) Ruby had a relationship with Oswald prior to the assassination.
2) Ruby had something to do with the assassination conspiracy.
3) Ruby was being paid off by someone.

THE STRANGE STORY OF ROSCO WHITE
INFORMATION, DISINFORMATION OR MISINFORMATION

In August of 1990, Ricky White held a news conference sponsored by the JFK Assassination Information Center in Dallas and the Assassination Archives And Research Center in Washington D.C. The news conference centered on the fact that Ricky White found his dead father's diary and other evidence in a military type canister and that this information revealed that his father was part of the assassination team in Dallas on November 22nd, 1963. The day before the news conference, Ricky White was interviewed by news reporter Earl Golz for the *Austin American Statesman*. Golz's report appeared in the Austin American Statesman the day before the news conference. Golz also published an account of the news conference on the following day. In the December edition of *Texas Monthly*, Gary Cartwright wrote an article about White. Information in this section was developed from the newspaper stories written by Golz and the magazine story written by Cartwright along with interviews I have had with J. Gary Shaw and Larry Howard of the JFK Assassination Information Center in Dallas, Texas and my own independent investigation and verification of this account.

Ricky White says that the diary clearly shows that his father, Rosco White, served in the Marines and got to know Oswald. It has been documented through other sources that White and Oswald both boarded the USS Bexar in San Diego in 1957 for a twenty two day trip to Japan. A photograph has been published by assassination researchers for years of a group of Marines in Japan in front of a tent. Oswald is in the photograph and so is a person who looks just like Rosco White. According to the White family, it's Rosco.

Ricky White was given a footlocker after his grandfather's death in 1982 that hand belonged to Rosco. Upon opening the footlocker, he found the following items in it:

Rosco White's Diary
Rosco White's Service Records
AN Unmarked Safe-Deposit Key
Receipt for $100,000 in negotiable bonds

Ricky White would pick up the diary and read it now and then but he says it wasn't until four years after his father's death that he read entries about November 22nd, 1963.

Ricky White claims that the dairy for that time clearly shows that Rosco White was part of a three man assassination team. The diary stated that there were six shots fired, two by Rosco White. Rosco White was behind the wooden fence on top of the grassy knoll and had a code name of Mandarin. His first shot hit the President in the throat. His second shot hit the President in the head. Of the other two assassins, one was located in the Records Building and used a code name of Saul. The third assassin was located in the Texas School Book Depository Building and used a code name of Lebannon. The diary also said that Mauser rifles were used in the assassination. Ricky White remembers his father giving him two rifles after the assassination in Dallas. One was an Argentine rifle and the other a 7.65 Mauser.

Ricky White says that the dairy shows that Oswald knew of the assassination plot but didn't fire any shots. Oswald was told to bring his rifle to work on November 22nd and to build a sniper's nest with boxes in the sixth floor window. All three assassins had an assistant who's job was to disassemble the rifles and carry them away.

The Diary also stated that Rosco White and Oswald had plans to escape together after the assassination and go to Red Bird Airport in South Dallas. Their driver was J.D. Tippet who didn't know anything concerning the plot. While driving the two in south Dallas, Tippit heard radio reports of the assassination and started to suspect that his two passengers were involved. Oswald became distressed and jumped out of the car. White got out of the car and shot Tippet with a pistol when Tippit told him he would have to take White downtown. Ricky White says that the diary stated:

"I killed an officer at 10th and Patton."

Upon reading the revealing entries for November of 1963, Ricky went to his mother's house and told her about it. According to Ricky, she acted as if she knew about the assassination and her husband's involvement in it all the time. The basic problem in this is that Ricky White doesn't know what happened to the diary. In 1988 he contacted Midland District Attorney Al Schorre about a key Ricky thought belonged to a safety deposit box that was among his deceased father's belongings. He thought his father may have left money behind and Ricky wanted to find it. He asked the district attorney's office for help. In telling his story to Schorre, he mentioned the diary. Schorre contacted the FBI.

The FBI presented itself at Ricky White's home in Midland, Texas. The agents asked Ricky to gather up his father's things and come to the Midland FBI office for an interview. He stated that the FBI made copies of the belongings except the dairy. But, after the interview, FBI agent Tom Farris came back to the house and stated that he had inadvertantly left his notebook in the box of documents Ricky had earlier taken with him to the FBI office. Agent Farris looked through the box and apparantly obtained his notebook. It was a few days later that Ricky White says he noticed that the diary was missing.

The only people who read the diary were:

Ricky White
Geneva White (Ricky's mother)
Tricia White (Ricky's wife)
Denise Carter (a family babysitter)

According to the JFK Assassination Information Center, Ricky White was the only known person to have read the November 63 accounts in the diary although many others can testify to the existance of the diary.

Records show that Rosco White obtained employment with the Dallas police on October 7th, 1963, about seven weeks before the assassination, as a clerk and photographer. He worked for the department until October 19th, 1964. However, sources located within the department in Gary Cartwright's *Texas Monthly* article reveal that White's personnel file contained no references. On the day of the assassination, Rosco White was assigned to the identification section of the Dallas Police Department.

Ricky White stated that after the assassination, he and his mother were sent to Paris, Texas to stay with his mother's parents and the diary states that Rosco White with the other two assassins went to Dripping Springs and stayed in a hideaway house for awhile.

In 1971, Rocso White was killed in an explosive fire that took place during employment at M&M Equipment Company. Reverend Jack Shaw visited Rosco White in the hospital several times before he expired. Shaw has stated that Rosco told him he didn't think that the fire was an accident and that he saw a man running from the fire. Reverend Shaw also states that he had acted as a counselor for both Rosco and Geneva White in the past. Rosco told him that he was troubled as he had lead a double life, had killed people in the past and that he felt that his family was in danger.

After Rosco's death, his wife, Geneva White, moved back to Paris Texas. The day of Rosco White's funeral a man who's name has only been given as "Bill X" by the White family, delivered a package of photographs. Geneva White locked these photographs in a file in her bedroom. One day Ricky broke the lock and looked at the photographs. He said that it contained about 40 photos concerning evidence of the assassination. One was a photograph of Oswald in his backyard holding the rifle. Another one was of Oswald's body in the morgue. In 1975, Geneva White's house was burglarized and the package containing the photos was taken. The FBI arrested three men in Florida a few weeks later who had the photographs. The FBI turned them over to the Senate Committee who finally turned them over to the House Select Committee On Assassinations. The package of photos was eventually returned to Geneva White. The three men arrested? Acording to a letter Geneva obtained from the Senate Committee, the men were to have been tried in Dallas, Texas but no one has ever been able to develop any more information on either the three men or the trial.

Ricky White states that sometime after he had discovered the evidence about the assassination in the diary, he located a military type canister in the attic of his grandparent's house in Paris. The canister contained what looked like secret cables and a hand written note verified to be in Rosco White's handwriting concerning the elimination of witnesses and news clips of 28 witnesses involved in the Kennedy assassination who had died under strange circumstances. The three cables are as follows:

```
Navy Int.
Code A MRC
Remarks data
1666106
NRC VDC NAC
(illegible) 63

Remarks Mandarin: Code A
Foreign affairs assignments have been cancelled. The next assignment is to eliminate
a National Security threat to world wide peace. Destination will be Houston, Austin or
```

Dallas. Contacts are being arranged now. Orders are subject to change at any time. Reply back if not understood.

C. BOWERS
OSHA

NAVY INT.
CODE A MRC
REMARK data
1666106
Sept. 63

Remarks Mandarin: Code A
Dallas destination chosen. Your place hidden within the department. Contacts are within this letter. Continue on as planned.

C. Bowers
OSHA
RE- rifle code AAA destroy/on/

NAVY INT.
CODE A mrc
Remark data
1666106
NRC VDC NAC
Dec. 63

Remarks Mandarin: Code G:
Stay within department, witnesses have eyes, ears and mouths. You (illegible) do of the mix up. The men will be in to cover up all misleading evidence soon. Stay as planned wait for further orders.
C. Bowers
RE-rifle Code AAA destroy/on/

John Stockwell, a former CIA task force chief, looked at the cables and stated that he thought there was a 90 to 95% probability that they were genuine.

Gary Shaw, director of the JFK Assassination Research Center in Dallas stated that Ricky White was given both a polygraph test and a PSE test and passed both.

What is even more curious about this whole story is that Rosco White's wife, Geneva White went to work for Jack Ruby as a hostess for a few weeks just before the assassination. A photograph of herself with Jack Ruby was published in a 1988 edtion of Time Magazine. According to Geneva, Rosco took the photograph.

Geneva says that she overheard her husband talking in Ruby's office about a plan to murder Kennedy. Mrs. White stated in an interview with Gary Cartwright that Ruby caught her listening and told her that if she ever revealed anything he would hurt her children and torture her. Rosco White said that Geneva would have to undergo a series of shock treatments to erase memory from her brain.

Evidently Geneva White has had many shock treatments and she claims she's a dying woman with all sorts of illnesses. In May of 1990, she claims she located another diary found between the pages of some of Rosco White's books. She turned the diary over to the Reverend Shaw and a private investigator by the name of Joe West. Evidently she had received over $5,000 for the diary from the two. West and Shaw held a press conference about the new diary but it was later proven to be a fake.

Joe West was working, at one time, with the JFK Assassination Information Center in Dallas, Texas. West is a Houston based private investigator. Without the knowledge of J. Gary Shaw's center, West had gone to Geneva White's home and obtained the fake diary. Without checking it out, he held a press conference in Houston. If the purpose of the second diary was to discredit the whole story, it seems to have worked. Ricky White has stopped talking about it. According to Larry Harris, a researcher at the JKF Information Center, Ricky White's wife has, "yanked the telephone out of the wall." The news media has stopped the talk shows and articles on the Rosco White story.

I spent a considerable amount of time on developing Joe West's connection to the Rosco White story and his defection from the JFK Assassination Information Center. According to the information I developed, several people close to the center indicate that they did not trust Joe West from the the start of his association with it. I have always admired J. Gary Shaw's twenty-eight year search for the truth in the Kennedy assassination which he has financed himself. Despite many beliefs that the center is out to profit from the Kennedy Assassination, my investigation concluded that the center and J. Gary Shaw has never developed any major profits and that, in fact, J. Gary Shaw has provided funding for his ongoing projects out of his own pocket, most of which has never turned a profit to pay him back. The center has always been under funded. Joe West came along and was willing to work on projects without pay and cover his own expenses.West has been described by several sources as a rather flamboyant person who wears expensive clothes and jewelry. I believe that, although people within the center didn't trust him completely, this was somewhat overlooked. West was a certified legal investigator through the National Association Of Legal Investigators and a state licensed private investigator who was willing to work at his won expense without pay. Who could ask for anything more.

Evidently, West talked Ricky White into letting him retain possession of the secret cables he had found. After West's connection to the Shaw group was cut, the group of people who had funded Ricky White had to sue West to get the cables back. Ricky White believes that the second diary was made up by his mother and sold to West because Mrs. White needed money.

Joe West is from Houston Texas and was involved, at one time in his life, in raising bond money for church groups. He also was involved in group travel projects in which he organized travel for groups of people traveling outside the United States. According to my sources, West is known to have made remarks that he had developed CIA contacts during his foreign travel projects. Through a tip prodived to me by J. Gary Shaw, I have been able to verify that Joe West is a member of an organization called the Association Of Former Intelligence Officers which will only let people join the orgnization who have been involved in government intelligence work. The bulk of the membership is made up of ex-federal intelligence officers. It is my conclusion then, that Joe West most likely did some sort of federal intelligence work at some point in his life.

If the Rosco White story is a missing piece of the puzzle that belongs to the Kennedy

Assassination, it fits perfectly. In studying Ricky White, you will find that he is not an assassination buff. He is just not the type of person who has studied the event and I do not see how he could have made the whole thing up. Three other witnesses confirm that the diary existed and that Rosco White wrote about being the gunman behind the fence. Details of the account fit perfectly into the puzzle. The White link with Oswald in the military, White's employment with the Dallas Police and the Dripping Springs safehouse account can all be corroborated.

I located an Austin resident who would rather not be named that told me that he rented a cottage on some farm property in 1970's. This source stated that he was walking around the area one day and entered an old barn. Inside the barn, this source located two boxes of files that contained letterheads from the Texas State Attorney's office and that these files concerned the Kennedy Assassination. The barn has since been torn down. Of course, the files in question could be unrelated to the White account of the safehouse in Dripping Springs but it sure seems to fit. The cottage was located in an isolated area that could not been observed from the main highway and the address was in Dripping Springs.

In 1991, I spoke with J. Gary Shaw one of the founders of the JFK Assassination Information Center in Dallas, Texas again concerning the Dripping Springs incident. Shaw told me that both he and Ricky White had interviewed an elderly man in Dripping Springs by the name of Earl Albrecht who recalls the safehouse. According to this source, he can remember both Rosco White and Lee Oswald being in the area the months before the assassination and can recall Rosco White being in the area with two other individuals right after the assassination.

J. Gary Shaw also told me that he had completed an indepth study of Rosco White's background in both the military, his time with the Dallas Police Department and his activities after leaving the Dallas Police Department. White's military background and travels have been paralleled by Shaw and Shaw states that documentary evidence clearly shows that Oswald and White were both on the USS Bextar that went to Japan. Both were stationed in the general area of the famous U-2 spy plane base. Shaw also noted that both Oswald and White have travels during a six month period while overseas that closely parallel each other. Oswald would leave for one location by one means of transportation and White would end up in the same place a few days later using a different mode of transportation. They would both be in the same location for a few weeks and then one would leave to return to the main base. A few days later, the second one would, again, take a different mode of transportation and end up back in the same place.

Shaw and the JFK Assassination Information Center also has documentary evidence that proves Rosco White worked for the Dallas Police Department during the time in question. The file on White is very strange. Some of it appears to be missing including his original employment application. The records of White going through the police academy are in tack. He obtained high scores. However, the information in the file contains gaps. Shaw states that he has interviewed several police officers who also question the file. Their remarks center on the fact that no references are shown and that these references and the original employment application must have been removed from the file as it was and still is the policy of the Dallas Police Department to check out applicants very closely. Either someone removed these documents or they never existed.

Several of the top experts who have studied this issue and talked both formally and informally at the 1991 Assassination Symposium in Dallas, Texas in November indicated that the CIA had a covert policy to place their own agents within various police departments in the United States. Naturally, if this is what occurred, Rosco White wouldn't have what you would call a regular personnel file showing a personnel investigation completed by the Dallas Police but a file would exist much like the file now in possession of the JFK Assassination Research Center. Since Rosco White didn't have any previous official law enforcement experience and since his employment with the Dallas Police was for a very brief period of time, part of which occurred during the time of the Kennedy assassination, it's all very strange.

I believe that it is relevant to note that J. Gary Shaw is one of the most well known, respected and honest assassination researchers in the country. He seems to be the glue that holds together the various fractions within assassination circles and is known as the man who can smooth over arguments between assassination researchers. Mr. Shaw is also one of the most knowledgeable persons on the Kennedy assassination I have ever had the pleasure to meet. He had spent the last twenty eight years looking into the subject on his own. Shaw is a practicing architect who has spent the overwhelming majority of the last twenty eight years of his spare time researching the Kennedy assassination with little or no pay for his efforts. My own feelings about Shaw is that he isn't now or ever was in it for the money, he's only looking for the truth. Shaw is cautious, skeptical and above board and it took awhile for me to get him to open up and talk to me which is understandable. Assassination research has been riddled with misinformation, disinformation, sensationalizm in the name of dollars and down right lies all of which Shaw had muddled through for twenty-eight years.

Is the Rosco White story valid?

OTHER POINTS TENDING TO CONFIRM THE ROSCO WHITE STORY

> *1) Many witnesses stated that shots came from behind the fence on top of the grassy knoll and this is where the diary says White was standing when he fired the shots.*

> *2) The Diary says that White hit the President in the throat and the head. Attending physicians thought the throat wound was a wound of entrance and the Zapruder film suggests that the head wound was from the front.*

> *3) One witness who saw activity behind the wood fence, suggested a person running with a rifle. Another saw a man who relayed a rifle to another man dressed as a railroad worker who disassembled the rifle and placed it in a railroad tool box that is consistent with the White story. These eyewitness accounts fit the Rosco White story perfectly.*

> *4) The diary shows that Oswald knew of the conspiracy but didn't*

fire any shots. This is consistent with the paraffin tests done on Oswald at the Dallas police station and my reverse speech analysis on Oswald which we will get into in the next few chapters.

5) The diary stated that there were two other assassins and this is consistent with the known facts when you consider the evidence concerning the Records Building across the street from the School Book Depository and witnesses who saw two men other than Oswald in the sixth floor window of the School Book Depository.

6) The diary says that Oswald and White were to be driven to Red Bird Airport by officer Tippit. Mrs. Roberts, Oswald's landlady, stated that during the few minutes Oswald was in his room, she recalls a Dallas police car pulling up to the curb at the house and honking the horn three times. The Dallas police car had two people in it. One of them had to have been officer Tippet.

7) Several witnesses said that two people where present at the Tippit shooting and this could have been Oswald and White.

8) Federal authorities seized a plane at Red Bird Airport that had it's motors running and was ready for take off. The plane was placed in a hanger and locked up. No other information in known about this incident.

9) There is documented evidence and a photograph that White's wife worked for a short time for Jack Ruby and it appears that Ruby knew Rosco White.

10) The diary described the assassination weapons as Mausers which is what the weapon found on the sixth floor of the School Book Depository Building was first identified as by the Dallas police.

11) Rosco White worked in the evidence section of the Dallas police department which could explain the strange backyard photograph and the confusion over the description of the rifle.

12) It's well documented that Geneva White has had a number of shock treatments.

13) The other backyard photograph found in the possession of the White family is clearly documented and no other explanation has ever been revealed as to why White would have a previously undiscovered backyard photograph.

154

14) At least one witness confirm the Dripping Springs safehouse story .

15) Both a polygraph test and a PSE test shows that Ricky White is telling the truth.

16) The number of shots is consistent with many witnesses who say that the number of shots is between, "four and six."

17) The testimony of Jean Hill, Gordon Arnold and the Newmans tends to ad weight to the White story.

18) The Badgeman Photograph tends to ad weight to the story.

19) The fact that an attempt was made to discredit the White account, in my opinion, ads weight to the the White account.

20) The witness who rented an isolated cottage in Dripping Springs and saw some assassination files in an old barn ads weight to the story.

21) It has been confirmed that White worked for the Dallas Police Department concerning the time period in question coupled with the fact that he had no prior police experience ads weight to the White account.

22) J,. Gary Shaw has confirmed the Oswald/White linkage in the military through his parallel study of unexplained travels. My resaearch tends to indicate that Oswald's unexplaned travels were for intelligence purposes which would mean that the White travels were for the same thing. This squares with the Rosco White story.

Based on the above, I believe the Rosco White story because it generally fits into the puzzle of things and I do not believe that Ricky White had enough knowledge about the assassination to plan such a hoax. Also, I do not believe that Ricky White's mother has the mental capacity to plan such a hoax. I also tend to feel that the fake diary incident Joe West presented was a setup. In fairness to Joe West, I would like to state that he is an accomplished investigator and has been awarded the Certified Legal Investigator designation through the National Association Of Legal Investigators which is not easy to obtain and is considered one of the most prestigious designations within the private investigative industry. However, I suspect that somehow, the fake diary could have been a frame.

On of the problems with the Kennedy assassination is the tremendous amount of misinformation and disinformation presented by both pro-conspiracy people and by anti-conspiracy people.

Throughout this work I have presented a great deal of evidence that reveals coverup information regarding an assassination conspiracy. In all fairness, I would also state that, over the years, there have been dozens of writers and researchers who have sensationalized conspiracy theories that have no basic merit. Some of this has resulted from the fact that much has been published by people who have no investigative experience or knowledge to investigate such matters. I will call this misinformation. On the same hand, I believe a number of things have been planted on purpose to discredit an assassination conspiracy. I will call this disinformation. Trying to sort out fact from fiction and disinformation from misinformation can be confusing. One has to wade through this approach when looking into the Rosco White story.

Did the Rosco White story start out as disinformation or misinformation? When you look at the motives and personality of Ricky White, I believe that the story started out as sincere. His first basic concern was to locate the safety deposit box that went with the key he had found. That has been verified. Was the problem then with Joe West? I believe that Joe West started out with a sincere interest in developing the truth. Was the fake diary disinformation to discredit the Rosco White story by Joe West? I do not believe that it was. I believe that it was misinformation by Mrs. White, Ricky's mother who apparently has mental problems and her excitement and need for funds to pay medical bills was the prime motivation. She simply attempted to recreate the diary from her memory and then told West that it was a second diary that she had located. I believe that Joe West became a victim. However, he should have taken the diary given to him by Geneva White to the JFK Assassination Information Center who would have studied the information and determined it to be a fake instead of defecting from the center and holding a press conference without checking out the diary first. The fact that he didn't smells too much like a frame to me but who is doing what to whom is murky. The relevant point is, despite the fake diary news conference held by Joe West, the Rosco White story still holds water. The problem is that the fake diary incident has tended to discredit the other relevant parts of the story in the eyes of the news media. What makes me so suspisious about the fake diary being a frame is this is the exact mode of operation engaged by people who specialize in disinformation.

THE TRAMP PHOTOGRAPHS AND
OTHER STRANGE MISSING LINKS

Right after the assassination, the police and sheriff's department made a search of the area behind the picket fence on top of the grassy knoll. As I have set out in other chapters, many witnesses and law enforcement officials encountered men who produced Secret Service Identification. The relevancy of the secret service identification witnesses and local law enforcement officials encountered becomes highly relevant as the tramp photograph story develops but, at this stage, it's important to point out that the official government version is that no secret service agents were in the area right after the assassination and the dozens of witnesses and local law enforcement officers who encountered them were mistaken.

As the local police combed the area behind the fence, they noticed that a train with a string of box cars were in a stationary position on the railroad tracks ready to take off. The police held the train to search the box cars. In the ninth box car, they located three men in what, at first, appeared to be tramps. These men were escorted from the box car to the sheriff's office which involved walking through part of the plaza area. During this escort, several photographs of the three men were taken.

For many years, the tramps in the photographs were a mystery. Neither the Dallas police or the sheriff's office had any record of their arrest. Assassination researchers began to study the photographs of the tramps. Several puzzling facts became obvious from a study of the photographs.

> A) The three tramps were not handcuffed and the officers escorting them were doing so in a very casual manner. The tramps did not seem to be under arrest.

> B) The clothes and general appearance of these three men upon very close observation would indicate that they were not really tramps. Although they were dressed in what could be described as work clothes, the clothes appeared to be clean and unworn unlike the clothes typical of a tramp. They had fresh haircuts and were clean shaven. The leather on their shoes were not worn. No visible holes in either their clothes or shoes were noted.

Until recently, the three men in the photographs have not been identified. Some researchers thought that one of the tramps might be E. Howard Hunt but photographic experts concluded that the man that looked like E. Howard Hunt was not him.

In 1980, Charles V. Harrelson was tried and convicted for a 1979 murder-for-hire killing of Judge John Wood of San Antonio, Texas who was probing organized crime and it's links to narcotics traffic. Harrelson was convicted and is serving three life sentences at the penitentiary in Marion, Ill. Harrelson has stated that he was the tall tramp and was present at the Kennedy assassination and played a role in the assassination but has retracted those statements. However, facial expert Janice Gibson who works under contract for the Houston Police Department concludes that the tall tramp is Charles V. Harrelson and long time photographic expert Jack White tends to indicate the same thing.

In late 1991, a man by the name of Chancy Holt walked into the JFK Assassination Information Center in Dallas, Texas and confessed to being the older tramp in the photograph. Holt's story was checked out by the center and also checked out by Dallas retired private investigator John Craig. He was interviewed for some seventeen hours by both John Craig and J. Gary Shaw. Both Shaw and Craig have conducted extensive background investigations on Holt.

Holt describes his story as follows. He stated that he was involved as a contact agent for the CIA. He was instructed to forge fake secret service identification cards and secret service pins and show up in the area behind the picket fence on the morning of the assassination. Holt stated that he had no prior knowledge of the assassination and didn't know the reason for his instruction to show up in the area behind the wooden fence with the forged identification cards. Holt says that he was provided with a key to the parking lot behind the wooden fence and entered it in an Oldsmobile. The vehicle meets the description of Sam Holland who was the railroad worker working in the railroad tower. Holt says he was instructed to wear work clothes. After the assassination, Holt stated that he went to the ninth boxcar in the railroad yard where he ran into the other two men in the tramp photograph. Holt says that the three men were instructed to stay in the box car while the train pulled out but the boxcar was searched by local law enforcement officers and they were found. The local police officers were shown CIA identification and the three men were then asked to walk over to the sheriff's office. Holt says that he was only present for a few minutes and was then released. Upon his release, he made his way to Redbird Airport in South Dallas and boarded a small plane that flew him out of the area. What is interesting about the Redbird Airport thing is that Redbird Airport is mentioned in the Rosco White story. This small airport is located in the general direction that Oswald was traveling after the assassination.

Craig claims that he interviewed people at Redbird Airport. His investigative interviewing confirmed that a plane was hangered and took off at about the time that Holt says he left. It has also been established that a hanger at the airport had been guarded with a plane inside with the engines running and the guards would let no one inside.

Holt's background was checked out by both J. Gary Shaw and John Craig. Craig indicated at the JFK Assassination Symposium in Dallas, Texas in 1991 that his background check reveals all kinds of links to intelligence agencies. Assassination researcher J. Gary Shaw also checked into Holt's background and concluded that Holt has intelligence links. Holt was tried a few years ago for a California murder and was found not guiltly. During the trial, it was brought up that Holt had ties to the CIA. The judge obtained what he termed as classified documents that he would not give to the jury but concluded that the Holt connection to the CIA is correct.

Craig and Shaw both describe Holt as a "career criminal" who was involved in a great deal of covert activites for U.S. intelligence. According to Craig, Holt said that he has been involved in all kinds of criminal acitvity but, because he also did work for U.S. intelligence, he was always able to get out of any trouble he got into but now the CIA will not protect him.

In June of 1965, the Houston police department was contacted concerning the whereabouts of an elderly couple as they had not been observed for a number of days although their son had been observed. The Houston police went to the elderly couple's home located in a residential section of Houston. The police approached the home and knocked on the door. They thought that they had heard a noise inside but no one answered the door. Upon entering the home without anyone answering the door, the police began to comb the inside of the house. In an upstairs room, the Houston police found a radio that was not commercially available but was known to be used by federal government agencies. At first, the Houston police thought that nothing appeared wrong. Then an officer opened the ice box and found the remains of the elderly couple cut up in pieces. The Houston police put out an all points bulletin for the son, Charles Frederick Rogers. The Houston police believe that Rogers was in his upstairs room right before they had checked on his parents. A fan was found on and a fresh meal was found in the room.

The background of Charles Frederick Rogers is very strange. According to sources within the Houston police, retired investigator John Craig and assassination researcher J. Gary Shaw, Charles Frederick Rogers is a covert agent within U.S. intelligence. Craig states that his investigation shows that Rogers is still alive as he has witnesses who have spotted him outside the United States. Craig also claims that Rogers was input into the NCIC FBI computer by the Houston police right after he became a missing suspect in the murder. Craig also says that during the years, the Houston police had believed that Rogers was on file as a suspect on the NCIC computer system. However, according to Craig, the FBI computer was checked after the Holt story broke and the Houston police became puzzled as to why Roger's name was not showing up. Craig says that the Houston police input the name of Charles Frederick Roger into the NCIC computer again but, for some unknown reason, the FBI will not place the name of Charles Frederick Rogers in the database.

The police facial expert, Janice Gibson, mentioned earlier has concluded that the men in the tramp photographs are:

> 1) Charles Frederick Rogers: wanted in connection with his parents
> murder and has ties to US intelligence.

> 2) Chancy Holt: The individual who has confessed to being the man
> in the photograph and says used to be a contact agent for the CIA.

> 3) Charles Harrelson: Who has confessed to being in the photograph
> but who has retracted that statement and who is currently serving a
> life sentence in Marion, Ill. for a murder-for-hire charge on Judge
> John Wood.

Photographic expert Jack White stated before the Select House Committee On Assassinations that he felt as if Harrelson was one of the three tramps in the photograph," unless Harrelson has an identical twin."

Gibson stated during the assassination symposium that Charles Frederick Rogers is wanted in Houston in relationship to his parent's murder but he has not been located. In 1975 he was legally declared dead. Craig and Gibson indicate that the Houston police believe that Rogers murdered his parents after they had found out about the tramp photograph and attempted to confront Charles Rogers with this information.

During the period of time that Oswald was passing out Fair Play For Cuba flyers in New Orleans, a local television station filmed his activity. A man looking like Chancy Holt shows up in one of these photographs. Holt has stated that the photograph is him and that he was instructed to take Fair Play For Cuba brochures, which he had made up, to Oswald during this time period. Photographic and facial police expert Joyce Gibson did an analysis of these photographs and concluded in a presentation at the 1991 JKF Assassination Symposium in Dallas, Texas that the New Orleans photograph is Holt. She said that, "In my opinion, it is him."

Both J. Gary Shaw and John Craig told me that they have other evidence that links Charles Frederick Rogers to the assassination. Craig interviewed the manager of the Winter Lane Skating Rink in Houston, Texas, the place were David Ferrie traveled to the day after the assassination and showed the manager a photograph of Rogers. According to Craig, the manager said that Rogers had been observed on numerous occasions in the building but, like David Ferrie, never went ice skating. Like Ferrie, he waited by a payphone during the times that he was in the building. It has also developed that Rogers was involved in the Civil Air Patrol in Houston at the same time that David Ferrie was involved in the patrol in New Orleans. According to Shaw and Craig, these two civil air patrols often came into contact with each other during flights between the two cities.

According to Craig whom I interviewed with a group of assassination researchers in November of 1991 in Dallas, Texas, Chancy Holt stated that he took twelve sets of identification to Dallas, Texas with him on November 22nd, 1963. Nine of these sets of fake identification were Secret Service identification which consisted of printed Secret Service cards, cases and pins. These items were made at the last minute as the pins used by Secret Service agents are color coded and the actual color to be used on any given day is not determined until as close as possible to the event they are going to be used for.

In my investigation of this story, I found some holes in it. John Craig stated that he was not or never has been a member of the National Association Of Legal Investigators although he says that he is a retired legal investigator in Houston, Texas. Craig told me in Dallas that he never joined the organization because they were not active in the Houston area during the time that he practiced legal investigation. Being very familiar with the National Association Of Legal Investigators, I can state that they have been active in all areas of the United States since the mid 1960's and they offer the only nationally recognized certification for legal investigators (Certificated Legal Investigator, C.L.I.) in the nation. Craig also stated that he had worked with the CIA in the past and was employed by them in the past. I interviewed a prominate investigator in Houston who worked very closely with Craig and this investigator told me that Craig has absolutely no ties to federal intelligence organizations. Another piece of information surfaced when I contacted another prominate private investigator in the Houston, Texas area. This source stated that the Holt story and Craig's connection to it are, "not credible". However, this source could not provide any hard information concerning why.

According to Craig, Holt stated that he was instructed to provide Oswald with the Cuba flyers so that the Camp Street address would not appear on them. However, the Camp Street address was placed on the flyers with a hand stamp and there is documentation of Oswald being the person who purchased those flyers from a local printing company. According to Craig, Holt says that he dealt with a badge company by the name of Lasco in San Fransisco, California in his procurement of fake identification. Craig stated in November to me that Lasco is, "the largest badge manufacturer in the United States." Being a badge dealer myself, I know that Lasco is not the largest badge manufacturer in the United States and that Blackinton holds that honor. When questioned on the badge maufacturer topic, Craig replyed that he was just passing on information given to him by Holt.

After the interview with Craig, I contacted J. Gary Shaw to determine a few things about the Holt story. I wanted to know how Craig got involved in the case and if Holt had contacted his center before Craig was involved or after. Shaw told me that he had no knowledge of Craig before the time that Holt came forward. He also stated that he contacted Craig because he had read an article in a newspaper that Craig was writing a book about Charles Frederick Rogers. I was very concerned about the Holt story and kept thinking about what happened to the Rosco White story when Houston private investigator Joe West produced a second Rosco White diary that proved to be false. Since both Craig and West are in the same city and since the attorney contact for Holt was in the same city, I was somewhat skepticial of the Holt thing and Craig's connection to it. However, after learning from J. Gary Shaw that Craig did not become involved with him and his investigation of Holt until after Holt came to Shaw's Assassination Information Center, and Shaw contacted Craig only after seeing his name in the newspaper concerning a book he was writing concerning Fredrick Rogers, I rested a little easier about the Holt story.

Based on the Rosco White story and the diminished credibility to it by the actions of Joe West, and the recent revelations provided by Mark Lane in his book *Plausible Denial*, I am still somewhat reluctant about the Holt story. I tend to believe a great deal of it but photographic expert Jack White brought up the point that one of the tramps did not seem to have aged in twenty nine years at the assassination symposium in Dallas, Texas when facial expert Joyce Gibson presented her photographic evidence. As I dug deeper and deeper into this, I got to a point in which I didn't know who to trust.

The name of Mark Lane's new book, _Plausible Denial_, keeps sticking in my mind. Lane's book is based on his defense of Liberty Lobby in a defamation action brought by Howard Hunt on a story that was published concerning Hunt's presence in Dallas during the time of the assasination. Lane received a not guilty verdict for Liberty Lobby which I will go into a little later but the fact remains that Lane now sees a CIA connection to the Kennedy Assassination. If intelligence organizations were involved in the assassination of John Kennedy, wouldn't they attempt to discredit any information that would surface that was true? Wouldn't they attempt to engage in disinformation and plant false stories and leads to throw all the assassination researchers who are still working on the case down the wrong path? If I was in charge of keeping the truth about the Kennedy Assassination from surfacing, I would be planting all kinds of stories so the investigators who are working on them would travel down these deadend streets. After the investigators had spent months and months and thousands of dollars investigating the false lead, I would then discredit the story and show that it was false, then quickly plant another false lead for the assassination investigators to follow. I believe that this appears to be going on based on the history of the assassination and independent investigators who have followed those leads. Disinformation seems to be everywhere. Let me cite some examples.

Priscilla Johnson McMillan interviewed Oswald in his hotel during the time that he was, "defecting" to in the USSR. She also published a biography on Oswald which was copyrighted and published in 1977. She has also published two other books, _Khrushchev And The Arts_ and _The Politics Of The Soviet Culture_. She states that she is a journalist and writer and has denied any involvement with the CIA as a contact agent or employee. Many assassination researchers suspect that she might have been involved with the CIA. A background check reveals that she did, at one point in her career, work for the Department of State. Since she did live in the USSR for a number of years and she did write two books about aspects of Soviet happenings, I would conclude that it is highly likely that she, at the very least, had contact with the CIA. Her book _Marina And Lee_ was published in 1977 and appears to provide a glaring backup document to support the Warren Commission. What has always puzzled me is how she seems to just have appeared at Oswald's room when he went to the USSR and was attempting to "defect". She just happened to be in the right place at the right time. That's her explanation and, considering the fact that she ended up writing a biography on Oswald and Marina, I find it hard to swallow. Plausible Denial? Who knows. Marchetti, in his work, The _CIA And The Cult Of Intelligence_, points out that the CIA has sponsored many book publishing ventures when it is to their advantage.

During the late 1960's and early 1970's dozens of books and articles were published concerning all kinds of fringe theories about the Kennedy Assassination. Some of these theories are, at best, odd ball ideas. Some of these ideas can be summarized with headlines like: Neo-Nazi Links To Kennedy's Murder, Kennedy Still Alive And Well, Gunmen From The Sewer Covers In Dallas, Kennedy Hit By Stray Shot From Secret Service Agent.

In late 1989, I got involved with a prominate private investigator in the Washington D.C. area who told me that he was hired to look into the theory that the fatal headshot to Kennedy resulted from a stray bullet from a Secret Service Agent in the follow-up car. This investigator, who I would rather not name, had a file that contained photographs of the followup car showing Secret Service Agents with firearms in their hands which I had seen before. He also told me that he attempted to interview some of these agents at their homes and by telephone but that these agents never came out of their homes, would not answer the door and had all of their telephone calls screened, never returning any of his calls. This investigator also told me that he had a friend who had worked for the Secret Service during Johnson's term and Johnson told this agent that he didn't want to be hit in the back by a stray bullet like Kennedy had been. From the file that this investigator showed me, it was quite apparent that he had spent some time in the investigation of this lead. Due to lack of funds from his client, whom he never named, he had to close the file. I believe that this theory has since been disproven but it gives a good example of how many researchers are fed false leads and travel down deadend streets.

Recently I spoke with a source who, officially is a practicing journalist. However, this source appeared to have all kinds of odd ball leads and appeared to want me to check them out. He suggested that I look into Joseph Kennedy having vast land holdings in Cuba and a big party that went on in Phoenix after the assassination given by powerful businessmen. This source also indicated to me that he had intelligence connections and he suggested that I have the CIA edit this book. There are all kinds of fringe theories still floating around to this day. Recently, I have noticed a great deal of Neo-Nazi theories around and the theory that Kennedy was fired upon from the tops of sewer covers in Dailey Plaza. During the 1991 Assassination Symposium in Dallas, Texas in November, I noticed two researchers pull the covers off of the tops of the sewer covers and get down inside them.

In the mid 1980's I had some contact with the CIA when I started publishing manuals on various aspects of private investigation. In an interview on learning the business of private investigation for the Washington Post, my book, _The Physical Surveillance Training Manual_ was listed and published in the article. A few days after the story appeared, I got an order and a check from the Russian Embassy in Washington. Being the Patriotic American I am, I did not wish to give communists information on how private investigators or anyone conduct a physical surveillance in the United States so I contacted the State Department. The order and letter contained the name of an individual and a check. I reasoned that the person ordering the manual must be involved in Soviet intelligence work, otherwise why would he want a manual on conducting a physical surveillance. I had a name and the check contained a checking account number and the name of a bank. I wanted to forward this information to our government. The people at the Department Of State informed me that this area of responsibility would be with the CIA. I called the CIA and explained to several different people this situation. They did give me an address to send a copy of the check and the letter to and I sent them copies. In the package I sent them, I also enclosed a cover letter and stated that this might be an opportunity to engage in disinformation with the Russian Embassy. A few weeks later, I got a letter back that stated that the CIA did not engage in disinformation activity. I guess now that this was a plausible denial. A few weeks later, I noticed that two men appeared to be hanging around the same places I was. I never was able to determine who they were but I felt I was being followed by them. A few days later, I obtained an order for one copy of _The Physical Surveillance Training Manual_ from the CIA Library. What puzzled me the most is that I had just finished reading a copy of _The CIA And The Cult Of Intelligence_ by Victor Marchetti in which he has a whole chapter on propaganda and disinformation. Marchetti's book is the first book to be officially censored by the CIA and contains actual locations of where the CIA deleted sentences. Every page or so a paragraph starts to talk about this or that and then you come to an open space that states in bold type something like:

10 LINES DELETED

I really could not believe that all this was happening but I kind of thought it was quite amusing and funny. I was proud of the fact that I had sold one of my books to the CIA library in Langley and thought it was kind of funny that people in the Russian Embassy would be interested in a book on private investigation. A few days later, I got a telephone call from the Russian who had ordered the book. I had not, as of yet, sent it to him. He spoke broken English and stated that he had ordered the book for "his business." I made several other telephone calls to government officials in Washington explaining that I did not want to send them the book but they advised me to go ahead that it was really no big deal.

This all brings me back to the Roscoe White story and the Chancy Holt story. Although I believe both J. Gary Shaw and John R. Craig in their feelings that the Holt story has validity, further investigation needs to be done. I believe at the present time that the Roscoe White story is true. I believe Ricky White. I also believe that there is a strong possibility that Joe West's activity which has somewhat discredited the Ricky White story might have been set up. Altough I am unable to confirm it, several rumors exist that Joe West developed intelligence contacts during the time that the Roscoe White story was developing. It's speculation but the possibility exists that West's activity might be connected to disinformation. I know West called my office during the summer of 1991 after he found out I had an onging project on the Kennedy Assassination in the works. He told Bryan Luedecke, the NAIS office manager, that he had some information he wanted to share and I had some stuff he wanted to look at (likely the reverse speech technology). I purposely did not return his telephone call to see if he would call again. He didn't. Like Oswald's background, you run into smoke and mirrors. It becomes difficult to get a true picture of who is on who's side, who has what motivation and who is dong what to who.

PRIOR KNOWLEDGE OF AN ASSASSINATION CONSPIRACY

In order to pinpoint prime suspects of the assassination and develop more evidence that would prove the conspiracy, I felt that a study of any available evidence of prior knowledge of the assassination would point the investigation in the right direction. Like everything else about the assassination, one doesn't have to dig very deep to locate evidence of prior knowledge of the assassination. If an assassination plot existed, I reasoned that evidence of plans in other cities during the President's trips would be found as the conspirators would have several alternate locations to commit the crime. If the assassination was not a conspiracy and was the result of the lone nut -one gunman theory, no other plans would be found. My focus on looking into prior knowledge of the assassination became:

> A) *Prior knowledge might reveal prime suspects.*
> B) *Prior knowledge for plans of other plots in other locations*
> *would tend to prove that the assassination was the result of a*
> *conspiracy.*

A) A study of any existing prior plots on the President's life could be studied to develop prime suspects for the assassination conspiracy that was brought to a successful conclusion in Dallas,Texas. If evidence of other attempts to assassinate Kennedy in other cities could be found, I would assume that they could all be related as one major overall plan. The reasoning behind this concerns the fact that, in the planning stages of a conspiracy to assassinate the president, the people who planned it would have to first study the trips that the President would be taking to develop the right opportunities and several locations would likely be decided upon. A number of locations and alternative opportunities would be carefully plotted out. This is exactly the procedure detailed in a once secret government study done on assassination in a document titled *Selective Assassination As An Instrument Of National Policy* reprinted by both Paladin Press and Loompanics.

Although determining the exact conspirators is foggy when you contain the events in Dallas on November 22nd, 1963, I reasoned that, if evidence of other plans for an assassination could be located in other cities in the President's travels, details of these plans could be closely examined concerning these events that might shed some light on prime suspects.

B) If evidence of other plans for a plot to assassinate the President could be found in other cities on other trips of the President, then Oswald could not have acted alone. How could a man who couldn't afford to support his family have financed such a plan that involved a number of possible locations. Oswald couldn't even afford a dumpy apartment for his wife and child and was living in a rooming house that cost him a mere few dollars a week. He was working in a job that paid minimum wages and didn't even have a car. Of course, pro-lone nut proponents will state that this line of thinking can be flattened because there may have been a plot to assassinate Kennedy which was totally separate from Oswald's activity but I find this no more plausible than the Select Committee's implication that there may have been two separate lone gun nuts in Dealey Plaza neither having any knowledge of the other which turned into a remarkable coincidence.

My major focus became to study any and all evidence that would indicate there were other plans in other cities to assassinate the president. What I found was that all of it had already been documented through previous government investigations and work done by previous assassination researchers but it was never brought together and considered in the focus I had developed. I didn't have to dig deep to find the information I was looking for.

According to the Select Committee On Assassinations, in March of 1963, the President had planned a trip to Chicago. Right before the trip, a postcard was sent to the White House warning that the President would be assassinated while riding in a motorcade. Extra protection and beefed up security was provided during March trip and no unusual incident occurred.

In October of 1963, Kennedy was planning another trip to Chicago which would involve a motorcade and attendance at an army-air force football game. Abraham Bolden was working for the Secret Service and uncovered a top secret investigation being conducted concerning a plot to assassinate Kennedy by four Cubans during the trip to Chicago. Because of the information developed in the secret investigation, the presidential trip to Chicago was canceled. Bolden was the first black appointed to the United States Secret Service and he was appointed by President Kennedy. After the assassination in Dallas, agent Bolden attempted to come forward and inform the Warren Commission of the Chicago plot. Instead, Bolden was taken from his assignment in Washington and flown to Chicago were he was held incommunicado for several days. Bolden claims that trumped up charges were filed against him concerning a bribe he made with two counterfeiters. Bolden was charged and convicted of these charges based on the testimony of the two convicted counterfeiters.

The Select Committee On Assassinations conducted investigations into the Bolden incident and learned that Bolden received an FBI teletype stating that an attempt to assassinate the President would be made on November 2nd by a four man team using high powered rifles. Bolden also stated that he became aware of the Secret Service investigation and surveillance of these four men by monitoring Secret Service radio channels in his vehicle and he had observed one of the subjects being detained in the Chicago office.

November 2nd, 1963, the Secret Service arrested a man be the name of Arthur Vallee. Vallee was known to have made remarks against Kennedy's foreign policy. He was in possession of an M-1 rifle, a handgun and 3,000 rounds of ammunition which were all found in his automobile. He had requested November 2nd off from work which was a time period when Kennedy was to be in Chicago. The November 2nd trip to Chicago by Kennedy was canceled. Vallee, like Oswald, was a Marine veteran. He had a history of mental problems and was known to be an expert marksman. He was a member of the John Birch Society. Vallee was released from custody on the evening of November 2nd.

On November 9th, 1963 a Miami undercover police officer, William Somerset, recorded a conversation with one Joseph A. Mitleer in which Milteer described a plan that was being worked out to assassinate Kennedy. Milteer was a leader in a right wing political organization called the States Rights Party. Somerset had infiltrated the organization and was covertly recording his conversation with Milteer in connection with his undercover investigation on the States Rights Party. Milteerer said in the recording that the assassination was in the planning stages and that Kennedy would be killed with a high powered rifle from a high building during a motorcade and that somebody will be picked up right after the assassination to throw the public off the track. Milteer was an ultra rich right-wing thinking person with views that mirrored such organizations and people as the John Birch Society and the ultra-conservative circles of business people in the oil business.

The undercover tape recordings of Milteer's remarks were turned over to Miami Police Captain Charles Sapp who informed the FBI. The President was planning a trip to Miami on November 18th. Originally a motorcade through Miami had been planned but the motorcade was canceled at the last minute. Four days later, the motorcade in Dallas went as planned. During the House Select Committee On Assassinations investigations, a transcript of the Somerset and Milteer conversation was put into the record. It went like this and I quote:

SOMERSET: I think Kennedy is coming here November 18 to make some kind of speech. I don't know what it is, but I imagine it will be on TV.

MILTEER: You can bet your bottom dollar he is going to have a lot to say about the Cubans, there are so many of them here.

SOMERSET: Well, he'll have a thousand bodyguards, don't worry about that.

MILTEER: The more bodyguards he has, the easier it is to get him.

SOMMERSET: What?

MILTEER: The more bodyguards he has, the easier it is to get him.

SOMMERSETT: Well, how in the hell do you figure would be the best way to get him?

MILTEER: From an office building with a high powered rifle.

SOMERSET: They are really going to try to kill him?

MILTEER: Oh yea, it is in the working.

SOMERSET: Hitting this Kennedy is going to be a hard proposition. I believe you may have figured out a way to get him, the office building and all that. I don't know how them Secret Service agents cover all them office buildings everywhere he is going. Do you know whether they do that or not?

MILTEER: Well, if they have any suspicion, they do that, of course. But without suspicion, chances are that they wouldn't.

Milteer was apparently in Dallas on November 22nd and watched the motorcade from Houston Street about a block away from the School Book Depository Building. Somerset has stated that Milteer contacted him in the morning on November 22nd, 1963 and stated that Milteer told him he was in Dallas and Kennedy would never be seen in Miami again. Photographic expert Jack White located a photograph of a man standing on Houston Street that had a remarkable likeness to Milteer. The photograph was blown up and Jack White made an indepth study of the photograph. His conclusion is that the man in the photograph is Milteer. Milteer was questioned by the FBI on November 27th and denied making any statements concerning the assassination. As you will see in a few paragraphs, Milteer was not the only person that migrated from Miami to Dallas. Milteer died in a suspicious heater explosion accident in February of 1974.

On November 17th, 1963, William Walter was working as a communications officer in the New Orleans FBI office. He claims that a cable came in concerning a plot that was uncovered to assassinate Kennedy in Dallas, Texas on November 22nd, 1963. Walter has stated that he notified the proper authorities of the cable that evening, filed it in it's proper place and went home. At the time of the assassination, Walters was eating lunch in New Orleans when he heard the news of the assassination. Walters rushed back to the bureau office and located the file with the cable. Walters decided to make a copy of the cable to keep in his own possession which he did. He states that he checked the bureau file a few days latter and the cable was missing. During the 1976 Senate Intelligence Committee hearings chaired by Senator Richard Schweiker, Walter presented a copy of the contents of the cable. The cable became public knowledge when Mark Lane obtained a copy of the cable under the Freedom Of Information Act during the Garrision investigation. The copy states and I quote:

URGENT: 1:45 AM EST 11-17-63 HLF 1 PAGE
TO: ALL SACS
FROM: DIRECTOR

THREAT TO ASSASSINATE PRESIDENT KENNEDY IN DALLAS TEXAS NOVEMBER 22 DASH TWENTY THREE

NINETEEN SIXTY THREE. MISC INFORMATION CONCERNING.

INFORMATION HAS BEEN RECEIVED BY THE BUREAU. BUREAU HAS DETERMINED THAT A MILITANT REVOLUTIONARY GROUP MAY ATTEMPT TO ASSASSINATE PRESIDENT KENNEDY ON HIS PROPOSED TRIP TO DALLAS TEXAS NOVEMBER TWENTY TWO DASH TWENTY THREE NINETEEN SIXTY THREE. ALL RECEIVING OFFICES SHOULD IMMEDIATELY CONTACT ALL CIS, PCIS LOGICAL RACE AND HATE GROUP INFORMANTS AND DETERMINE ID ANY BASIS FOR THREAT. BUREAU SHOULD BE KEPT ADVISED OF ALL DEVELOPMENTS BY TELETYPE. OTHER OFFICES HAVE BEEN ADVISED. END AND ACK PLS.

If the Walters story is correct, no record exists of the FBI doing a thing about the incident.

One of the strangest accounts concerning prior knowledge of the assassination came from a prostitute by the name of Rose Cheramie. On November 20th, Cheramie was found beat up on the side of a road by Louisiana State Police Lieutenant Francis Fruge. Fruge took Cheramie to a local state hospital near Eunice, Louisiana. Cheramie informed both Fruge and Doctor Bowers at the hospital that she had been driving with two Latins from Miami to Texas and had overheard the Latin men discuss a conspiracy to assassinate Kennedy. After an argument started between Cheramie and the two Latin men, she was thrown from the car.

Lieutenant Fruge did not pay much attention to the Cheramie story as she appeared to be under the influence of drugs. After the assassination, Lieutenant Fruge became concerned with Cheramie's foreknowledge of the assassination and went back to the hospital to interview her. Charamie further stated that she worked for Jack Ruby and the two Latins also worked for Jack Ruby. Cheramie also stated that she had observed Oswald and Ruby together in the past. Fruge informed the Dallas police of the Cheramie story but stated before the House Select Committee On Assassinations that they did not seem interested in it as they already had Oswald as the prime suspect. Cheramie was killed in a hit and run accident in November of 1965.

Evidently, Cheramie and the two Latins were not the only people traveling from the Miami area to the Texas area in the days before Kennedy's Texas trip. Marita Lorenz, a person involved with the CIA and the Miami Cuban refugees, also made a trip by vehicle from the Miami area to Dallas, Texas with Cubans about the same time. The Lorenz account was detailed in a civil action brought by E. Howard Hunt and explained in Mark Lane's recently published work, *Plausible Denial*.

It is relevant to refresh our memory about Dealey Plaza witnesses giving descriptions of "Latin" men walking towards the assassination site, appearing in the sixth floor window and leaving the assassination site just after the assassination.

On October 4th, 1963 Dallas attorney Carroll Jarnagin was out on the town with a local "exotic dancer" that went by the name of "Robin Hood." The couple were having a time going from one club to another. At 10:00 P.M. that entered the Carousel Club and sat down at a table. A few minutes later, a man walked into the club and demanded to see Jack Ruby. Jack Ruby came out and sat down in a booth with the man. Jarnagin overheard their conversation. The stranger said that he was using the name H.L. Lee and had just gotten in from New Orleans. Ruby and Lee talked about some type of murder for hire and Ruby asked this Lee if he could do it without, "hitting the Govonor." Ruby said something about doing it from the roof of a building. The man named Lee looked over at Jarnagin who was staring at the two and asked Ruby who he was. Ruby remarked that the person was an FBI agent. At that point, "Lee" got up from the table and walked out. The following day, Jarnagin contacted the Texas Department Of Public Safety and told them about the incident.

After the assassination, Jarnagain noted that the man who had been in Ruby's club was Lee Oswald. He wrote out a report of the conversation he had witnessed and mailed it off to J. Edgar Hoover in Washington by certified mail. He was interviewed by several law enforcement people and his story has remained firm.

PROTECTION OF THE PRESIDENT

You will note that we have four events that indicate prior knowledge of an assassination. Two FBI warnings were telexed, one specifically concerning the Dallas trip. According to the Select Committee on Assassinations, between March and December, the Secret Service had custody of 400 threats concerning Kennedy's life. The protection of the President in Dallas Texas did not seem to be beefed up. The motorcade route was not examined carefully. If it would have been, the hairpin turn from Houston onto Elm Street would have been noticed and the Texas School Book Depository Building would have been guarded with all windows being closed and locked.

If one checks out Dealey Plaza, one will find that the only way to get onto the Simmons Freeway from Main Street is to make a right hand turn from Main Street onto Houston and then make the left hairpin turn onto Elm Street. The Simmons Freeway is entered just past the Triple Overpass. Although Main Street and Elm Street come together like one side of a fork just before the roads go under the Triple underpass, a small curb or grade exists between Elm Street and Main Street on the other side of the underpass. This would not permit one to travel down Main Street to enter the Simmons Freeway because the ramp can be accessed only by Elm Street. Although the first plans printed the route without the right turn onto Houston and the hairpin turn onto Elm, the plan was evidently changed. The reasoning officially being that the motorcade needed to get onto the Simmons Freeway which could not be accessed from Main Street because of the curb.

My examination of the area is different. Instead of the hairpin turn onto Elm Street, it would have been much safer for the motorcade to go directly down Main Street and a small wooden plank could have easily been put in position for the motorcade to have gone from Main Street to Elm Street on the other side of the Triple underpass instead of making the hairpin turn on Elm Street next to a seven story unguarded building. Anyone could have looked at the area and noticed that the hairpin turn and the Elm Street Plaza area would have been a perfect ambush site from the grassy knolls on each side and the tall buildings in the background. This caution could have prevented the assassination.

The FBI had an open file on Oswald. They had a threatening letter from him and knew that he was working in the School Book Depository Building. After the assassination, the fact that the FBI had a file on him and the fact that they had received a letter from him was apparently covered up for obvious reasons. This information should have been turned over to the Secret Service. The telex that went out about an assassination threat should also have been turned over to the Secret Service.

From photographic evidence at the time of the assassination, I have always wondered about the sluggish reaction of the Secret Service. The driver of the open presidential vehicle hit the brakes after the first shot rang out which was the exact opposite of what agents are trained to do. The open presidential vehicle came to almost a complete stop. When I interviewed Jean Hill, one of the closest witnesses to the assassination, she said that the presidential vehicle slowed down to almost zero miles per hour. It was only after the fatal headshot that the vehicle speeded up. If the Secret Service agent as a passenger in the front of the Presidential vehicle would have thrown himself on top of Kennedy the instant the first shot rang out and if the driver would have hit the gas instead of hitting the brakes, the President might not have received the fatal headshot. It is questionable if the first shot the president took would have been nonfatal.

Another thing that has always puzzled me is the sluggish reaction of the Secret Service men riding directly behind the President in the follow-up car. At the moment of the first shot, they all seemed to freeze. When the full uncropped version of the James Altgens photograph is studied, the back door the the Vice Presidential vehicle has opened. Two Secret Service men positioned on the north running board of the Secret Service follow-up car look towards the rear. The two on the other side look at the back of the president. All are frozen. What's the problem?

The problem is that all these men who are supposed to be protecting the President were up until the wee hours of the morning in a place called the Cellar in Fort Worth. Some were likely drinking. What they were doing there is not exactly known but the bar is owned by a friend of Jack Ruby's.

Based on the FBI cable from the Bolden account, the FBI cable based on the Walter account and the information from undercover officer Somerset, the weight of the evidence tends to show that J. Edgar Hoover had prior knowledge of an assassination plot. The fact that Hoover successfully covered up the fact that the FBI had an open file on Oswald also adds a great deal of weight to Hoover's foreknowledge. The fact that there is evidence which would tend to indicate that Oswald was a paid informant of the FBI and that Jack Ruby was a one time paid informant of the FBI adds even more weight. The fact that Hoover's FBI disregarded and threatened witnesses who provided information that would tend to indicate a conspiracy and did not support the lone nut-one gunman theory as Hoover announced within hours after the assassination also tends to support the hypothesis that Hoover knew about the assassination. The fact that FBI agent Regis Kennedy took the Beverly Oliver film and never returned it supports an FBI coverup and tends to corroborate the hypothesis that the FBI had prior knowledge of the conspiracy to assassination Kennedy. I will cover Hoover's motive about not reporting the uncovered plot to assassinate the President under the motive section but I believe all of these facts, when linked together, would tend to conclude that Hoover found out about the assassination conspiracy and did nothing about it.

Oswald was apparently an open file within the Dallas FBI office. The local FBI office knew Oswald was in Dallas, knew he was a one time defector to the Soviet Union, knew he was married to a Russian, knew of his activities with the Fair Play For Cuba Committee, knew he was arrested in New Orleans and knew he was working in the School Book Depository Building which was on the Presidential motorcade route. The Walter cable would also suggest that, at least Hoover, knew that a plot existed for an assassination attempt in Dallas. However, during the planning and advance stages of the President's trip to Dallas, the FBI did not turn this information over to the Secret Service. If information would have been provided to the Secret Service, security measures could have been taken that might have prevented the assassination as it had been done in Chicago and Miami. Instead, security was rather lax and some of the Secret Service men assigned to protect the President were up until the early morning hours in a bar owned by a friend of Jack Ruby's.

Our original question and focus concerning evidence of plans to assassinate Kennedy in other locations of the country would rule out the lone nut-lone gunman theory is a reality beyond a reasonable doubt. In March of 1963, beefed up security was provided during a Chicago trip. In October of 1963, another trip by Kennedy to Chicago was canceled. A trip to Miami in November was altered and a motorcade canceled. All of this activity concerned known assassination attempts.

Our question concerning a prime suspect points towards men described as Latin. The Bolden account concerns Cubans in an attempted assassination. The Milteer/Somerset recordings reveal information about anti-Castro Cubans. The Walters FBI cable talks about a "militant revolutionary group" which fits the description of the anti-Castro Cubans. Both the Cheramie and Lorenz accounts describe men as Latins. Eyewitness accounts of the assassination place men described as "Latin" walking into the assassination site, in the sixth floor window and walking away from the assassination site. Oswald can be linked to the anti-Castro Cubans during his activity in New Orleans. Jack Ruby can be linked to the group through his gunrunning activity and his connection to organized crime which had plans to assassinate Castro sponsored by the CIA. At the same time, the CIA can be linked to the anti-Castro Cubans whom they actually covertly sponsored.

Based on the focus of this section, I would conclude that the militant anti-Castro Cubans were involved in the assassination who's covert activity was sponsored by the CIA and that both Oswald and Ruby as well as organized crime can be linked into this group. I would also conclude that J. Edgar Hoover uncovered the assassination plot and did not report his findings to the Secret Service.

THINKING ABOUT A CONSPIRACY MOTIVE

If John Kennedy was assassinated as the result of a conspiracy, then some sort of motive must have been involved. I wanted to focus in on motive for several reasons. Of course a motive must be established in any murder case but I felt that exploratory investigation and research in this area could give more weight to the evidence already known and help pinpoint the investigation in the right direction. By exploring possible motives, one could see if the other two requirements (means and opportunity) were present. Looking at different motives, we could also see if Oswald and Ruby would fit into these pieces of the puzzle. Before we move to motive, let us look at the evidence that we currently have developed about Oswald and Ruby :

> A) We have fairly well linked OSWALD to an intelligence connection. I believe that has been established. However, to go beyond that fact and attempt to develop the exact nature of his intelligence activity is almost impossible. You run into what is best determined as "smoke and mirrors." You cannot tell exactly who it is that Oswald is working for although I believe that we can state with certainty that Oswald was involved in intelligence work.

> B) I believe that we have established that RUBY was somehow involved in organized crime. Like Oswald, his exact relationship to organized crime cannot be shown as we, again, run into "smoke and mirrors."

> C) I believe that we have established beyond a reasonable doubt that Oswald and Ruby had a relationship before the assassination.

> D) Beyond a reasonable doubt, I believe that we have also established that RUBY murdered OSWALD to silence him and that he was ordered to do so.

> E) Beyond a reasonable doubt, authorities were attempting to marshall the evidence that would indicate a lone gunman theory.

The way in which investigation into this area works is to develop a hypothesis and then look at facts that would fit into that hypothesis that would either prove or disprove the theory. That is, once a hypothesis is worked out, you then seek to develop evidence that:

> A) *Would tend to add weight to the hypothesis*
> B) *Would tend to disprove the hypothesis*

I believed that we could first, explore possible motives, see if means and opportunity would fit into the puzzle and then see if we could link Oswald, Ruby or both of them into the chain of evidence. The exploratory investigation then, was to search for various general motives and:

> A) *See if means and opportunity were present.*
> B) *See if Oswald and/or Ruby could be linked into the motive by their known associations.*
> C) *Look at the motive from the eyes of the assassination conspiracy planners to see if it fit.*

I began to explore the issues Kennedy was involved with in his Presidency to see if they would fit into this line of thinking. I identified the following areas of concern in relationship to this approach:

> *THE CIVIL RIGHTS MOVEMENT*
> *THE CUBAN CONNECTION*
> *THE ANTI-INTELLIGENCE ESTABLISHMENT*
> *THE WAR ON ORGANIZED CRIME*
> *INTERNAL AFFAIRS*
> *THE VIETNAM WAR*
> *THE OIL DEPLETION ALLOWANCE*

THE CIVIL RIGHTS MOVEMENT

This civil rights movement was in full swing during the Kennedy administration. Although my study of Kennedy's involvement in the civil rights movement makes me believe that he was, at first, very hesitant to become involved in it for obvious political reasons, he supported it. Through his brother, the attorney general, the administration supported blacks having the right to enter white college campuses and rights of blacks to protest and march without violence in the south.

Martin Luther King Jr., the leader of the civil rights movement, was not well liked within the FBI. Hoover placed wiretaps on his telephone and attempted to discredit him. Although the Kennedy administration went along with the wiretapping of King, Hoover had come to the administration with some evidence that King's organization was infiltrated by communists. King was cut down by an assassin's bullet after the Kennedy assassination and the House Select Committee On Assassinations stated in it's findings that:

> *"The committee believes, on the basis of the circumstantial evidence available to it, that there is a likelihood that James Earl Ray assassinated Dr. Martin Luther King, Jr. as a result of a conspiracy."*

Dr. Philip H. Melanson covers the King assassination in his book, *The Martin Luther King Assassination: New Revelations On The Conspiracy And Cover-up, 1968-1991.* The Melanson book, I believe, establishes beyond a reasonable doubt that King was murdered as the result of a conspiracy.

Activities of the civil rights movement during the Kennedy administration was, for the most part, run by the justice department through the attorney general's office. Robert Kennedy headed this activity as attorney general. Of course, history shows that Robert Kennedy was shot down by assassination while attempting to obtain the democratic nomination for President. Researcher Dr. Phillip H. Melanson reveals in his book, *The Robert F. Kennedy Assassination: New Revelations On The Conspiracy And Cover-Up,* that Bobby Kennedy was assassinated as the result of a conspiracy. Robert D. Morrow, in his work, *The Senator Must Die,* also reveal startling evidence that Robert Kennedy was assassinated as the result of a conspiracy. After reading and studying the works of Robert Morrow and Dr. Phillip Melanson, I believe that they both show beyond a reasonable doubt that Robert Kennedy was murdered as the result of a conspiracy.

So the three leaders of the civil rights movement, President John Kennedy, Attorney General Robert Kennedy and Doctor Martin Luther King all died as the result of a conspiracy. At the same time, we have J. Edgar Hoover who appears to not have supported the civil rights movement of the American black. I draw this conclusion by studying the written and published works of:

172

J. EDGAR HOOVER: The Man And The Secrets: By Curt Gentry
THE BOSS: By: Arthur Theoharis and John Cox
THE DIRECTOR: By: Ovid Demaris
THE LIFE OF J. EDGAR HOOVER: Secrecy And Power: By:
Richard Powers

Robert Kennedy, John Kennedy and Dr. Martin Luther King were all assassinated most likely as the result of a conspiracy and all three were the top leaders of the civil rights movement. I believe that this would tend to throw a great deal of weight on the hypothesis that the JFK assassination conspiracy might have had something to do with the civil rights movement.

OSWALD's activity in Clinton, La. in which he stood in line during a civil rights movement that resulted in a registration drive for blacks tends to provide a linkage between OSWALD and the civil rights movement. It has also been established by studying the FBI program COUNTERPOL that American intelligence had infiltrated many of the activities of the civil rights movement in the 1960's.

The major reason that I conclude that the civil rights movement had little, if nothing, to do with the Kennedy assassination is that the person who took Kennedy's place in history, Lyndon Johnson got many of the civil rights programs through congress and there is enough evidence to point to the fact that Johnson was able to get successful passage were Kennedy might have failed.This smashes the motive in pieces. I also concluded that, if the civil rights programs of the blacks was an issue in the assassination, the KKK would become the prime suspect in such a hypothesis. Although the KKK had a capacity for violence, I do not feel that they had the means or the opportunity to pull off such an event. Based on this reasoning, I scratched civil rights from the list.

THE CUBAN CONNECTION

In looking at the Cuban connection to the assassination of President Kennedy, three events took place during his administration that dealt with Cuba. They are:

A) THE BAY OF PIGS
B) THE CUBAN MISSILE CRISIS
C) THE COVERT ATTEMPTS BY THE CIA TO MURDER CASTRO

The Bay Of Pigs involved a covert attempt by Cuban Refugees to take Cuba by force. This operation was sponsored by the CIA. This program was already in place when Kennedy became president and was started during the Eisenhower administration. Eisenhower's vice president, Richard Nixon, was in charge of this program. Nixon was in Dallas the morning of the assassination. The Bay Of Pigs invasion of Cuba was at first supported by the Kennedy administration and the covert action went forward. Cubans landed on the beach to execute their plan. At the last minute Kennedy refused to provide the needed air support for the invasion and the assault was a bloodbath for the Cubans wishing to take back their homeland. Kennedy was blamed for it's failure by both the intelligence community and Cuban soldiers of fortune. Kennedy ended up firing Allen Dulles, director of the CIA, for the event and this infuriated both the Cubans involved in the attempted overthrow of the Castro government and people within the CIA.

The Cuban Missile Crisis was started when U-2 aircraft (U.S. Spy planes) flew over Cuba and photographed launch sites being built of nuclear missiles which were being supplied to Cuba by the Soviet Union. Kennedy went public with the information and a confrontation between Kennedy and Khrushchev developed. Kennedy set up a naval blockade of all Soviet Ships bound for Cuba and it appeared that the world was at the blink of nuclear war. Khrushchev backed down and the United States and the Soviet Union entered an agreement that the Soviet Union would withdraw all nuclear missiles from Cuba in exchange for a US promise not to invade Cuba again. Kennedy agreed to this publicly which further infuriated the Cuban people in the United States with plans to take back their homeland.

During the Kennedy Administration, it has also surfaced that the CIA had covert operations going on that involved attempts to murder Castro, attempts to ruin the Cuban economy and attempts to discredit Castro. Although these covert actions were not known at the time of Kennedy's assassination and were not uncovered until many years later, there is evidence that would indicate that both the President and the President's brother learned of these covert operations and attempted to put a stop to them. It has also been established since November 22nd, 1963 that the CIA was using members of organized crime to execute these covert operations against Castro.

In the first several months of Lyndon Johnson's administration, he had John McCone, the director of the CIA, in his office almost every day. The reason for these daily meetings, according to Nathan Miller's *Spying For America* was Johnson's obsession with the idea that Fidel Castro had assassinated Kennedy in retaliation of the United States government's attempt to assassinate him.

Linkage to the assassination of John Kennedy to the Cuban connection is found both with Lee Harvey Oswald and Jack Ruby. Oswald is found working for the photographic firm that was involved with the photographs taken by the U-2 spy plane that developed the information that revealed that Cuba was building nuclear missile ranges. Oswald's linkage to both pro and anti-Castro groups is found with his intelligence activities in New Orleans. His involvement with the U-2 spy planes while in the Marines and his possible involvement in the Gary Powers U-2 flight over Russia in which Powers was shot down adds more weight to Oswald's involvement. Ruby's unexplained trips to Cuba and his apparent deception over those trips developed by the Select Committee On Assassinations which concluded that Ruby made at least six trips to Cuba and those trips were for reasons other than pleasure links Ruby to Cuba.

I also feel that the Cubans being trained in paramilitary invasion techniques by the American government developed the means to commit assassination. The fact that their activity was covert and hidden within the intelligence community of the United States, the fact that they were covertly being supplied with weapons and ammo and the fact that they were being trained to kill are all contributory factors for this belief.

THE WAR ON ORGANIZED CRIME

The Kennedy Administration conducted a war against organized crime that was headed by the President's brother and attorney general Robert Kennedy. Again, in this issue, history reveals that Robert Kennedy was cut down by an assassin's bullet seeking his brother's old position of power and again we find Hoover involved in this issue.

Robert Kennedy actively sought inditements on members of organized crime like no other attorney general has done before or since. The House Select Committee On Assassinations made a study of the Justice Department's involvement in it's fight in organized crime and found the following:

> A) The number of attorneys assigned to investigate and prosecute members of organized crime went from just over ten when the Kennedy administration took office to over sixty in 1963. After Kennedy was assassinated, that number started to drop back down and by 1966 the figure had dropped back to forty-eight.

B) The days spent in the field by federal investigators involved in the investigation of organized crime was less than one thousand in 1960. After the Kennedy administration came to power, that figure shot up to 6,177 by 1963. After the assassination the figure again started to drop and by 1966 was only 3,480.

C) The number of days in court concerning organized crime figures also jumped during the Kennedy administration. In 1960 that number was about 61. By 1962 it rose to 329 and by 1963 it had jumped to 1,081. After the assassination, it declined until the figure was below 800 in 1966.

D) The number of days in Grand Jury also jumped when the Kennedy administration came into power and then declined after the assassination. In 1960 the figure was about 100, in 1961 518, in 1962, 894 and in 1963, 1,353. After the assassination the figure dropped. By 1964 it was 677 and by 1966 it was way back down to 373.

Robert Kennedy had Carlos Marcello, the alleged crime boss of New Orleans, deported and was in an ongoing battle with Jimmy Hoffa who was placed in jail during the Kennedy administration. At the same time J. Edgar Hoover, director of the FBI was consistently stating that there was no such thing as the mafia in the United States. In both *Secrecy And Power* by Richard Powers and *J. Edgar Hoover* by Curt Gentry, Hoover attempts to cut off the Kennedy investigations into organized crime.

I believe that we have established beyond a reasonable doubt linkage between Jack Ruby and organized crime. Solid linkage between Oswald and organized crime is not made. However, it is important to point out that there is evidence of his uncle and surrogate father that would suggest that the uncle was involved with the Marcello operations in New Orleans.

I believe that organized crime had both the means and opportunity to carry out an assassination. History proves that gangland style murders were common place within organized crime and the capacity for violence is present. Both the ability and skill to commit the crime and the ability to procure the necessary tools are present.

INTERNAL AFFAIRS

I believe that it is quite interesting to note the boundaries of the American press today as compared to those boundaries in the 1960's. Today the press deliberately investigates the private and personal lives of public figures. The 1960's seem to be a different age with a different set of rules with boundaries which precluded such reporting.

Presidential candidate Gary Hart had his chances ruined as the Democratic nominee as a result of an affair. Congressman Wilbur Mills, one of the most powerful men in the Congress had his power base yanked out from under him as the result of an alleged relationship he had with an exotic dancer. The Supreme Court nomination of Clarence Thomas was endangered by alleged sexual comments and his alleged willingness to date Anita Hill even though he was single at the time of the incident. Due to the flying rumors about President Kennedy's womanizing, I thought it would be both interesting and relevant to look at this issue and see if it could have had anything to do with his assassination.

During President Kennedy's early years, he entered the Navy. One of his first assignments was within the office of Naval Intelligence in the nation's capitol. Kennedy started seeing a reporter who worked for the Times-Herald by the name of Inga Arvad. Arvad was a Danish and attractive woman who was under surveillance at the time by the FBI as she was suspected of being a German spy. Apparently she had, at one time previously, had close ties to high ranking German officials.   The FBI, during it's surveillance activities of Arvad, obtained tape recorded conversations between Kennedy and and Arvad. It's r belief that if this story would have broken during the political campaign to reach the Presidency, Kennedy would not have been elected. It is my feeling that the American public would have been outraged that this Presidential candidate would permit himself to get involved in such a compromising position. But the age of journalism worked under a different set of boundaries in those days.

There is much documented evidence that Jackie Kennedy wanted a divorce from John Kennedy because of his indiscretions. Apparently, Kennedy's father, Joe Kennedy, struck up a deal with Jackie Kennedy to stay married to his son in exchange for a large allowance so the incident would not affect him politically. So life went on as usual in the eyes of the public while Kennedy apparently had many affairs with other woman during his marriage to Jackie.

Judith Campbell was apparently one of the President's mistresses. Campbell relates many exchanges and details between her and the President in her book, _My Story_, published in 1977. Campbell was also in contact with Sam Giancana during the time that she was seeing the President secretly. Giancana is an alleged mobster boss. Hoover found out about the affair Campbell was having with the chief executive and her link to organized crime and told the President so. After Hoover's secret file of the Campbell affair became known to the President, he cut it off.

In the published works, _A Woman Named Jackie_, by C. David Heymann and _A Question Of Character_, by Thomas Reeves,   the authors point to many of the affairs John Kennedy had while he was married to Jackie Kennedy both before and during his Presidential Administration. During the White House years, Jackie was off on a great deal of extended trips including month long yachting vacations with Aristotle Onassis. As soon as Jackie would leave on here trips, a steady stream of females were coming to the White House for "internal affairs."

One of the most publicly known affairs the President had was with Marilyn Monroe. This affair is well documented in the published works of Sandra Shevey, _The Marilyn Scandal_, Anthony Summers' work _Goddess_, _The Secret Lives Of Marilyn Monroe_, _The Marilyn Conspiracy_ by Milo Speriglo, _Who Killed Marilyn_, by Tony Sciacca and in both _A Woman Named Jackie_ by David Heyman and _A Question Of Character_ by Thomas Reeves.

The John Kennedy and Marilyn Monroe affair went on during the time that Kennedy was President. At one of Kennedy's birthday parties which was a public tribute to the President, Marilyn Monroe got up on the stage and sang a sexy happy birthday Mr. President in a skin tight outfight. The President was grinning from ear to ear. Evidently, the President ended the Marilyn affair for fear that it would become public knowledge and hurt him politically. He sent Bobby Kennedy in to talk with Marilyn about the affair. Evidently, Bobby was swept off his feet by the sex godess Marilyn Monroe and had an affair with her himself. Milo Speriglio, a well known and respected private detective and a person known well to this author conducted many years of investigation into the Marilyn Monroe Conspiracy and provides evidence in his two books on the subject that Marilyn Monroe was being wiretapped and the Kennedys had something to do with her death.

Apparently, Robert Kennedy got into the same trap that his brother did with his affair with

Marilyn. Marilyn was relating to others that Bobby planned to divorce his wife and marry her. Marilyn's loose tongue was likely the result of her instability and drug abuse. The attorney general cut off his affair with Marilyn and Marilyn threatened to make both her affair with Bobby Kennedy and John Kennedy public at a news conference the weekend after her untimely death. Instead of her press conference which was to occur on the following Monday, she became a homicide victim on the Friday night or early Saturday morning of that weekend. Although her death was ruled a suicide from a drug overdose, both Milo Speriglio and Tony Sciacca provide evidence that would lead one to believe that Monroe's death was not a suicide and that witnesses in the neighborhood saw Robert Kennedy enter the Monroe home on the day in question.

I have spoken with my fellow investigator Milo Sperigilo on this subject on many occasions and he has always related to me that the Marilyn Monroe homicide was a conspiracy and that there is significant linkage between the murder and the Kennedys to suspect them.

Three of the Kennedy "internal affairs" could have involved covert spying using Kennedy to obtain information. Inga Arvad, a suspected German spy was involved with Kennedy during a period of time when he was working in Naval Intelligence. The Judith Campbell affair took place during a time when Kennedy was President. At the same time that Campbell was carrying on an affair with the President, she was in communication with Sam Giancana, a mafia boss who was involved with the CIA's attempts to assassinate Fidel Castro. The Monroe affair with John Kennedy provides a thread of evidence back to organized crime also. According to Milo Sperigilo and Tony Sciacca, Monroe's home was bugged and there is some evidence which would point to the wiretapping being done by organized crime, perhaps Jimmy Hoffa in an attempt to develop information that discredited the Kennedys.

I believe that it is important to note that no evidence has surfaced that would indicate that any of these affairs had anything to do with Kennedy's death. However, the Arvad, Campbell and Monroe affairs were obvious national security risks and the probability of other unknown affairs that might have been a security risk are a possibility. Linkage back to organized crime is present in both the Campbell affair and the Monroe affair with regards to her house being wired. From the eyes of various American intelligence organizations, I believe that they saw the President's "internal affairs" as a national security risk and I believe that this may have been a contributing factor in the assassination although it was not the sole motivation.

THE ANTI-INTELLIGENCE ESTABLISHMENT

Two of the earliest political appointments Kennedy made after being elected to the Presidency concerned our intelligence organizations. He announced that the current director of the CIA, Allen Dulles and the current director of the FBI, J. Edgar Hoover would remain in office in his administration. However, there is a great body of evidence that points to Kennedy's dislike, and distrust of the these organizations and an overwhelming body of evidence that indicates that the President intended to keep a pre-occupation with intelligence organizations and wanted to maintain better control of them.

Kennedy fired Allen Dulles after the Bay Of Pigs incident. Many Dulles top aides also got the ax when Dulles was pink-slipped as the Kennedy administration began to clean house. The President commented that he would, "splinter the CIA in a thousand pieces and scatter it to the winds." After the Bay Of Pigs incident, Kennedy opened investigations on CIA activities and started actions to back up his scattering to the winds statement. This involved:

Budget Cuts

Station Chiefs being put under the direct control of Ambassadors who reported to Kennedy.
Transferring paramilitary operations to the Pentagon.
Creating the Defense Intelligence Agency to take over previous functions within the CIA.

It has also become general knowledge that the President wanted to appoint his brother, Bobby Kennedy , as head of the CIA. However, Bobby Kennedy didn't like the idea and thought it was a bad political move so the President instead appointed John A. McCone as CIA director and unofficially made Bobby Kennedy the administration's watchdog on the agency.

The Kennedy administration was clearly outraged when he learned of covert operations that involved attempts to assassinate Castro and was clearly upset over the assassination of the leader of South Vietnam which, many researchers on the subject have suggested a CIA involvement.

The CIA had sponsored the Cuban refugees who were attempting to overthrow the Castro government and had many manhours of contingency plans involved in this activity. During the Cuban Missile Crises, Kennedy publicly promised that he would not attempt a US invasion of Cuba. Heads must have flew within the CIA when this became publicly known policy.

The Kennedy administration had an ongoing battle with J. Edgar Hoover. By Hoover's actions concerning Martin Luther King and the entire civil rights movement at the time, one would tend to infer that he was not in favor of the civil rights of black Americans that the Kennedy administration was. Hoover's continued denial that organized crime existed in the United States and the Kennedy administration's apparent war on organized crime was also in conflict. The attorney general's office apparently felt like the FBI stonewalled some of the investigations involved in the war on organized crime.

Hoover had always had direct access to the President. When the Kennedy administration came into power, Hoover was instructed that he would have to go through the attorney general, Robert Kennedy, to obtain access to the oval office. Hoover was apparently outraged. When you look at the history of the FBI before the Kennedy administration, you find that, although the FBI was technically under the office of the attorney general, Hoover had always operated the agency somewhat independently and had always had direct access to the President. The Kennedy administration attempted to curtail Hoover's independence and cut off direct access to the White House. Hoover was told he was to go through the attorney general to reach the oval office. Shortly after taking over the office of attorney general, Robert Kennedy called Hoover's office one day and was told by Hoover's secretary that he was not in. Kennedy apparently found out that Hoover was in his office taking a nap. Robert Kennedy then had a telephone line installed directly from his office into the office of J. Edgar Hoover bypassing Hoover's secretary. This apparently infuriated Hoover.

In 1963, rumors began to circulate that Hoover would be replaced in Kennedy's second term. Hoover would reach the age of seventy which was mandatory retirement age in January of 1965. The rumors were that the Kennedy administration had no plans to exempt Hoover from retirement. It is interesting to note that Johnson did exempt Hoover from retirement but left the option open to rescind the exemption at any time. Unlike the Kennedys, Lyndon Johnson and J. Edgar Hoover were good friends. Johnson lived next door to Hoover during his years in the Senate and Hoover was often a Johnson dinner and breakfast guest. Hoover was also liked by Lyndon Johnson's young girls who often called him uncle and it's apparent that the Johnson/Hoover friendship continued after Johnson became Vice President. It is also interesting to note that one of the first things Hoover did after the Kennedy assassination is remove the direct line that went from Hoover's office to Robert Kennedy's office.

Assassination researcher Penn Jones Jr. has stated that he developed information that Hoover made a secret trip from Washington to Dallas on November 21st, 1963 and spent the night at the estate of Clint Murchison Sr. Jones claims to have interviewed a chauffer who picked Hoover up at the airport and drove him to the Murchinson estate.

What is even more strange is the FBI's apparent prior knowledge of an assassination plot on Kennedy that was in the works. You'll recall two cables that went out indicating an assassination plot we covered in an earlier chapter as well as the covertly tape recorded incident between Milteer and Sommerset. Based on the Hoover's strong motive to see Kennedy out of office, the apparent prior knowledge of a plot to assassinate Kennedy and the FBI coverup of the conspiracy that followed the assassination as well as the coverup concerning Oswald's connection to the FBI, I believe that the weight of the evidence indicates that Hoover likely had prior knowledge of the plot to assassinate Kennedy and then failed to take any action that would stop the assassination.

Kennedy often made off the cuff remarks concerning both the FBI and CIA and indicated that these agencies would be reorganized in his second administration. The President felt the various intelligence agencies had gone out of control and needed to be brought back into a stricter line of command. There is a large body of evidence which would indicate that Kennedy planned to place all of the intelligence organizations of the United States under one agency which could better be controlled from the Oval office.

The linkage of Oswald's ties to the intelligence community are significant. It's also been established that Ruby was a one time FBI informant. His connections to organized crime are significant. The linkage between organized crime and the CIA in covert operations as it related to Cuba have been established as well as Oswald's Cuban connection. We have closed the circle on this issue.

One of the most interesting things about the CIA and the Kennedy assassination is Garrison's trial in New Orleans of Clay Shaw. Garrison attempted to show a connection between Shaw and the CIA. Although Shaw was found not guilty at the trial, most of the jury members have publicly stated that they felt as if Garrison had proven beyond a reasonable doubt that Kennedy was assassinated as the result of a conspiracy. In more recent years, better evidence has surfaced that would point to a connection between Shaw and the CIA.

An even more interesting court case resulted in 1985 when Mark Lane was hired by Liberty Lobby to defend them in a civil action brought on by E. Howard Hunt. The civil action involved an article written by Victor Marchetti concerning Hunt's connections to the Kennedy assassination and the possibility of Hunt being in Dallas during the time that the assassination took place. Hunt was suing for Defamation. Hunt won the action against Liberty Lobby and Liberty Lobby appealed the action. Mark Lane was retained as attorney for the defendant for the second trial.

Lane called a witness by the name of Marta Lorenz who had, at one time, been romantically involved with Fidel Castro. Lorenz was told by CIA people that Castro planned to murder her so she defected from Castro, came to the United States and began working for the CIA. The CIA story that Castro had planned on murdering Lorenz was likely deceptive as the CIA had a strong motivation to recruit Lorenz. Lorenz was later used in failed attempts to murder Castro with poison pills. She was sent back to Cuba and did continue a relationship with Castro but could not carry out the murder. She was again brought out of Cuba for fear that Castro would find out what she was up to.

During the Hunt Vs. Liberty Lobby trial, Lorenz was placed on the stand and stated that she worked for the CIA but was not able to talk about any of the assignments she had been given. Her testimony revealed that Hunt was a paymaster for some of the covert operations run out of Miami and used a codename. She also related a story in which she traveled with several people in the group by car from Miami to Dallas. She stated that she was in Dallas one day before the assassination and stated that she was in the company of E. Howard Hunt. She also stated that she observed Jack Ruby in the hotel room with the other people involved. Lorenz stated that she was not told the nature or substance of the covert plan under way in Dallas one day before the assassination but requested that she be returned to Miami as she did not want to become involved in it. Her request was granted and she was put on a plane bound for Miami on November 21st, 1963.

Hunt claimed that he was in Washington D.C. the morning of the assassination and was with his wife during the afternoon hours shopping for Chinese food. Hunt stated that he heard of the assassination on the car radio while he was parked outside a grocery store while his wife was inside obtaining the food. Hunt also stated that he spent late Friday afternoon and the the following weekend with his children and family watching the Kennedy assassination events unfold on television. Hunt produced one witness who stated that he saw Hunt drive by a restaurant on the day of the assassination. Hunt's wife did not testify because she has since expired. Hunt did not have any of his children testify and Mark Lane pointed out in cross-examination that one of Hunt's claims in the action is that he experienced trouble with his children having to convince them that he was not in Dallas.

The jury ruled in favor of Liberty Lobby. Hunt therefore lost his defamation action on Liberty Lobby which resulted from an article that suggested that Hunt was in Dallas on November 22nd, 1963. I am not going to suggest that Hunt was in Dallas on November 22nd, 1963 and I'm not going to conclude that Hunt was in Dallas on November 21st, 1963 either. Instead, I refer the reader to Mark Lane's new book, _Plausible Denial_ which reveals Mr. Lane's involvement with this case. _Plausible Denial_ is excellent reading and I highly recommend you do so. I would also recommend _Rush To Judgment_, Lane's first book. However, I believe that it is out of print but I would take the time to check in a used book store.

The CIA was very compartmentized and very secretive even within it's own circles. Assignments, especially in the area of covert activities were very controlled as to the information given out. Things were so secret and information given on such a restricted need to know only basis that individual operatives who were actually carrying out assignments didn't even know the overall plan or purpose of the activity they were performing. I doubt that the CIA overall had a contingency plan to assassinate Kennedy. However, individual agents working with the CIA likely had a strong motive as well as the means and opportunity to plan the assassination.

THE VIETNAM WAR AND THE MILITARY INDUSTRIAL COMPLEX

During the Presidential campaign, Kennedy harped on a missile gap that existed between the USSR and the USA. After taking office, Kennedy felt that intelligence reports were overstating the number of missiles the Soviets had implying that the overstatement was done with the motivation to improve the defense and intelligence budgets in the United States. There is a great body of evidence that would indicate that Kennedy's second administration would have attempted to contain and control military spending. There is also evidence that points to a total withdrawal of troops from Vietnam.

During the later part of Kennedy's administration, the United States had about 16,000 troops in Vietnam. Kennedy came to believe that US involvement in the Vietnam war should be reduced. Only three weeks before he went to Dallas, he had signed orders to start withdrawing troops. The first withdrawal would be 1,000 and all troops were to be out of Vietnam by 1965. Two days after

Kennedy's assassination, Lyndon Johnson rescinded the withdrawal and eventually accelerated the war. The rest is history. Kennedy was turning into a dove. Johnson turned into a hawk. Thus, the great body of evidence would point to the fact that, if Kennedy had lived, US involvement in the Vietnam war would not have continued from the standpoint of providing troops but, because of his death, US policy concerning the war went in the other direction.

One of the most interesting things about the Vietnam war during the early 1960's is that the CIA was substantially involved in it covertly. This concerned Kennedy to the point of placing covert activities under the control of the ambassador. When one studies the murder of Diem, possible CIA involvement could have been involved. It's apparent that CIA people forged or created false cables after Kennedy's assassination that attempted to blame the Diem murder on the Kennedy administration, when, it fact, the body of evidence really pointed away from the Kennedy administration and pointed more towards the CIA.

THE OIL INDUSTRY AND JOHN KENNEDY: Texas is an oil state. A tax credit was given to the oil industry often referred to as the oil depletion allowance. There was much concern within the oil industry about Kennedy's apparent desire to change the oil depletion allowance and this outraged people in the oil industry. One of the primary leaders of oil in Dallas was H. L. Hunt. Both Ruby and Oswald can be linked to the Hunt office. Ruby visited the Hunt office the day before the assassination. Oswald wrote a hand written letter to H.L. Hunt asking that his position be explained to him that surfaced in thew 1970's. Both Lyndon Johnson and John Connally politically supported the needs of the oil industry as both were well known politicians from the oil state. James Reston, Jr. points out in his work, *The Lone Star: The Life Of John Connally*, which is a well well researched work that both Johnson and Connally had become very concerned with Kennedy's views on the oil depletion allowance to the point that they felt Kennedy could loose Texas in the next Presidential election if he started verbalizing his desire to do away with the tax credit.

One of the most fascinating links between the oil industry is it's close association with the CIA. Most oil businesses involved overseas contacts and business dealings that became rip for CIA interest and there is reason to believe that some CIA covert activities used the oil industry as cover.George DeMohrenschildt, a person with close association to Oswald during the months before the assassination is a good example. Demohrenschildt was described by the Warren Commission as a petroleum engineer and was supposed to have been involved in geological work to search for oil in his worldwide travels but his connections to the CIA have been solidly established and a great deal of his travel as a scout for oil was likely a CIA cover.

You will recall that Oswald's wife had moved in with Mrs. Pain who's relatives worked for The Agency For International Development. DeMohrenschildt had also worked for AID. AID had some involvement with the oil industry and firm ties to the CIA.

There is significant links between Ruby, Oswald the CIA and the oil industry and the oil industry in the United States had a motive to remove Kennedy from power. As a group by itself, however, I do not believe that they had the means or opportunity to assassinate Kennedy.

WHAT COULD HAVE BEEN: What if John Kennedy had not been cut down by assassination in Dallas? What if he would have lived to seek another term of office? Would Robert Kennedy have been placed at the head of the CIA? Would our involvement in Vietnam had been different? Would Kennedy had retired J. Edgar Hoover? Would the war on organized crime continue by the Justice Department? Would Kennedy have completely reorganized all of the intelligence organizations into one agency? The answer to these questions, in my opinion, are a likely yes!

Could Kennedy have been re-elected? Let us take a look at the situation as we know it. Hoover was in possession of secret files on the Arvad, Campbell and Monroe Affairs and likely had other information in his secret files about Kennedy. He learned that the Kennedys didn't plan on extending his mandatory retirement in the second Kennedy administration. Would Hoover have leaked these files to the Republicans who could have used them to defeat Kennedy? I believe that those files would become a key and Hoover would have released them to save his own neck for Hoover must of reasoned that the faith of Kennedy's second term coming to pass concerned whether or not the files would remain secret or revealed publicly.

Would the American public put up with a President who, had in the past, endangered national security by having an affair with a suspected German spy and an affair while President with a woman who was likely reporting to members of organized crime? Would the public stand for the affair with Monroe and the apparent wiretapping of her private moments with the President by organized crime? I do not believe that the American public would have tolerated the President of the United States committing the crime of adultery let alone with females who were spying on him.

Naturally, if Kennedy was not assassinated and obtained the democratic nomination, Lyndon Johnson would not have been in that election as a Presidential contender and there remains a question concerning his appearance on the ticket as the Vice President. There was some talk of dropping Johnson from the ticket in Kennedy's second term. If that had happened, it would have likely been the end of Johnson's career. It has often been said and I will repeat it here that Johnson had more to gain by the assassination of Kennedy than any human being in the world. However, I have found no creditable evidence that Johnson had anything at all to do with the assassination although there is enough evidence to now show that Johnson didn't believe the Warren Commission's findings anymore than Mark Lane did. In fact, during Johnson's remaining days at his ranch near Johnson city, he stated hinting that he thought that elements within CIA might have been involved and then suddenly died of a heart attack.

I have always been fascinated with the rule of physics which states that an object in motion tends to remain in motion and I have always applied this to the politics of the Kennedys in the 1960's. If John Kennedy had lived, would we have had a twenty-four year block of Presidents with Kennedy as their last name? If Kennedy had lived and had been elected to a second term, what could have happened after that term? Would Bobby Kennedy then run for the Presidency? Would Bobby Kennedy win the Presidency, serve two eight year terms and then hand the office over to his younger brother Ted Kennedy? Succeeding history certainly reveals that both Bobby and Teddy wanted to become President just like their older brother. Bobby Kennedy was assassinated attempting to win the office. Ted Kennedy tried to win the nomination unsuccessfully but was defeated by Jimmy Carter as Teddy developed his own problem that resulted in the death of a young female and developed other problems involving "internal affair" at a period in time when the press was no longer willing to look the other way.

In summarizing the individual issues involved during the Kennedy administration, we developed the following five possible motives:

> 1) J. Edgar Hoover was going to be retired in the second term of Kennedy. Instead, Johnson came into office and Hoover remained as head of the FBI. Hoover's secret trip to Dallas the day before the assassination appears suspicious.

> 2) With Hoover out of the way, the Justice Department would be free to use the FBI to investigate organized crime and an all out war on organized crime would be declared. Instead, Johnson came into office and the Justice Department's preoccupation with stamping out

organized crime diminished.

3) The Intelligence organizations, especially the FBI and the CIA were going to be re-organized under one agency and more control of these agencies would be placed under the executive branch. Instead, Lyndon Johnson came into power and left the intelligence organizations the way they were.

4) Kennedy was ready to start pulling back commitment to Vietnam and all advisors would be out of the area by 1965. Kennedy has already signed orders to start removing Americans. Instead, Johnson came into power, rescinded the withdrawal order and accelerated the war.

5) Kennedy's refusal to provide air support with the Bay Of Pigs and his promise not to invade Cuba during the Cuban Missile Crisis angered the Cuban Refugees and people within the CIA who were involved in the covert actions.

LINKING IT ALL TOGETHER:

There is significant linkage between many of the motives we have explored. The intelligence community, the Cuban issues and organized crime can all be directly linked together and the "internal affairs" can indirectly be linked to organized crime. The CIA was deeply involved with the Cuban refugees and sponsored them in their efforts to overthrow the Castro government. The CIA was also involved with organized crime in their attempts to murder Castro. The Affair of Campbell can be traced back to organized crime and the Monroe affair can indirectly be linked with the wiretaps of her home. Oswald can be linked both to the intelligence community and the Cuban issues. Ruby can be linked to organized crime and organized crime can be linked to the CIA during this period of time concerning attempts to murder castro. The CIA was deeply involved in covert activity in Vietnam and strong evidence would suggest that they were involved in the murder of Diem. The fact that CIA people attempted to place the blame of Diem's murder on Kennedy by forging state department documents after Kennedy's assassination is further evidence pointing in the direction of the CIA. There is substantial evidence that Hoover successfully marshalled the evidence presented before the Warren Commission and cloaked much of the information on Oswald and the Kennedy assassination. As part of the federal intelligence community, the FBI had strong ties to the CIA. In every instance, the trail leads back to the CIA.

As I stated earlier, I do not believe that the CIA, as an overall agency, was at the top of the organizational structure the planed the assassination of the President. I do believe that a small group of people within the CIA, without the knowledge and consent of the CIA in general was involved. Segments of organized crime, the Cuban Refugees and right-wing international money people in private business were involved. It's also apparent that Hoover's domestic intelligence monitoring uncovered the assassination plan but Hoover kept in quite choosing to do nothing hoping that after the assassination, his friend Lyndon Johnson who seceded to the Presidency would not force him into retirement which is exactly what transpired.

CONCLUSION: THE ASSASSINATION CONSPIRACY
AND COVER UP

In chapters one and two we looked into a basic overview of the assassination and the government investigations that took place. We find that the first recorded words of police officials (Police Chief Curry's radio transmission seconds after the shots rang out) point to the railroad yards behind the picket fence. The first eyewitness accounts on television pointed to the grassy knoll area from the Newman accounts. The first inditement documents of Oswald stated that he was involved in a conspiracy and the federal government placed pressure upon the Dallas authorities to have any remarks about a conspiracy removed. Rumors of a conspiracy were flying throughout the world. The new president and the Department Of Justice were apparently interested in subduing rumors of a conspiracy and wanted something issued that would dispel the conspiracy theory. Johnson set up the Warren Commission which successfully stopped many other governmental bodies from starting an official investigation into the assassination.

The Warren Commission marshalled the evidence to fit the lone gunman theory and issued it's conclusion that three and only three shots were fired from the sixth floor window of the School Book Depository Building and that Oswald fired all three shots. Other government investigations revealed that the wounds on Kennedy presented by the Warren Commission were not in the right location, that the CIA withheld information relevant to the assassination and that the CIA was involved with organized crime in attempts to assassinate Castro. In 1976, the House Of Representatives formed the House Select Committee On Assassinations and the committee overruled the Warren Commission and concluded that Kennedy was assassinated as a result of a conspiracy. The House Select Committee On Assassinations determined that at least one of these shots had been fired from the knoll and picket fence area.

In a study of activity in the grassy knoll/picket fence area, eyewitness accounts and photographic evidence are found that describe suspicious activity in the knoll and picket fence area. Nineteen witnesses, two photographs and one home movie point to evidence that would indicate shots from the grassy knoll. Two witnesses place Ruby at the assassination site. Several of these witnesses provided descriptions of men around the knoll/picket fence area and those descriptions tend to corroborate each other. Each piece of the evidence developed concerning this activity tends to corroborate the entire body presented.

In other developed and organized data we find that Oswald was not the lone assassin in the sixth floor of the School Book Depository, the magic bullet theory of the Warren Commission doesn't make much sense and that the other evidence pointing to Oswald's guilt as the lone gunman doesn't add up. We covered time studies that would indicate Oswald could not have been on the sixth floor alone and fired all three shots. We also developed eyewitness accounts and photographic evidence that tends to show more than one person involved in shots fired from the sixth floor window. The witnesses who provided descriptions of the men in the sixth floor windows do not match Oswald's description at all. In exploring ballistics evidence, we find that the magic bullet theory developed to explain the lone gunman theory doesn't hold water because: the trajectory doesn't track out, the testimony of Connally doesn't fit, the Zapruder film does not support the theory, and the recovered bullet could not have done all the damage because of it's condition and weight. The facts concerning who's stretcher the magic bullet was found on tend to show that the bullet was either picked up somewhere else and placed on an unrelated stretcher or it was planted. We also find several witnesses and one photograph that would tend to show that Ruby was at Parkland Hospital. In the absence of any other motivation, the fact that Ruby lied about his presence at Parkland Hospital would tend to indicate that he planted the magic bullet.

In exploring other forensic evidence, we find that the paraffin test on Oswald does not prove he fired a rifle, a great deal of controversy exists concerning the actual murder weapon, the empty shells recovered don't fit into the puzzle properly, the fingerprint evidence appears to be a frame, and blood found on the sidewalk on the north side of Elm Street is a mystery. We also find evidence that the wounds of the President's body are completely inconsistent with the magic bullet and lone gunman theory and there is substantial evidence that the forensic evidence concerning the President's body is not consistent. There is also evidence that would tend to indicate that the famous backyard photographs of Oswald are fakes and that other shots were fired.

Concerning the developed facts surrounding Oswald after the assassination up until the time of his arrest, we find a number of facts that do not make sense from the lone assassin standpoint. He hung around the School Book Depository for several minutes and then walked out the front door. He walked past several bus stops and then boarded a bus traveling back towards the assassination site. He exited the bus and walked over to the bus station were he started to get into a cab but asked another bystander if she wanted his cab. Oswald was dropped off near his rooming house by the cab driver. I find if difficult to believe that a person who just murdered the President of the United States would linger around the murder site, walk several blocks and then board a bus traveling back towards the murder site, exit the bus near the murder site, walk another few blocks and then casually offer his cab to another party. Whatever transpired from the time Oswald left the School Book Depository Building until the time he entered his rooming house remains a mystery to me. Upon Oswald entering his rooming house, a patrol car with two men pulled up to the house and honked it's horn. Oswald was only in his room for a few minutes and left through the front door. The last time he was observed, he was standing at a bus stop but the only bus coming by this stop was traveling back downtown towards the assassination site. Somehow, Oswald went in the other direction.

Time study reveals that Oswald could not have walked from his rooming house to the murder site of officer Tippet. Several witnesses saw more than one person fleeing the murder site. The recovered shells were first described as being fired from an automatic weapon which Oswald didn't have and both the shells and bullet fragments recovered from the body of Tippit would tend to indicate that they came from two different weapons. At least one witness indicates that Ruby may have been present at the movie theater during Oswald's arrest. Oswald attempted to discharge his handgun while he was being arrested but the gun misfired due to a bent pin. If the pin was bent at this time, how could it have been working perfectly a few minutes before when he allegedly murdered officer Tippit.

The background studies of Oswald and Ruby indicate that Oswald was involved in intelligence work and that Ruby was involved in organized crime. The next chapter reveals beyond a reasonable doubt that Oswald and Ruby had a relationship before the assassination. The communications links between Oswald and Ruby were both overt and covert. This investigation developed several cutout and dead drop communication chains in the covert area and also developed ten witnesses who could place Ruby and Oswald together in an overt manner. Ruby's deception in that he did not know Oswald would tend to implicate him in the conspiracy.

The Garrison investigation and inditement of Clay Shaw shows that Garrison was on the right track and the Rosco White story is consistent with all evidence presented. Garrision was getting ready to firm up a case on David Ferrie who can be linked to Oswald but Ferrie mysteriously died. Ferrie's death was ruled a suicide but Garrison developed evidence that would tend to point towards a murder. Ferrie was linked to Oswald, the CIA and organized crime. Upon Ferrie's death, Garrision indited Clay Shaw for conspiracy in the President's murder. During the trial, Garrison established the fact that Kennedy's assassination was the result of a conspiracy in the eyes of the jury. The government attempted to discredit Garrison and attempted to block out of state subpoenas. Although Shaw was found not guilty in Garrison's case, later evidence provides more solid establishment that Shaw had significant ties to the CIA. The Rosco White story is consistent with all other established evidence in the case.

Running through the entire body of evidence is consistent cover-up of any evidence that would point towards a conspiracy. The fact that the FBI had an open file on Oswald was covered up and FBI agent Hosty was ordered to destroy evidence. The recovered rifle, first reported as a Mauser changed make, brand and model. The palm print stated to be found on the rifle conflicts with FBI documents and first reports given by the Dallas police that no relevant prints were located. The first inditement of Oswald naming him as part of a conspiracy was changed upon pressure from the federal government. The evidence relating to Oswald's trip to Mexico was, at first, covered up. The newspaper ad Oswald allegedly ordered the rifle from was changed. The paraffin test that revealed negative results on Oswald's cheek was suppressed. Investigation after the Warren Commission indicate that the bullet wound on the president's back was not in the right location. There is considerable evidence to show that the backyard photographs with Oswald holding the murder weapon are fakes and that the license plate of the Walker House has been removed from the photo between the time it was found by the Dallas police and the time it was entered as evidence in the Warren Commission. The written statement made by officer Baker concerning Oswald drinking a coke was simply crossed out and the evidence abandoned. The House Select Committee on Assassinations concluded that the FBI failed to investigate the possibility of a conspiracy. This committee also concluded that the CIA failed to share it's information and suppressed information concerning the Kennedy Assassination. Witnesses were asked not to talk and many witnesses who had information that indicated a conspiracy were not called upon to testify. The Zapruder film was suppressed for many years and lies about Kennedy turning around in his seat were published. When the Zapruder film finally made it's way into the public, it appears that significant frames have been tampered with to cover up evidence. The Oliver and Arnold photographic evidence was confiscated and has disappeared. Descriptions of the President's body from the time it was illegally taken from Parkland Hospital without an autopsy until the time that the autopsy was done in Washington are in conflict. Other evidence concerning the coffin and the way the president was placed in the coffin are inconsistent. This evidence tends to point towards the fact that sometime and somewhere between Parkland Hospital in Dallas and the Bethesda Naval Hospital in Washington, the body was altered. Two members of the commission, Richard Russell and Hal Boggs and the President himself, Lyndon Johnson all stated in the years after the Warren Commission that they did not believe that Oswald had acted alone in the assassination.

Reverse Speech reveals and uncovers new evidence about the Kennedy assassination. The analysis concludes that Oswald was not the lone assassin and most likely didn't fire the shots. However, it indicates that he had some knowledge of and connection to the assassination. Reverse speech also reveals that Wade thought there was a problem with the evidence with Oswald and that Oswald was not the sole person involved in the assassination. The knowledge about Curry's remarks through reverse speech also indicates that he was not exactly comfortable with some of the evidence. Further remarks made by Wade to the news media indicate that he was not telling the truth when he stated that he did not know Jack Ruby. Comments made before the press by both Chief Curry and Detective Lovell indicate that some sort of payoff took place with Ruby. The reversals found in Ruby's last press conference tend to corroborate the reversals of a payoff or ransom made by Chief Curry and Detective Lovell. Ruby's reversals also indicate that he was telling the truth when he stated that the truth about the assassination has not come out. Reverse Speech also corroborates the fact that a relationship between Ruby and Oswald was present before the assassination in the Conorto analysis. The fact that Ruby introduced Oswald to both Confronto and Oliver as a CIA agent provides the solid proof developed through the Footprints Of Intelligence study that defiantly concludes that Oswald was involved in intelligence work.

In exploring motive we find that organized crime, the Cuban Refugees, and fractions within the CIA all had strong motives to remove Kennedy from office and that these groups can all be linked

186

together in various covert activity. We also develop a strong motive of J. Edar Hoover. In exploring the evidence totally, I do not believe that either Johnson or Hoover were directly involved in the assassination conspiracy. I do believe that the weight of the evidence tends to show that Hoover had foreknowledge of the assassination and did nothing about it.

SUMMARY: PUTTING WHAT WE KNOW TOGETHER

1) NUMBER, LOCATION AND SPACING OF SHOTS: Based on this investigation, more than one person was involved in the assassination of John Kennedy which means that the assassination was the result of a conspiracy. Based on this investigation, between four and six shots were fired. These shots were not evenly spaced and at least two of these shots were almost on top of each other. The shots were fired from the area of the School Book Depository Building, The grassy knoll behind the picket fence area on the north side of the plaza and probably from the Records Building.

2) COVER-UPS: Based on this investigation, various individual government agencies were involved in a cover-up of the actual facts concerning the assassination. Film was taken and never revealed. Other film was altered and suppressed. The events revealed in the Zapruder film were lied about. Some witnesses were threated, others were flatly told not to talk and still others disappeared some dieing under stranger circumstances. The FBI withheld information that it had a file on Oswald and destroyed evidence. The CIA withheld relevant information concerning evidence of Kennedy's assassination.

3) THE FATAL HEAD SHOT: Based on this investigation, the fatal shot came from behind the picket fence and the weight of the evidence based on Ricky White's testimony and his polygraph and PSE testing along with the photographic evidence of the badgeman photograph would tend to show that Rosco White was the rifleman behind the fence. Based on the tramp photograph and Chancy Holt's statements, and evidence from both the Ricky White story as well as evidence that surfaced during the civil trial of E. Howard Hunt Vs. Liberty Lobby, the weight of the evidence would tend to show that members of intelligence organizations and members of the Cuban refugee group were involved.

4) OSWALD'S INTELLIGENCE ACTIVITIES: Based on this investigation, Oswald was involved in intelligence work. The exact nature of that intelligence work can not be concluded but the weight of the evidence tends to show that Oswald was involved in intelligence work as a CIA contract agent, an FBI informant or both.

5) OSWALD'S INVOLVEMENT IN THE ASSASSINATION: The weight of the eyewitness testimony tends to show that Oswald was not in the sixth floor window. Brennan, the only witness to testify officially that Oswald was in the sixth floor window could not identify Oswald in a police line up, kept changing his mind about being able to identify Oswald, made statements about Oswald being in the sixth floor window that are inconsistent and failed a PSE test. Time study of Oswald's location in the School Book Depository Building tends to show that he could not have been in the sixth floor window at the time of the assassination. The weight of the evidence would also tend to show that if Oswald murdered officer Tippit, another person was with him and the weight of the evidence tends to show that this other person was the person who shot Oswald. The paraffin tests tend to conclude that Oswald did not fire any shots. Both PSE testing and Reverse Speech analysis conclude that Oswald had some involvement in the assassination but that he did not fire any shots.

5) JACK RUBY: Based on this investigation, Jack Ruby was involved with organized crime. Based on the information developed in this investigation, Ruby is implicated in the conspiracy, was likely present at the assassination site while the assassination was taking place, was likely

present at Parkland Hospital, likely planted the magic bullet and most likely murdered Oswald so nothing about the conspiracy would come out. Based on information developed in this investigation, Ruby was involved in some sort of payoff with individual officers of the Dallas police. Reverse Speech analysis confirms Ruby's involvement in the assassination.

6) THE RUBY/OSWALD CONNECTION: Based on the information developed in this investigation, Jack Ruby and Lee H. Oswald had a relationship before the assassination. Substantial evidence shows that Oswald and Ruby were in communication both covertly and overtly before the assassination. Reverse Speech analysis confirms the connection.

7) HOOVER'S KNOWLEDGE: Based on information developed in this investigation, the weight of the evidence tends to show that J. Edgar Hoover, through his monitoring and investigative activities uncovered a plot to assassinate Kennedy and had the motive, means and opportunity to cover it up.

8) ORGANIZATIONS INVOLVED: Based on information developed in this investigation, individual members of organized crime, the intelligence community and the Cuban refugees can be linked together and had the means, motive and opportunity to take action on the President.

RESEARCH SOURCES AND ADDITIONAL INFORMATION

Note: This list gives you instant access to other information concerning the Kennedy Assassination and acts as a list of research material the author drew upon to compile the investigation found in the body of Missing Links. Any serious assassination buff will want to purchase, read and study at least some of the material listed here. For a start, I suggest you at least read the first eleven works listed below.

ONE: BOOKS STILL IN PRINT ON THE JFK ASSASSINATION AND OTHER RELATED MATERIAL

BEST EVIDENCE: Disguise And Deception In The Assassination Of John Kennedy: By: David S. Lifton. Carroll & Graft Publishers, Inc., 260 Fifth Avenue, New York, New York, 10001. ISBN: 0-88184-438-1. Copyright 1980 with updated edition in 1988. Best Evidence contains the author's study of the physical evidence of the president's body and offers startling evidence that the body was altered from the time it left Dallas until the time the autopsy was performed at Bethesda Naval Hospital in the Washington D.C. area. Thoroughly researched and documented. The newer edition contain actual autopsy photographs that have been suppressed for years that reveal further evidence that both the body and photographs were altered.

ON THE TRAIL OF THE ASSASSINS: My Investigation And Prosecution Of The Murder Of President Kennedy; By: Jim Garrison. Copyright: 1988. ISBN 0-941781-02-X. $19.95. (Released in November 91 in paperback) Sheridan Square Press, 145 West 4th Street, New York, New York 10012. Garrison was the DA in New Orleans at the time of the assassination. This book contains information on his investigation of David Ferrie and Clay Shaw and their connection to the Kennedy Assassination. It's also the book the spurred the movie by director Oliver Stone. Very well written containing a great deal of unanswered questions.

PLAUSIBLE DENIAL: Was The CIA Involved In The Assassination Of JFK?: By Mark Lane. Copyright 1991. ISBN 1-56025-000-3. $22.95. Thunder's Mouth Press, 54 Green Street, Suite 4S, New York, N.Y. 10013. Lane provides information pointing to possible CIA's involvement in the JFK Assassination. His new book involves his defense of Liberty Lobby who was sued by E. Howard Hunt over an article they did that indicated that Hunt was in Dallas on November 22nd, 1963.

CROSSFIRE: The Plot That Killed Kennedy: By: Jim Marrs. Copyright: 1989. ISBN: 0-88184-524-8. $25.95 Carroll & Graft Publishers, Inc., 260 Fifth Avenue, New York, New York, 10001. Jim Marrs has put together one of the best recent books on the Kennedy assassination. He has been researching the events for twenty years and teaches a course on assassination at the University of Texas.

HIGH TREASON: The Assassination Of President John F. Kennedy What really Happened. By: Robert J. Gorden and Harrison Edward Livingstone. Copyright: August 1989. ISBN 0-941401-02-2. Hardcopy: $21.95. Softcover: $16.95. The Conservatory Press, 212 Emily Lane, Boothwyn, Pa. 19061. High Treason is another very good work that explores all the issues of a conspiracy and cover-up concerning the assassination of John Kennedy. The book contains sixty-six pages of photographs.

REASONABLE DOUBT: By: Henry Hurt: Copyright: 1985. ISBN: 0-30-004059-0. Holt, Rinehart and Winston, 383 Madison Ave., New York, New York 10017. Hurt explores evidence that points away from the lone gunman Lee Oswald theory and goes deep into Oswald's ties to the intelligence community. Another excellent work that's hard to put down.

ACT OF TREASON: BY Mark North: Copyright: 1991, ISBN 0-88184-747-X ($26.95) Carroll & Graft Publishers, Inc., 260 Fifth Avenue, New York, New York, 10001. North's book is interesting and focuses in on the fact that Hoover had prior knowledge of the assassination and did not act on the knowledge which I tend to agree with. The book is well researched.

CONSPIRACY: By Anthony Summers. Copyright: 1980, ISBN: 0-07-062392-9. McGraw-Hill Book Company, New York, New York. Summers' work sets out compelling evidence of a conspiracy and then focuses in on the Cuban connection. Another work this author has read more than three times.

CONTRACT ON AMERICA: The Mafia Murder Of President John F. Kennedy: By: David Scheim: Copyright: 1988. ISBN: 0-933503-30-X. $19.95 hardcover. Shapolsky Publishers, Inc., 56 East 11th Street, New York, N. Y. 10003. A very good work on the organized crime connection to the Kennedy Assassination.

MAFIA KINGFISH: Carlos Marcello And The Assassination Of John Kennedy, By: John H. Davis. McGraw-Hill Book Company, New York, New York. Copyright 1989. ISBN 0-07-015779-0. Well researched work that tunes in on New Orleans Mafia Crime Boss Carlos Marcello's connection to the JFK assassination.

FINAL DISCL SURE: The Full Truth About The Assassination Of President Kennedy. By: David W. Berlin. Copyright 1988. ISBN 0-684-18976-3. $19.95. Charles Scriber's Sons. Macmillan Publishing Company, 866 Third Ave., New York, N.Y. 10022. Berlin was counsel to the Warren Commission. Although Berlin sticks by the general findings of the Warren Commission, his book goes into cover-ups by the CIA and NSC. I still do not agree with Berlin's general findings at all but it's interesting reading.

CONSPIRACY OF ONE: The Definitive Book On The Kennedy Assassination: By Jim Moore. Copyright: 1990. ISBN: 0-962219-2-7. $24.95. The Summit Group, 1227 West Magnolia, Fort Worth, Texas. Moore explains in his book how he first became an assassination critic of the Warren Commission but was later converted to support it's findings. He has worked very closely with the Sixth Floor- a museum in the former School Book Depository Building now open to the public. Although this author does not agree with the findings of Moore, his book is well written and interesting.

SPY SAGA: Lee Harvey Oswald And U.S. Intelligence: By: Philip H. Melanson. Copyright: 1990. ISBN: 0-275-93571-X. $21.95. Praeger Publishers, One Madison Avenue, New York, New York. 10010. Spy Saga is must reading for assassination buffs. Melanson presents compelling evidence that Lee Oswald was a U.S. intelligence operative and I don't see how anyone could doubt it after reading this work.

WHO KILLED JFK? The Kennedy Assassination Cover-Up, The Web: By: James R. Duffy. Copyright 1988. ISBN: 0-86299-561-2. $14.95. Shapolsky Publishers, 136 West 22nd Street, New York, New York, 10011. Duffy is an attorney who takes a close look at Lee Oswald compiled from government records.

CONSPIRACIES, COVER-UPS AND CRIMES: By Jonathan Vankin. Copyright, 1991 ISBN: 1-55778-384-5 (24.95) Paragon House, 90 Fifth Ave., New York, New York,

10011. Explores assassination theory in the United States as well as different types of cover-ups.

THE SQUAD: The U.S. Government's Secret Alliance With Organized Crime, By: Michael Milan. Copyright: 1989. ISBN 0-944007-52-X. $19.95. Shapolsky Publishers, Inc. 136 West 22nd Street, New York, New York. 10011. This book is written by a man in hiding who uses a pen name claiming he was a member of a hit squad of professional killers recruited by J. Edgar Hoover. Milan claims in his book that one of his assignments was to travel to Dallas and hit one of the men who was the gunman who killed Kennedy. Although no supporting evidence to back up his claims are given, it's interesting reading.

MEDIOLEGAL INVESTIGATION OF THE PRESIDENT JOHN F. KENNEDY MURDER: By Charles G. Wilber, Ph.D. Copyright 1978. ISBN 0-398-03679-9. Charles C. Thomas Publisher, Bannerstone House, 301-327 East Lawrence Ave., Springfield, Illinois. Wilber is a practicing forensic pathologist who takes a close look at the forensic evidence in the Kennedy assassination. His work has become a classic.

A QUESTION OF CHARACTER: A Life Of John F. Kennedy. By: Thomas C. Reeves. Copyright 1991. ISBN: 0-02-92565-7. ($24.95) The Free Press, 866 Third Ave., New York, New York, 10022. A very critical look at the character and political career of John Kennedy.

J. EDGAR HOOVER: The Man And His Secrets: By: Curt Gentry. Copyright: 1991, ISBN: 0-393-02404-0. $29.95. W.W. Norton & Company, 500 Fifth Ave., New York, New York. 10110. Highly critical review of Hoover's career as the director of the F.B.I. with well documented chapters on how he covered up things pertaining to the Kennedy Assassination.

UNSOLVED: GREAT MYSTERIES OF THE 20TH CENTURY: By: Kirk Wilson. Copyright 1990. ISBN: 0-88184-470-5 ($18.95) Carroll & Graf Publishers, Inc., New York, New York. A kind of directory with chapters on famous unsolved mysteries. The work contains information on the assassination of John Kennedy, the death of Marilyn Monroe and the disappearance of Jimmy Hoffa.

A WOMAN NAMED JACKIE: By: C. David Heymann: Copyright 1989. (Papaerback edition: $5.95) Signet, 1633 Broadway, New York, N.Y. 10019. Traces the life and times of Jackie Onassis. Includes much information on her marriage to John Kennedy, his affairs during their marriage, her desire to obtain a divorce, her secret yachting vacations with Onassis during the time that she was first lady and some details of behind the scenes politics.

SPYING FOR AMERICA: The Hidden History Of U.S. Intelligence: By Nathan Miller. Copyright: 1989. (Paperback Edition $5.95) Dell Publishing, 666 Fifth Ave., New York, New York 10103. Traces the complete history of U.S. intelligence gathering in the United States from the birth of our nation. Includes information on the relationship of Kennedy and the CIA during his adminstration. Also contains a chapter on Lyndon Johnson's relationship.

REVERSE SPEECH: A New Investigative Frontier: By Ralph Thomas. Copyright: 1991. Contains manual and cassette tape. ($35.00) Thomas Publications, P O Box 33244, Austin, Texas 78764. Contains information on this author's ten month study of Reverse Speech as an investigative technique and how to use it as such.

REVERSE SPEECH: Hidden Messages In Human Communications: By: David John Oates. Copyright: 1991. ISBN: 0-941705-18-8. ($29.95) Knowledge Systems, Inc. 777 W. Morris Street, Indianapolis, In. 46231. Contains information from the founder and developer of Reverse Speech on how he discovered and developed Reverse Speech into a science.

THE LONE STAR: THE LIFE OF JOHN CONNALLY: By: James Reston, Jr. Copyright 1989. ISBN 0-06-016196-5. ($25.00) A biography on John Connally containing a chapter on his account of the Kennedy assasination.

THE CRISIS YEARS: KENNEDY AND KHRUSHCHEV: 1960-1963: By Michael R. Beschloss. ISBN: 0-06-016454-9. ($29.95) Edward Burlingame Books, New York, N.Y. Contains very good information on the conflicts between Kennedy and Khrushchev.

JFK WANTS TO KNOW: Memos From The President's Office, 1961-1963. Edited By: Edward Claflin. (1991) ISBN 0-688-08846-5 ($22.95) William Morrow And Company, New York, N.Y. Contains Presidential memos and documents of the Kennedy adminstration.

TWO: VIDEOS AND CASSETTE TAPES IN PRINT

JFK CONSPIRACY: Narrated by Edwin Newman (Two hour two cassette tape collection) $15.95. Audio Renaissance Tapes, 5858 Wilshire Blvd., Suite 205, Los Angeles, Ca. 90036. Interviews with key players and witnesses relating to the Kennedy Assassination.

OSWALD NEW ORLEANS RADIO INTERVIEWS: Cassette tapes of both radio interviews purchased from The Collector's Archives, Box 2, Beaconsfield, Que., Canada, H9W 5T6.

RUSH TO JUDGMENT (VIDEO) Mark Lane. MPI release. A black and white 100 ...inute video of Mark Lane interviewing witnesses. Lane states in the video that this is a legal brief for Lee Oswald.

REASONABLE DOUBT: (The Single-Bullet Theory.) Video production by Chip Selby and Mike Selby. (1988) WhiteStar, 121 Highway 36, West Long Beach, NJ 07764. Phone (908) 229-2343. Evidence presented smashes the single bullet theory and contains interviews with several leading authorities on the subject.

BEST EVIDENCE: The Research Video. By: David Lifton. Copyright 1990. Rhino Home Video, 2225 Colorado Ave., Santa Monica, Ca. 90404. Goes along with the book, Best Evidence. Contains interviews with key witnesses and provides evidence that the body was not the same from Dallas to Washington DC.

FAKE: By Jack White. (1990) ($26.00) Jack White, 301 West Vickery, Fort Worth, Texas 76104. Jack White is a photographic expert that has studied photographic evidence relating to the Kennedy Assassination for years. This video concerns the famous backyard photographs and reveals evidence that points to a forgery.

THE MANY FACES OF LEE HARVEY OSWALD: By Jack White. (1991) $26.00. JFK Video, 301 West Vickery, Fort Worth, Texas, 76104.

THE SIXTH FLOOR: (1989) Dallas County Historical Foundation. 411 Elm Street, Dallas, Texas 75202. Phone (214) 653-6659. A video historical account of the Kennedy assassination and the Texas School Book Depository Building.

ZAPRUDER FILM: ENHANCED VERSION PREPARED FOR THE HOUSE SELECT COMMITTEE ON ASSASSINATIONS. United States Archives, Washington, D.C. This enhanced video version of the Zapruder Film contains slow motion, still motion and blowups.

THREE: OTHER RESEARCH MATERIAL

THE SIXTH FLOOR: John F. Kennedy And The Memory Of A Nation: Copyright: 1989: The Dallas County Historical Foundation, 411 Elm Street, Dallas, Texas 75202. $2.95. A sixty-two page booklet on the Kennedy Assassination and the Texas School Book Depository Building put out by the people who run the 6th Floor.

THE ASSASSINATION STORY: A book of newspaper clippings concerning the Kennedy Assassination from The Dallas Morning News and The Dallas Times Herald. Published by American Eagle Publishing Company, P O Box 750, Dallas, Texas.

JFK QUICK REFERENCE GUIDE: By: Martin Brazil. $12.95. Purchased through the JFK Assassination Research Center, Dallas, Texas. This guide is an outline and summary of data concerning the JFK Assassination.

FIFTY-ONE WITNESSES: The Grassy Knoll: By Harold Feldman. Copyright: 1965. A long article that appeared in the March issue of Minority Of One and several other publications. The study is an indepth study of fifty-one witnesses in the assassination area who stated that they thought the shots had come from behind the fence. Can still be obtained from The Collector's Archives, Box 2, Beaconsfield, Quebec, Canada, H9W 5T6.

WHEN THEY KILL A PRESIDENT: An unpublished manuscript by former Dallas Deputy Sheriff Roger D. Craig. The manuscript describes how Craig was run out of the Sheriff's department and blacklisted for not going along with official findings. Craig is no longer alive.

NOVEMBER 22ND THE DAY REMEMBERED AS REPORTED BY THE DALLAS MORNING NEWS: Copyright: 1990. $11.95. Taylor Publishing Company, 1550 West Mockingbird Lane, Dallas, Texas 75235. Contains dozens of photographs and news reported concerning the assassination.

FOUR DAYS: The Historical Record Of The Death Of President Kennedy. Compiled by United Press International and American Heritage Magazine. A coffee table type book containing an historical record of the assassination with many photographs.

LIFE MAGAZINE: February 21st, 1964. A feature story on Lee Oswald containing the famous backyard photograph on the cover.

LIFE MAGAZINE: November 25th, 1966. A feature article on Governor Connally's examination of the Zapruder Films titled A MATTER OF REASONABLE DOUBT.

LIFE MAGAZINE: November 24th, 1967. Feature articles on why Kennedy went to Texas and The Last Seconds Of The Motorcade with photographs taken by nine bystanders.

TIME MAGAZINE: November 28th, 1988. A feature article called J.F.K.'s Assassination: Who Was The Real Target?

TEXAS MONTHLY: December 1990. Feature story about Rosco White.

TEXAS MONTHLY: November 1991. Feature story on the Oliver Stone movie.

MANCHESTER: New Hampshire's Magazine: An interview with Ricky Don White.

FORGIVE MY GRIEF: By: Penn Jones. Penn Jones was a small town newspaper owner who owned the Midothian Mirror in Midothian Texas. He was one of the few newspapers in the 60's who covered assassination stories from a critical point of view. Forgive My Grief is a compilation of newsclips that appeared in his newspaper.

SEARCH AND DISCOVERY OF THE SINGLE SHOT TO THE PRESDEINT'S HEAD: By: R.B. Cutler. A research paper the explores the different theories of the fatal headshot with diagrams. Cutler Designs, Box 1465, Manchester, Ma. ($5.00)

SOME TROUBLING QUESTIONS: Testimony Of Dr. Vincent Guinn: Contains summary evidence on Doctor Guinn's study of some of the forensic evidence and his testimony before the Select Committee On Asassinations. Published by: Wallace Milam, 360 Greenway Ave. Apt 4, Dyersburg, Tn. 38024.

CHIEF JESSE CURRY PERSONAL JFK ASSASSINATION FILE: A rare 133 page limited edition publication compiled by retired police chief Jesse Curry with many Dallas police photographs. (The author's thanks to former Dallas patrolman Jim Rattey for lending his autographed copy to the author for this investigation.)

DESTINY IN DALLAS: By R. B. Denson. A rare 64 page monograph published in 1964 by the private investigator who was hired by the Ruby defense team.

DEALEY PLAZA BLUEPRINT: Prepared and published on November 20th, 1990. A full sized blueprint of the assassination site with witnesses chartered and their opinion of the direction of shots.

FOUR: OUT OF PRINT BOOKS
Note: You may be abe to locate some of these works in a used bookstore.

THE DAY KENNEDY WAS SHOT: By: Jim Bishop. (1968) A well researched historical account of the Kennedy Assassination.

THE DEATH OF A PRESIDENT: By William Manchester.(1967) Another historical account on the assassination and funeral. Excellent to the minute time line coverage.

MARINA AND LEE: By: Priscilla Johnson McMillan: (1977) An excellent research work of the life of Lee and Marina Oswald based in part on hours of interviews with Marina.

OSWALD'S GAME: By: Jean Davison: (1983) A well documented account of Lee Oswald.

LEGEND: The Secret World Of Lee Harvey Oswald. By: Edward Jay Epstein. (1978) A well researched account of who Oswald was and what his life really consisted of.

ALEK JAMES HIDELL, ALIAS OSWALD: By: W.R. Morris and RB Cuteler (1985) An interesting account of Oswald who wasn't the assassin and Alek James Hidell.

RUSH TO JUDGMENT: By: Mark Lane. Paperback edition by Dell Publishing. Copyright 1966. Signed copy by Mark Lane. Lane was one of the first Warren Commission critics and the first to write a book on the JFK Assassination Conspiracy. Lane is an attorney who was retained by Oswald's mother to defend him before the Warren Commission. His work, Rush To Judgment, is highly important reading for assassination buffs. Although it was published in 1966, the evidence presented is overwhelming and this author believes this work should still be in print. If you can find a copy in a used bookstore, buy it no matter what the price.

THE ASSASSINATION TAPES: An Electronic Probe Into The Murder Of John F. Kennedy And The Dallar Coverup.(Copyright 1975) Another rare work conducted by former CIA agent George O'Toole that is the result of his PSE testing on key players in the assassination. If you can find a copy buy it! It took me many months to locate one.

THEY KILLED THE PRESIDENT: By Robert Samanson. (1975) A very well researched account that JFK was murdered as a result of a conspiracy.

PORTRAIT OF THE ASSASSIN: By Gerald R. Ford and John R. Stiles. Published in 1965 by Simon And Schuster. Since Ford sat on the Warren Commission and became President of the United States, this book has become a collector's item. It was also an issue in his confirmation hearings when he became Vice President as the issue was raised that he released information in secret documents in this work. Although I can not agree with all of Ford's findings (as the name of the book implies) , it is interesting reading.

INQUEST: By: Edward Jay Epstein. (1966). Epstein's book was the first book on the market the explained the whys and hows of the Warren Commission and the flaws in the official report.

THE ASSASSINATION CHAIN: By: Sybil Leek and Bert Sugar. (1976) Critical review of all recent assassinations of political figures and the official government findings on them. Includes research on the assassinations of John Kennedy, Robert Kennedy, Martin Luther King Jr. and George Wallace.

THE KENNEDY ASSASSINATION AND THE AMERICAN PUBLIC: Social Communication In Crisis: By: Bradley Greenberg and Edwin Parker. (1965) A study of new coverage of the JFK assassination and public opinion.

A MOTHER IN HISTORY: By: Jean Stafford. (1966) A mass market paperback based on several interviews Stafford had with Marguerite Oswald, the mother of Lee Harvery Oswald.

THE OSWALD FILE: By: Michael Eddowes. (1977) Another mass market paperback revealing evidence of a conspiracy that point to at least two gunmen with good research on the background of Oswald.

COINCIDENCE OR CONSPIRACY? Bernard Fensterwald, Jr. (1977) A mass market paperback containing information on hundreds of biographies of people and suspects surrounding the JFK assassination. Describes over 200 people who provided revealing information of a conspiracy and cover-up.

GOVERNMENT BY GUNPLAY: Assassination Conspiracy Theories From Dallas To Today. Edited by Sid Blumenthal and Harvey Yazijian of the Assassination Information Bureau. (1967) From Dallas to Watergate, this little mass market paperback is well researched on assassination theory.

THIRTEEN DAYS: A Memoir Of The Cuban Missile Crisis: By Robert F. Kennedy. (1969) Mass market paperback. Details concerning the actions in the White House during the Cuban

Missile Crisis.

THE CIA'S SECRET OPERATIONS: By Harry Rositzke. (1977) Hardback book on espionage, counterespionage and covert action of the CIA in the 1960's and before.

A THOUSAND DAYS: John F. Kennedy In The White House. By Arthur Schlesinger, Jr. (1965) A historical account (favorable) of the Kennedy Presidency.

J.F.K.: The Man And The Myth: By: Victor Lasky. (1977) mass market paperback . Critical review of Kennedy.

HOOVER'S F.B.I.: By William W. Turner. (1971) Mass market paperback. Former FBI agent gives critical review of the FBI and Hoover.

THE RUBY OSWALD AFFAIR: By Alan Adleson. (1988) Adleson was hired by the Jack Ruby family to handle his estate after Ruby's death. This is an excellent and interesting account with much insight into Jack Ruby.

AND WE ARE ALL MORTAL: By George M. Evica. Copyright 1978. University Of Hartford.

WHITEWASH: By Harold Weisberg: Dell Books. A critical look at the Warren Commission.

UNNATURAL DEATH: Confessions Of A Medical Examiner: Michael M. Baden, Ivy Books, New York, New York. Mass market paperback. Baden is a retired chief medical examiner for the city of New York. His book explores forensic investigation of murder and covers the Kennedy Assassination.

CORENER AT LARGE: Thomas T. Noguchi, M.D. Mass market paperback, Pocket Books. Forensic pathologist challenges the verdicts of the most controversial murders including JFK.

MY STORY: Judith Exner: (1977) Paperback . Judith Exner's affair with John Kennedy and her involvement with the mob.

WHO KILLED MARILYN? And Did The Kennedys Know? By: Tony Sciacca. (1976 papaerback) Covers the death of Marylin Manroe and Monroe's affairs with both John and Robert Kennedy.

THE MARILYN CONSPIRACY By: Milo Speriglio. (1986 papaerback edition) Pocket Books. Milo does an excellent job on explaining the death of Monroe and the affairs of John and Robert Kennedy with her. He also includes revealing information that Monroe was murdered with links to the Kennedys.

IT DIDN'T START WITH WATERGATE: By Victor Lasky (1977) Describes political dirty tricks before Watergate and contains information during the Kennedy Presidential campaign and adminstration.

AMOUNG THOSE PRESENT: By: Nancy Dickerson (1976 paperback edition) Interesting account of Dickerson's coverage of four Presidents from Kennedy to Ford. Covers Kennedy's perception of woman as sex objects and revealing information concerning the relationship between Kennedy and Lyndon Johnson.

JFK: THE MAN AND THE MYTH: By: Victor Lasky (Paperback Edition). An early account of some of the stuff not covered on Kennedy by the press during his adminstration.

TO MOVE A NATION: The Politics Of Foreign Policy In The Adminstration Of John F. Kennedy. By: Roger Hilsman. Copyright 1967. Rare book.

THE POLITICS OF LYING: Government Deception, Secrecy and Power. By: David Wise. Copyright: 1973.

WHO KILLED KENNEDY: By: Thomas Buchanan. Published in London England in 1964.

MAFIA, U.S.A. By: Nicholoas Gage. Copyright: 1972. Contains information on organized cime in America.

FIVE: OFFICIAL U.S. GOVERNMENT REPORTS

Two government investigations, the Warren Commission Reports and the Select Committee On Assassinations were used in the compilation of Missing Links. Aside from the volumes produced by these two reports, abridged editions have been published by various U.S. Publishers and can sometimes be located in used book stores.

THE WARREN REPORT: The Warren Report was published by the U.S. Government Printing office and abridged editions by several commercial publishers. The U.S. Government Printing Office published 26 volumes. Bantam Books published a mass market paperback of the findings titled Report Of The Warren Commission On The Assassination Of President Kennedy. Several commercial publishers including Doubleday, McGraw Hill and The Associated Press published hardbound copies of the summary findings. Several other commercial publishers published highlights of key witness hearings. Some of these books can still be found in used book stores.

REPORT OF THE SELECT COMMITTEE ON ASSASSINATIONS: First published is a multi-volume series by the U.S. Government Printing Office. Findings published commercially by several U.S. publishers. The most widely circulated commercial printing was The Final Assassinations Report, a mass market paperback published by Bantam Books.

SIX: COMPUTER SOURCES

During the course of doing the work involved in Missing Links, I used a modern investigative technique that involved a computer and a modum. By contacting various online networks of information, I have been able to keep track of newspaper and magazine stories that involve the Kennedy Assassination and quickly develop other items in print. I used the following sources for this technique:

COMPUSERVE INFORMATION SERVICES: Both Iquest and Executive News Service.

WESTERN UNION'S EASYLINK: Infomaster.

I also used some computer searches that helped link together pieces of information and help locate organizations, people, and services in regards to the Kennedy Assassination.

SEVEN: ORGANIZATIONS

ASSASSINATION ARCHIVES AND RESEARCH CENTER: 918 F Street, N.W. Suite 510, Washington, D.C., 20004. Phone (202) 393-1917. A hub of independent research material. A massive collection of research material used by researchers and writers.

JFK ASSASSINATION INFORMATION CENTER: 603 Muniger #310, P O Box 40, Dallas, Texas, 75202. Phone: (214) 871-2770. The center is located near the assassination site. The center is another major hub of research and investigation activity. Vistors can go through the exhibts and see films. The center is activily involved in onging research work into the Kennedy assassination. The giftshop sells books, videos and other related items. The center also sponsors a yearly assassination symposium.

LAST HURRA BOOK SHOP: 937 Memorial, Williamsport, Pa. 17701. Phone: (717) 327-9338. A book dealer that deals in hard to find and out of print books on anything that relates to JFK and the assassination. These people are very helpful. Highly recommended.

THE PRESDIENT'S BOX BOOKSHOP: P O Box 1255, Washington, D.C. 20013. Another book dealer that deals in hard to find and out of print books on all Presidential assassinations.

THE COLLECTOR'S ARCHIVES: Box 2, Beaconsfield, Que., Canada, H9W 5T6. This organization sells hard to locate books, videos, cassette tapes, research papers and unpublished manuscripts as well as photographs related to the assassination.

THE THIRD DECADE: State University College, Fredonia, New York, 14063. The Third decade is a very good newsletter under the editorship of Jerry Rose on the Kennedy Assassination that covers book reviews, points of view and new evidence as it breaks. Highly recommended.

THE CUTOUT COMMUNICATIONS CHAIN BETWEEN LEE OSWALD AND JACK RUBY

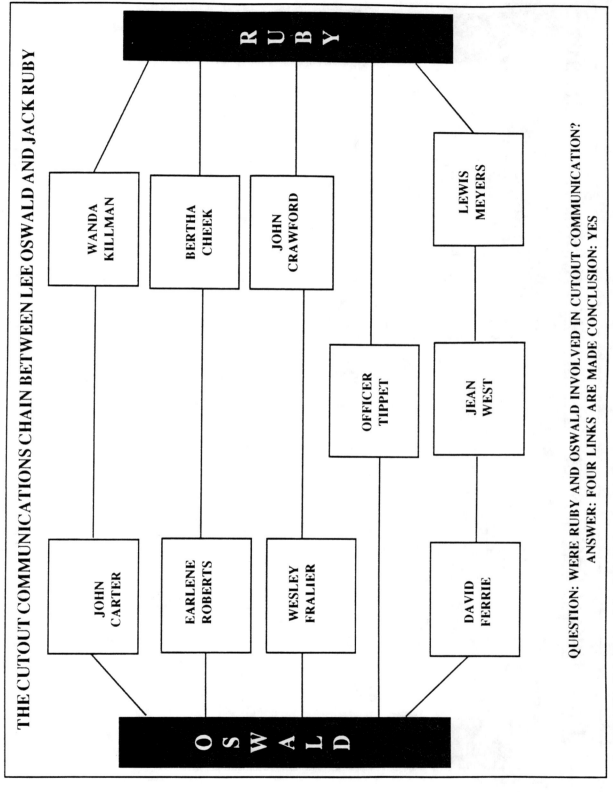

QUESTION: WERE RUBY AND OSWALD INVOLVED IN CUTOUT COMMUNICATION?
ANSWER: FOUR LINKS ARE MADE CONCLUSION: YES

DEAD DROP COMMUNICATIONS BETWEEN OSWALD AND RUBY

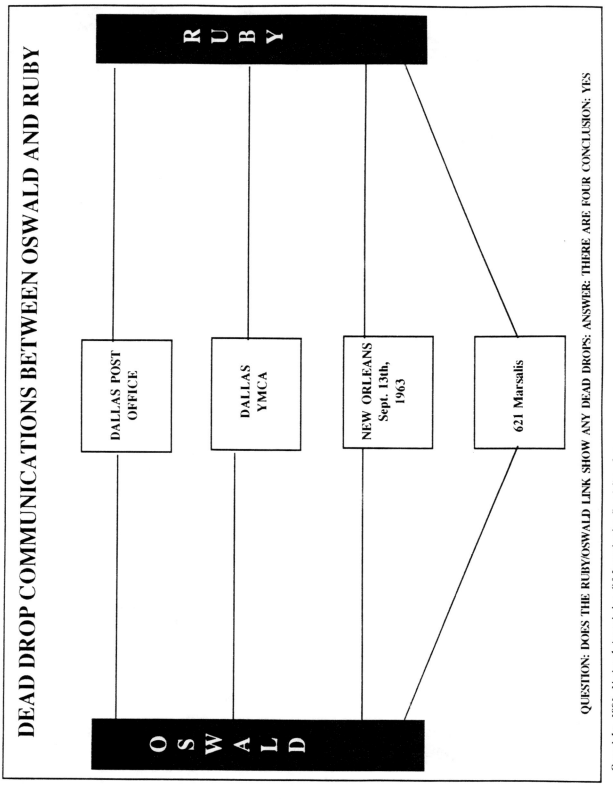

QUESTION: DOES THE RUBY/OSWALD LINK SHOW ANY DEAD DROPS: ANSWER: THERE ARE FOUR CONCLUSION: YES

WITNESSES PLACING RUBY AND OSWALD
IN DIRECT COMMUNICATION

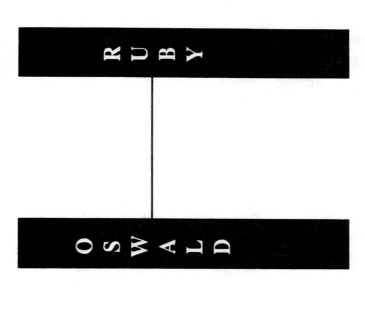

1) RAYMOND KRYSTINK

2) MADELEIAR BROWN

3) RAYMOND CUMMINGS

4) WILLIAM CROWE

5) BEVERLY OLIVER

6) JANET CONFONTO

7) KATHY KAY

8) WALTER WESTON

9) ESTER ANN MASH

10) CARROLL JARNAGIN

QUESTION: WERE RUBY AND OSWALD IN DIRECT COMMUNICATION?
ANSWER: TEN WITNESSES HAVE STATED THAT THEY WERE
CONCLUSION: YES

1) **CASTRO & CUBA:** Ruby made several unexplained trips to Cuba. Oswald was involved in attempts to travel to Cuba. The CIA was involved in covert activities in Cuba and assassination attempts on Castro.

2) **ORGANIZED CRIME:** Ruby was a member of organized crime. The CIA was in bed with organized crime in attempts to assassinate Castro. Organized crime was attempting to monitor Kennedy by placing females in his company. Kennedy was attempting to destroy organized crime.

3) **OIL INDUSTRY:** A letter has surfaced from Oswald to H.L. Hunt. Ruby visited the Hunt office the day before the assassination. The CIA was covertly involved with the oil industry. Kennedy threatened the oil depletion allowance.

4) **THE F.B.I.:** Oswald was likely an FBI informer. Ruby was a one-time FBI informer. The FBI is linked to the CIA as part of the overall American intelligence establishment. Hoover was going to be retired and hated the Kennedys.

5) **CUBAN REFUGEES:** Oswald was involved with this group which was covertly sponsored by the CIA. The Cubans were outraged for Kennedy's actions concerning the Bay Of Pigs. The FBI was monitoring Cuban Refugee activity using undercover methods.

6) **VIETNAM WAR:** The CIA was covertly involved in the Vietnam war and likely had something to do with the Diem assassination. Kennedy was withdrawing from Vietnam. The CIA forged cables that would point to Kennedy involvement in the Diem murder.

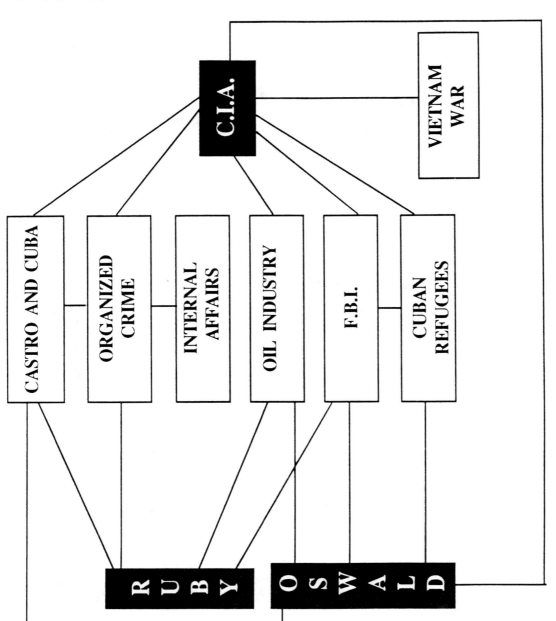

THE LINKAGE THAT TRACES BACK TO THE CIA